Greengrass Pipe Dancers

Crazy Horse's Pipe Bag and a Search for Healing

Lionel Little Eagle

To Jim &
Helen — Thank
You for your
friendship God
Bless you Both!
Lionel Little Eagle
06

Naturegraph Publishers

Library of Congress Cataloging-in-Publication Data

Pinn, Lionel Little Eagle, 1952-

   Greengrass pipe dancers : Crazy Horse's pipe bag and a search for healing/Lionel Little Eagle.
      p. cm.
   ISBN 0-87961-250-9
      1. Calumet bags. 2. Dakota Indians—Material culture. 3. Dakota Indians—Rites and ceremonies. 4. Dakota Indians—Religion. 5. Crazy Horse, ca. 1842-1877 I. Title.

E98.T6 P56 2000
306.6'997852—dc21   00-052385

Cover painting and illustrations
by Matt "Storms-In-His-Heart" Atkinson

Cover design by Albert Vanderhoof

Naturegraph Publishers has been publishing books on natural history, Native Americans, and outdoor subjects since 1946. Please write for our free catalog.

Naturegraph Publishers, Inc.
3543 Indian Creek Road
Happy Camp, CA 96039
(530) 493-5353

Books for a better world

Dedicated to Tamara Brown Pinn

May 6, 1952 - June 7, 1990

❧❧❧❧

A mother, a daughter, a sister, a wife,
An aunt, a friend, a nurse for life.

A gentle spirit of light and love,
A glowing lamp from up above.

A peaceful calm in a raging sea,
A blooming rose in God's eternity.

Sweet love of loves, Tamara Lynn

❧❧❧❧

With Respect and Honor to Crazy Horse's Pipebag

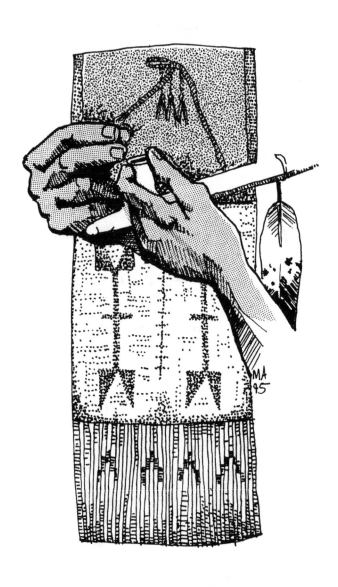

TABLE OF CONTENTS

ACKNOWLEDGEMENTS

I would like to thank all the people who have helped to make this book possible. In honor of that assistance, I humbly and lovingly offer the following: In memory of my beloved parents, Lionel and Una, for that precious gift of life and the opportunity to feel this good earth, I offer the chapter entitled "Top of the World." To my childhood guide and mentor, Truman Hill, who always encouraged me to write from the heart, I offer the chapter entitled "Mingling Spirits." To my brother, Kenny, I offer the chapter called "Drumming for Strength." To my sister, Wenonah, I gift the chapter called "Gathering Songs." To my son, Jody, and his daughter, Sierra Jade, I offer the chapter entitled "First Sweat." Jeremiah I offer to you the chapter "God's Big Toe," and to the symbol of Tamara's and my love, Travis, I present the chapter called "Cannupamony." To Tamara's children, Michael, Keith and in memory of Valerie, I offer with love the chapter called "Time To Dance." To my step-children, Ida, Nicole, Rebecca, Brenden, Brooke, Amiee, and Gabriel, I offer the chapter entitled "Council Tree."

To all the medical doctors and spiritual practitioners who gave so much of their knowledge to bring healing, I offer the chapter entitled "Truth." To my beloved grandmother, Lucy Marie, for her stories, I present "Going Home Again." To "Mom," Barbara Ann Black, and her entire family for making me a part of that family, I gift the chapter "Mother's Wisdom." To Keven Brown for his keen editor's eye and spiritual heart I offer the chapter called "Keven Brown Eagle." In respect and honor to all the four leggeds, swimmers and flyers, and to the plant and mineral kingdoms, I offer the chapter entitled "Can-Wanka, Mystery Tree." To all the twinkling golden stars of inspiration and friendship I offer "Eagle Dream." To Matt Storms-In-His-Heart Atkinson I present the chapter "Wambli Come to Greengrass." In memory of my Bahá'í father and teacher, Vinson Brown, I respectfully offer the "Dream Bag" chapter. To my dear Pinn and Norris relatives across this great Turtle Island I graciously give the chapter "Sweet Dreams." To my great grandfather, Joseph Charles, his descendants and to the Micmacs of Nova Scotia, I offer the chapter entitled "Micmacs in South Dakota." With respect and love, I offer the chapter called "Two Men Dancing" to the "Defenders of the little ones," Max and Barb Defender. To my dear great aunt Elsie Charles Basque I pass along the chapter called "Keepers of the Flame."

I would also like to acknowledge the many elders and medicine men and women who so graciously opened their hearts and souls to me and my work. Especially to the Old Coyote family, I offer the first chapter entitled "Rain Bugs in Paradise." To the Looking Horse family I offer the chapter called "Calf Pipe Story." To my dear friend, Marie Not-Help-Him, and her family, I present the chapter "The Lance Society," and to her mother, Celane, I share with great pride "Celane's Smile." In memory of Ellis Chips and in honor to the Chips family I offer "Yuwipi Time." With the greatest respect I offer Wallace Black Elk the chapter entitled "Crazy Horse Sweat." In memory of Frank Fools Crow I humbly offer the chapter entitled "Smoking with the Pope." In memory of my Micmac elder and counselor, Sam Bald Eagle, I offer the chapter "Sam's Council." To my warrior friend, Severt Young Bear, I offer the chapter called "Young Bear." In memory of and respect for the medicine man, Pete Catches, I offer the chapter called "Pete Catches' Medicine." With respect to all sun dancers past, present, and future I offer the chapter entitled "Moon of the Greengrass Sun Dance." To all the pipe carriers of all the families and nations I offer the chapter entitled "Coyote Smoke." To Shirley Calfrobe I gift the chapter entitled "Hey You," and in memory of her husband and my guide, Tom Calfrobe, I respectfully offer the chapter entitled "Listening to the Clouds." To Harry and Rufus Charger I offer the chapter "Dancing On." To Vincent Black Feather I respectfully give the chapter "Sun Dance Healing." In memory of a medicine man of the people, Martin Highbear, I share the chapter "Paha Sapa Council." To all of you who read these words with an open and understanding heart I offer, in a prayerful way, the chapter entitled "The Pipe Day, Releasing the Dance."

It is said that when the Creator closes one door, he always opens a new door. I am eternally thankful for that new door and new life's partner, my wife, Hilda Kumpf. To her I offer Little Eagle, forever.

INTRODUCTION

I write with the greatest love and respect for the Lakota and Dakota nations who are part of this story, but I write with absolutely no authority. The authenticity of this story is purely what I have experienced. When asked, I tell people that my heritage is Micmac and European, and if they look deeper, they will see that I am a simple member of the human race. That, above all, is my true heritage.

I have been fortunate and blessed for most of my life to be part of many Native American activities and ceremonies, to watch and learn, to speak out, and to hold my tongue when necessary. The backdrop of this story has a lot to do with these experiences. The story reflects what I know, not with any sanctioned authority, but just what I know intuitively. Although *Greengrass Pipe Dancers* is a true story, I do not claim that it is completely factual. I have utilized a number of direct quotes from conversations I have had or overheard, but such quotes are not exact. No cameras or tape recorders were present during such conversations or at the ceremonies in which they may have occurred. I did my best to take good notes when the opportunity allowed, but in larger part, I just sat down, recalled, and wrote this book from what I remembered. Good stories are like good recipes: sometimes you will add a few more grains of sugar, or substitute 2% milk for whole milk, or even leave out a part all together. The bottom line is what comes out and how it tastes.

To understand the story that I am going tell, the reader should know that there are five key elements to this story.

Tammy

The first key element is my late wife, Tamara. I called her Tammy. She was as gentle as a cool summer breeze, as kind and quiet as a floating leaf in autumn, as powerful and wise as the winter winds, as everlasting and beautiful as the cedar tree in spring. Tammy's life was not so complicated on the outside; it was the inside that roared with the intensity of a lion. She had experienced the heartfelt loss of her daughter, Valerie; the emotional turmoil of a marriage that did not work out; the all too familiar struggle of being a single mother with two sons; the tragedy of being the victim of sexual abuse; and finally the unforeseen affliction of a devastating disease called cancer at the young age of thirty-five. She also felt and recognized the glories and victories of her life: a mother's pride in her maturing and loving sons; the birth of a third son; scaling the mountains of education and training to acquire her calling as a registered nurse; the purity of a loving and supportive family; the reality and contentment of a strong faith; and the joy of a good marriage. These parts of her life defined what I knew and what I was allowed to love. I am eternally blessed.

The Healing

The healing we initially sought was from the cancer that Tammy had acquired. Being a nurse, Tammy was very familiar with the role and code of the medical institutions: to hope beyond hope. She accepted the reality of her tragic illness. Cancer has a way of motivating you toward the truth. We had carefully and diligently maneuvered our way through an incredible maze of treatments and therapies in an effort to capture the elusive cure. We eventually exhausted and then exited the trails of medical hope, knowing that when you leave one place, you must enter another. For us that new place was the spiritual essence of a fearless faith and the immeasurable grace of a loving God. This became represented to us in physical places like Greengrass, Pine Ridge, Eagle Nest Butte, Oglala, Porcupine, Wambli, the Badlands, Happy Camp, and Suquamish.

The People

Another significant part of this story manifested itself in the mysterious and powerful lives of the people who called these places home. A number of medicine men and women gave of their time, wisdom, and life to us in our efforts to gain the ultimate healing.

The Pipe Bag

The fourth significant part of this story deals with what some have called an artifact. To our family it is a stunning and life-changing pipe bag. A pipe bag is a pipe carrying implement used by many of the North American Indian tribes in the past and the present. It is usually simply constructed from deer or antelope hides, but often is decorated with various colored bead patterns, quillwork, and dyed horse hair. These bags would become the heirlooms of a family and treasures of a tribe. Often times many pipes would pass through a single pipe bag. Like a mother's womb, it contained life, and if you listened carefully enough, you could hear God's soft voice whisper wisdom through it.

☆   ☆   ☆

In the history of this particular pipe bag, in our family, there have been three different keepers. The first keeper was Dr. Henry Alexander Brown, who quietly kept the pipe bag safe for more than fifty years. It came to him under the most extraordinary circumstances. That story has been recounted by Dr. Brown's son, Vinson, in his book, *Warriors of the Rainbow.* However, the most complete telling of that story came when I asked Tammy to tell me how this precious gift found its way into her family. She was hesitant at first, but she eventually wrote down a

Keeper from 1896 - 1948

very detailed, slightly fictionalized account which succeeds in bringing the historical setting and human feelings of the pipe bag story to life. Dr. Brown's experience is such a significant part of the Greengrass Pipe Dancers story that I, respectfully, include it here to introduce you to the pipe bag and its first keeper.

The stagecoach bounced along the straight and forever roads of South Dakota. The grass was turning from green to golden. They had skirted the Badlands with their desolate cliffs and gullies and were now traversing a rolling prairie with occasional low hills and buttes. The year was 1895, and Dr. Henry Alexander Brown was making a new start in life. He had received his MD degree two years earlier and now sought to start his practice for the good of the people. He wondered for perhaps the hundredth time if he had made the right decision in coming to this place and to these people.

His first wife, Clarrisa, had left him, gone back to her parents, taking four-year-old Adeline with her. Clarrisa had never been the same after the death of their infant son. That had been his greatest failure. He was a doctor, yet his son had stopped breathing, and not all the training, not all the books, not all his efforts were able to save his life.

He had failed with Clarrisa. Their joyous young love had gradually diminished over five years of marriage. He did not know why she avoided his presence and shrank from his touch after their son died. And Adeline was Clarrisa's child. They spent their days together during the long hours required of a young doctor's practice.

Henry sold the empty house. A new doctor had come to take over his practice. "Become a ship's doctor," advised his Scottish mother as they sat together after dinner one evening. "You'll be able to travel all over the world, and the fascination of visiting new places will help you forget your pain."

Henry later told his best friend, Percival, as they sat together in the Canadian club, "I'd like to go to the most desolate place in the world. Somewhere where people are unfortunate dogs and I can see how lucky I am in comparison. That place could be Africa, India, or any other place for that matter."

"If you'd really like to go to the most desolate place on the face of the earth," said a bearded stranger who sat to their left, "you don't have to go even a thousand miles. If it is desolation that you seek, then go be a doctor on the Indian reservation at Pine Ridge in the new state of South Dakota. There you will find what you are looking for and much more."

"If I am going to make a new start," thought Henry Alexander as the stagecoach lurched over yet another rut, "then I will use the name Alex. I always thought it had a better sound." But not all his brave resolutions, college, marriage, or life as a doctor had prepared him for living on an Indian reservation in 1895. The times were extreme. The once pride-filled and free Sioux were now being hammered into the prairie grasses of South Dakota. They still felt the pain of Crazy Horses' assassination and the killing of Sitting Bull. Just beyond town, Chief Big Foot and his band of Minneconjous Sioux were massacred and buried in a mass grave. All this was fresh in the memories of the Sioux. They now lived in small shacks with tar paper roofs on the outskirts of town and other outlying areas. They wore white men's cast off clothing. It hung in tatters from their gaunt frames. Their dark eyes constantly sought the ground, and he could sense the hopelessness in their faces. They haunted the liquor store and the government commissary, and he watched them stagger homewards under the influence of alcohol or the burden of provisions.

The new doctor, Alex Brown, rented a small brick building in town and hung a shingle above the door. He bought a horse and a buckboard and was soon making calls in the neighboring areas, to the borders of the Badlands and the fringe of the Black Hills, and down into northern Nebraska. But his clients were not Indians. They were the soldiers who had remained to keep the peace, Indian police, stagecoach drivers, town merchants, mercenaries, and soldiers of fortune. He attended them in ill health and childbirth, and sometimes for the miseries of overindulgence. They flourished.

The first winter came and the snows fell. Alex and the local judge sat drinking coffee in the local cafe. Alex then noted, "I feel that as a doctor I should make some effort to help them," referring to the Indians.

"They don't want your help!" replied the scornful old judge. "Every winter they die like flies. They catch the measles and they die. They catch pneumonia and they die. They can't fight those diseases the way we can. Perhaps God meant for them to die out. Now that they've lost their land, they live like parasites. They have no contribution to make to our society. What reason is there for them exist?"

A man came panting into the cafe where Alex and the judge sat and announced his wife was having a baby. The next morning his office was filled with cases of coughs and sniffles and a sprained ankle, but in the late afternoon as darkness began to fall, Alex made his way across town to the Indian shacks. The familiar mourning chants assailed his ears. Heard closely, it sent a chill down his spine. He saw a few women carrying armloads of firewood or buckets of snow to melt for water, but none of them looked at him. A drunk lurched by. Finally, he approached a middle-aged woman and said, "I am a doctor. Can I help any of your people who are ill?"

The woman brought her eyes to the level of the top button of his coat and straightened her thin shoulders with a pathetic dignity. "You no do good here. Our medicine is gone. Our people they die quickly like little babies. One day they are among us. The next day they are gone to the spirit world. We make songs to mourn them. We make songs to send them on their way. We will be together with them before many moons go by. You go! I will tell our people. If they need a white man's medicine, they will come for you."

Alex walked slowly back to town. "I thought I knew pain," he said to himself. "People here say the Indians are savages. They say they have no feelings because their faces are expressionless. But there is pain in their death song, and it is greater than mine, because theirs belongs to a dying people who have been severed from their past and see no hope for their future."

The wood burner made the room behind his office cozy. The long-haired tabby that had adopted Alex sat in his lap as he sipped a cup of tea. The snow was too deep for any but the most desperate to venture forth; consequently business had been slow. He had not thought about such matters for a while, and even the distant wailing had become a customary sound that scarcely penetrated his consciousness. "Perhaps if I live here long enough I will become as callous as everyone else," he thought. He recalled his mother's advice to become a ship's doctor and it sounded better to his mind than it ever had before. "I've learned my lesson," he said aloud, "that others have worse pain than I. Perhaps it is time to move on when the roads are passable in the spring."

There was a knock on the door. Usually people walked into the office, but this time no one followed the knock. Alex opened the door and peered outside into the swirling snow. An Indian stood silently before him. He was taller than the average and his hair hung in neat braids on either side of his head, bound by red ribbon. His shabby coat was made of buckskin and had seen better days. His moccasins were whole and elaborately beaded. In all, he was the best dressed Indian that Alex had ever seen. With shoulders erect and head held high, he looked at Alex face to face. It was the first time Alex had looked into an Indian's eyes. They held no expression. "My son is dying," he said. "Come."

Alex put on his fur-lined coat. He picked up his black doctor's bag. Looking about him, he also gathered a blanket and pillow from his bed and a loaf of bread and some cheese from the cupboard. Then he followed the Indian out the door.

To his surprise, two horses were tethered beside the street. The Indian assisted him to mount stirrupless and they rode into the falling darkness. After a ride of several miles, the ghostly outlines of teepees were silhouetted by faint moonlight. The horses were given into the care of a man who appeared silently, and Alex followed his companion into the largest of the lodges. A small fire was burning in the center, and by its flickering light Alex could see a younger and an older woman. Then he became aware of the sound of shallow, labored breathing and saw a form huddled beneath a buffalo robe, still except for the effort to exchange air.

The boy was perhaps eight or nine years old and feverish. Alex could tell even before he listened to his lungs that he had a bad case of pneumonia. He asked the women for water, and it was silently proffered in a metal bucket with a dipper. He offered the boy sips slowly and then sponged his body as he thrashed and moaned. He rubbed an elixir rhythmically on his back and sponged him again. The women watched him surreptitiously. He thought, "It must seem to them as if I am performing a ritual, a white medicine man." The night proceeded slowly as he slept for brief intervals between attending to the boy. By morning the boy was worse. His lungs were filling with fluid which he was too weak to cough up, and he heard the dread sound of the death rattle in his chest.

Alex thought of his newborn son who had lived for one brief moment, had taken one breath and stopped forever. Yet he had loved him with all his heart. He thought of this boy's father. He realized that behind the man's stoicism there existed a love for this boy that had broken the bounds between the white man's and Indian worlds and had brought him here to allow him to prove himself as a doctor, to save the life of this child.

For two days and two more nights Alex worked on the Indian boy, always just one step ahead of death. He nibbled on the bread and cheese, slept in snatches, the women awakening him each time the boy's breathing got worse. His whole being became centered on the task of saving the boy. He did not know at which moment he ceased to worry about proving his worth as a doctor. He prayed as he hadn't done since childhood with a child's sincerity. He realized, as the boy hung by a thread between life and death, that this task was beyond the extent of his powers alone. The boy's father had not entered the lodge since the night he brought him here, but Alex knew that he was aware of all that transpired, and he waited.

On the morning of the third day Alex awoke with a jerk. Something was different! He knew what it was in an instant. The breathing was irregular. Sometimes the boy would take a long breath that ended in a sigh. Then he would cease breathing at all for a few seconds. He was dying. "No!" cried Alex. He jumped to his feet and then knelt down beside the boy. As he finished one last, sighing breath, Alex put his mouth to the boy's lips, pinched closed his nostrils and exhaled deeply, forcing air into his lungs. "Breathe!" he shouted. "Breathe!" Each time the boy stopped breathing, Alex breathed for him. After what seemed like an endless time, he realized the boy was breathing on his own. Then he coughed and Alex rejoiced at the sound, turning him on his side to help release the thick secretions. His eyes flickered open. He was breathing more easily now. The younger woman came forward and began to spoon sips of nourishing broth into the boy's mouth, which he swallowed. Alex looked up and saw the boy's father standing just inside the lodge. His arms were folded on his chest and his face was like carved stone. Alex slept.

When he awoke the boy was gone. Only the older woman was in the teepee. "Boy all right," she said reassuringly. She left and returned a little later with a bowl of stew and a bucket of warm water. "Eat! Wash!" she said, and Alex was again left alone. The stew tasted strange, but Alex was hungry and he ate it. "It might be horse, antelope, or even dog, goodness knows," he thought. He washed it down with several sips of the warm water before he used it for cleaning purposes.

The day was clear and cold. Five teepees stood in the center of the camp. They were made of tanned hides sewn together, and had designs painted around the base and upper parts. Smoke rose in thin spirals from the openings in the tops. The ground around them had been swept clean of snow and debris. In the center of the camp a community fire burned and over it hung a pot which smelled of the stew he had eaten. It was attended by the younger woman of the lodge. She smiled at Alex as he strolled through the camp and Alex smiled back. A few children were darting in and among the lodges, playing tag. They seemed healthy enough. Alex smiled as he watched them.

Gradually he became aware of another presence and looked around. The boy's father stood beside him. His face seemed gentle in the sunlight. They stood in silence for a few moments, surveying the camp. "They want us to live in little square houses," said the Indian. "Very few live in lodges any more, and we can't hold out forever. Soon we will live as the white man decrees and our own ways will be forgotten." He looked and turned to Alex. "You saved my son's life," he announced. He held out a handful of gold and silver coins. "I have white man's money to pay you."

Alex instinctively started to take the money, then he flung down his hand. "No!" he exclaimed. "The white men have taken enough from the Indians. It is time something was given back. I give you your son's life and I will take no payment for it. It is what I owe you."

The Indian looked taken aback. Then he beckoned to Alex. "Come!" They went back into the teepee. Inside were assembled the older woman, the younger woman, and the boy who was indeed on his way to recovery, although he had dark circles beneath his eyes and his expression was grave and haunting. There was also a younger girl of five of six whom Alex presumed to be the sister. The Indian spoke to the younger woman and she walked to a pile of belongings in a corner and brought forth a deerskin bag with a small amount of beadwork. From it he withdrew a pipe stem and then the pipe bowl. He attached the two objects together, making them one. He began ritualistically filling the pipe with tobacco, speaking softly as if praying. Once he had finished, the younger woman obtained a burning ember from the fire and held it over the bowl. The Indian drew deeply on the stem and soon the pipe was smoking strongly. He held it horizontally to the earth and proffered it to Alex. Alex accepted it, placed the pipe on his lips, and began to draw on it. He felt his throat and lungs expanding and being pressured; he quickly exhaled the smoke and handed the pipe back to the Indian, who once again smoked heavily from it, filling the lodge with smoke. He then handed the pipe to his young woman helper, who sat down holding it in a respectful way.

The Indian then gave instructions to the older woman. She walked to the pile of belongings and brought the boy's father another object wrapped in skins. The Indian uncovered it and held it out to Alex. It was about three feet long, made of soft hide, and beautifully beaded with white, blue, green, and gold beads. An extraordinary pattern of dyed porcupine quills graced the front and back sides accompanied with scattered reddish horse hair tassels. Although Alex did not know what it was, he held it respectfully.

"It is a pipe bag," said the Indian, answering his unspoken question. "It is used to carry our ceremonial pipe." He was silent for a long moment. Then he said, "This bag has a story. One winter the white soldiers were burning all the belongings the Indians held sacred. Among those objects were the belongings of some of our most beloved leaders. Medicine bags, pipes, drums, weapons, pipe bags, and many more things. They gouged the drums and broke the stems of the pipes. Then they made a great pile of our sacred objects and they set it on fire. I think they were afraid of those objects. Maybe the ghosts of the sacred ones lived in those things. This pipe bag was thrown on the very top of the pile. I can tell you that this bag once belonged to a great warrior of our people.

The soldiers were in front, standing around the fire. The Indians looked on from a little ways back. The women were wailing and mourning for our loss. It was then that I called upon the Mystery; I prayed for a sign from Wakan Tanka. I asked for a sign that would tell me that our people had not been forgotten. I began to sing my personal prayer songs and the women were silent. The flames leapt higher and higher. I continued to pray. I raised my arms upward toward the sky to draw the powers of the Creator. Then the whirlwind came. It blew dust and ashes around the soldiers. They were coughing and holding their hands over their faces. The whirlwind spiraled over the burning pile and picked the pipe bag off the very top, carrying it a ways off into a clump of bushes. We couldn't celebrate. We couldn't go get it then. We waited until nightfall when the soldiers were gone. Then I took it out of the bushes. It had not even been harmed. This was the sign that I had prayed for!"

"It is indeed sacred," said Alex. "But why do you give me something that is so precious to your people when I have desired not to be paid for my services?"

"I had a dream," said the Indian. "In the dream I was told to give this pipe bag to the first white man who did something kind for my family. I was also told that if I did this, it would bring good to my people in the future. So that is why I give this bag to you now."

Alex bowed his thanks. "It is a great honor. Because of your dream I will accept this sacred trust and do my best to keep it safe for your people."

The man who had taken the horses when they arrived escorted Alex home. People eyed Alex strangely as he rode through the streets with the Indian. The brick office seemed unreal, as though he had been gone for weeks. The cat was hungry and the half-empty cup of cold tea still rested on the table. The town judge came stomping into his office. "Where the hell did you go with those no-good Indians? Captain Jake's wife was in labor for two days before she finally gave birth and the midwife wasn't much help. Old lady Rasmussen broke her leg and the vet from White Clay had to set it, him half drunk at the time. I'll see you run out of town, Alex Brown, if you doctor those useless redskins again and leave us good Christian folk to suffer! It ain't right, I tell you! It just ain't right!"

Although the Indians did not call for his services again, Alex found that his business had indeed dropped off. There were fewer visits for cough medicine and chest liniment, no more friendly chats from the judge or anyone else for that matter. In the streets Alex was often glared at and, most of the time, given the cold shoulder.

When springtime came and the roads were passable after the melting snows, Alex boarded the stage. He was headed further west, bound for San Fransico Bay. Dr. Henry Alexander Brown was making another new start in life. He'd been at Pine Ridge for a little less than a year. He wondered how many new starts he'd wind up making.

As the stagecoach tilted around one of the few bends in the South Dakota road, one of the passengers exclaimed, "Look! There's Indians up there."

"Are they going to attack us?" the frightened woman exclaimed.

"Naw," answered a man on the same side of the stage, "it's just one man and a boy."

This caught Dr. Brown's attention. He leaned toward the window on that side of the stage. On top of a small butte he saw silhouetted against the sky, a man and a boy on horseback. They both wore feathers in their long, braided hair. As the doctor peered toward the two Indians, they both raised their hands at the same time and waved in his direction.

Surreptitiously, Alex let down the window and waved his arm in salute.

"Put that window up!" snapped the lady. ""You're letting the dust inside."

"Good-bye," said Alex softly. "May your son live to gladden your old age." He patted the black doctor's bag that reposed on his lap, with the pipe bag inside it. "I'll keep it safe for you, my friend."

☆   ☆   ☆

On the passing of Dr. Henry Alexander Brown in 1948, the pipe bag was entrusted to his son, Vinson Brown, who kept it for the next forty years. When he was five years old (in 1918), Vinson said that his father first showed him the pipe bag, and told him the story of how the Oglala Sioux chief had given it to him. When Vinson touched its soft doeskin, he felt a flame of wonder dart up his arm and into his heart. He then began to have a frequently recurring dream for the next four years. The dream was always the same. Vinson described his dream in *Warriors of the Rainbow*:

I seemed to be floating in the sky looking down at a land of many round hills. On the top of each hill was a group of Indians. Some of them were lying on the dry grass with their fingers digging the ground despairingly. Others lifted their arms hopelessly to the sky. Women were

Keeper from 1948 - 1988

huddled together, weeping. All were wearing old, cast-off white men's clothing, just rags. Their faces were filled with a deep sadness, and their skin seemed drawn over the bones, so that I felt both bodies and souls were hungry.

There seemed to be growing a strange light up in the sky. Looking up, I saw the sunlight flashing on the wings of a beautiful white bird, a dove. The dove circled down from the sky, its body and wings pure as new-fallen snow. Fluttering and circling, it came slowly, but there was a feeling about it of immense power, as if all that was in the sky centered upon it.

As the dove came near the top of one of the hills, a strange and remarkable thing happened. The Indians there suddenly sprang to their feet, gazing up at the dove. The white men's rags fell from their bodies and disappeared. Instead, they now lifted their heads proudly under handsome headdresses and their bodies were covered with clean buckskin that glittered with beads and with buckles of shell. Their faces glowed with happiness and joy. Their bodies arched like bows drawn back to send forth humming arrows. Then, to my amazement, they began to march up into the sky after the dove, marching with the springing steps of conquerors, like lords of the world.

As the dove dipped low again and again, other dark-skinned peoples rose joyously from hill after hill and marched up into the sky, following the beautiful white bird. I saw many costumes in my dream, but I did not know what they meant or what tribes they represented, only that feathers were waving, beads of many colors glittered, and brown arms gleamed with bronze and gold. Drums began to mutter, lifting and rolling into thunder, and pipes shrilled with triumph. Voices chanted ancient songs and shouted age-long cries of the peoples.

Slowly a bow formed in the sky, a rainbow of people marching to glory, a rainbow of unity, and a vision so marvelous in its sense of beauty and joy that I can never forget it nor hope to see anything its equal. Slowly, at the end of each dream, this vision of glory would fade away, but the promise of it always remained, the promise of a wonderful change coming.

When Vinson was nine years old he visited a Shoshone Indian reservation in Nevada. He found the Shoshone families there living in broken-down shacks, wearing old, cast-off clothing, and looking very sad. As he was young, he did not connect this experience to his dream, and because he did not understand, he said his wonderful dream stopped, but it had influenced the course of his life. Much later, in the 1930s, Vinson was living in a mountain jungle of Panama with a Guaymi Indian who still lived in the old way. He became so impressed with the Indian youth's spirituality that he began to search different religions to find a more universal truth than he had received from his Christian upbringing. He began to understand, more and more, how his own people had crushed and hurt the Indians, and what a great loss this was to both cultures.

Vinson discovered the "more universal truth" he was looking for some years later, after his return to the United States, while working in the Office of War Information. He found it in the Bahá'í Faith, a religion which had originated in Iran about a hundred years earlier. Its founder, Bahá'u'lláh, taught that the cultural diversity of the human family must be cherished, and that all religions are part of God's plan. But it wasn't until 1949, while on a lecture trip in the Southwest for the National School Assemblies, that Vinson finally understood the meaning of his pipe-bag inspired dream. He had told many Indians he met on his travels the story of his dream, but none were able to interpret it for him. Then, one day, while driving from Albuquerque, New Mexico, to Snowflake, Arizona, he met a tall young Otomi Indian striding along the road. Vinson offered him a ride, and, in the course of their conversation, told the young man about his childhood dream. The Indian's face suddenly shone with understanding. He told Vinson that the dove in his vision symbolized white men who would help the Indian people overcome their despair and feel pride in their own culture. He explained, "The fact that the Indians you saw in the sky were wearing the clothes of the ancient days meant that these white men would not make fun of or laugh at the old Indian culture and religion. Instead they would assist the Indians to be proud of their ancestors and get back the great spirit and knowledge the ancient people had" (*Warriors of the Rainbow* pg. 22).

Vinson had started his new publishing company, Naturegraph Publishers, in 1946, devoted to books on nature and the outdoors. By training, he was a biologist and naturalist, having received his M.A. in biology from Stanford University. He also had a degree in anthropology from the University of California at Berkeley, where he had studied under the famous anthropologist, Alfred Kroeber. Having had the privilege as a child of sitting on Ishi's lap, the last Yahi, having traveled with Kroeber to visit Indian tribes in northern California, and having met many Indians already, it is not surprising that Vinson's interests turned more and more toward Native Americans. In an attempt to fulfill his dream about the return of the Indian spirit,

Vinson most likely read every book ever written at the time about Indians.

In 1960, Vinson's eldest son, Kirby, also traveled to Panama, where he lived for the next two years. During Kirby's stay a large number of Guaymi Indians converted to the Bahá'í Faith, which they felt was a fulfillment of their ancient prophecies. On hearing this news through his son, Vinson's enthusiasm for both his newfound religion and Native Americans became a flame which never died for the rest of his life. The reader may wonder why he connected the Bahá'í Faith to the revival of Indian culture. This is because the central teaching of the Bahá'í Faith is the unity of humankind through the diversity of its component cultures. Vinson believed that this concept fulfilled the expectations of many religions including the prophecies of Native American tribes. His belief soon became manifested in the book *Warriors of the Rainbow: Strange and Prophetic Dreams of the Indian Peoples*, which he wrote with his Eskimo friend, William Willoya, and published in 1962. Their goal in this book was to help revive the return of the Indian spirit. This was the first of many Native American books to be published by Naturegraph.

After all these years, the words the Oglala chief had spoken to Vinson's father in 1895—"bring good to my people in the future"—took on new meaning. The pipe bag became a renewed source of inspiration for Vinson as he studied about Native Americans, visited them, and taught others about their culture and spirituality. He traveled thousands of miles to seek firsthand knowledge and understanding from the chiefs and medicine men of many Western tribes. He worked ceaselessly to inspire interest in the Indian culture through writing books, keeping up a large correspondence, giving public talks, and especially through his Indian council fires, which he held annually for over twenty years at Council Oaks, his home in Healdsburg, California, and later in Happy Camp, California. He invited Indian peoples from as many tribes as could make the trip; acquaintances he made on his travels. Vinson always carried file cards in his shirt pocket to jot down names and addresses of those who expressed an interest in Native culture. The pipe bag was always displayed with reverence at these meetings. Legends and stories were shared, songs were sung, games were played, crafts were displayed, and people danced to the beat of the big drum. These were weekends of fun, laughter and humor, purifying sweats, plenty to eat, and talks around the campfire.

Most rewarding from these gatherings were the lasting friendships that grew between once strangers of distant tribes.

In 1966, Vinson traveled to South Dakota to meet with Frank Fools Crow, one of the most respected spiritual leaders of the Lakota. He came to ask Fools Crow if he could help him go on a vision search on Bear Butte, a place sacred to the Lakota people. He also brought with him the pipe bag that had been given to his father. Fools Crow told Vinson that the vision quest was a very serious thing, and that he should take the next year to prepare for it, and come back the next summer. Vinson agreed. He also told Fools Crow that he would loan the pipe bag to him during that year to use in his ceremonies. Vinson wanted to know if Fools Crow could determine where the bag had come from and who had owned it.

The surprise came a week later when Vinson took his family and some boys to watch the sun dance of the Oglala Sioux at Pine Ridge. At the commencement of the dance, it was announced over the loud speaker that the pipe bag of Crazy Horse had been found. The pipe bag was hung on the central sun dance pole where the dancers could touch it to receive additional power. Later, Fools Crow came to Vinson and told him that the pipe bag, which he believed to have belonged to Crazy Horse, had been given to Vinson's family for a purpose, and that he should continue to guard it and use it only in sacred ways.

Vinson's wife, Barbara, recalls, "In our home, the pipe bag was kept in a specially made cherrywood case. It was treated as a sacred heirloom and always held a place of honor in the living room. We knew the pipe bag was sacred. Since we could not afford home owner's insurance, the pipe bag was our protector. One year near Healdsburg, a grass and forest fire was swiftly devouring everything ahead of it, and our place was in its path. All the fire engines were busy elsewhere, yet my faith in the pipe bag's protection didn't waiver. When the flames encroached our hillside, we fought back for all we were worth, swatting down flames with wetted gunny sacks, ignoring exhaustion. Although the fire burned 360 degrees around us, our home and Naturegraph building were barely singed as the inferno continued up the forested hillside."

Through the power of the pipe bag Vinson helped set the stage for the spiritual gatherings of many tribes which in later years were to become widespread. He was often a guest at these council fires, from Neah Bay, Washington, to Flagstaff, Arizona.

One of his favorite themes for these presentations was the visions and prophecies of the Native Americans and how they were fulfilled in the new religion of unity.

☆　　☆　　☆

In October of 1987, three years before his passing, Vinson entrusted the precious care and responsibility of the pipe bag to me, his son-in-law of Micmac heritage, and its third keeper in our family. I was also given instructions to utilize its energy to seek healing and to bring peace to a gentle lady named Tammy, my wife and his daughter. I knew that it was not going to be easy, but I also knew that it was going to happen. It came as quite a surprise and I felt I was not worthy of this honor, but I accepted it in deep respect and humbleness. *Greengrass Pipe Dancers* is the story of this period of my life.

Keeper from 1988 - 1991

I first became acquainted with Vinson though his book about Crazy Horse. It happened in the summer of 1978 I hung my hat in a lobby of a Houston, Texas library in my never-ending quest to learn more of my Indian heritage. I wandered through the aisles in the hope of finding some new reading material on the subject. After an hour or so of unsuccessful search I decided to ask the librarian for assistance. She was very polite and said she had a book that might be of interest to me. I followed her as she walked purposefully to a shelf. She moved her finger along the third row from the top and suddenly exclaimed, "*Crazy Horse, Great Upon the Mountain*, by Vinson Brown." She placed it in my hands and said with a smile, "Try this one." Then she returned to her desk. Little did I know as I thumbed through the pages that this book would eventually be so important in my life.

It was during a Council Fire in 1980 that I first met Vinson coming down a path through the woods from his home with his wife, Barbara. In his arms he cradled a case. He set it up against a tree and called for everyone to draw near. When the case was opened, I beheld a beautiful and venerable pipe bag. He announced that this was the pipe bag of Crazy Horse! My heart filled with excitement and amazement. People moved closer as he continued to talk about it. But I found myself frozen in my steps. The pipe bag of Crazy Horse seemed so powerful to me, I feared coming any closer. During intervening years I attended other of Vinson's Indian events, but my awe of the pipe bag never faded.

The Dance

The fifth significant element of the Greengrass Pipe Dancers story is the dance itself. I have always felt that life was a dance, and during the course of my life I have been able to confirm that feeling. I have also been able to see, for the first time, that there is more to the dance than meets the eye or touches the heart. It seems that everyday I am given a new version of the dance, a new step to learn. For much of my life I was limited to the physical dance of life, but now I have been blessed with the greatest dance of all: the dance of afterlife to which belong dancing spirits of energy. Energy is produced through movement. When you have a constructive and purposeful movement, then you have the dance. The Oshu devotees of Africa feel strongly that the physical is there to serve the spiritual, and that the dance is a soulful dialogue with our ancestors. A dancing body opens the gateway between this world and the world of spirit.

Throughout my life I have been exposed to many forms and styles of dance. Both through my conscious and subconscious efforts I have always tried to understand and learn the many variations of the dances of life. When I was a youth in Alabama, I attended the local church, and what stands out in my memory are the fantastic and, at times, fanatical dances we performed together. Standing on benches, tables, and each other we made an effort to reach a moment of spiritual ecstasy and glory, a moment of closeness to God.

One of the mysteries of the dance is how it makes people feel. Love, sadness, and the blues are inspired by the dance. However, due to a lack of understanding, some dances arouse suspicions and for some represent change and rebellion. The know-it-all people who frown and classify dances as the "devil's work" are still alive and well today. But, the next time you see a new and different dance, look closely and you will observe the mystery at work; the child becomes a giant and the man becomes a bear. The mystery of the dance becomes alive and real, right in front of you. Look even closer, if you dare, and you may recognize your own fears or realize your own dreams in the mirror of the dance.

Enlightenment is sought and often achieved through the use of the dance. Many people throughout the world have built their tradition, culture, and even religion around the dance. I think of the trancelike movements of the whirling dervishes of the Middle East; the exacting and poised movements of the Japanese Kabuki dancers; and the grace and power of the Russian Kirov Ballet. It is true that dances such as these have evolved and expanded from the original movements. From that development has come the splendid and stunning spectacle of the dance performance. Years and years of hard and dedicated training is necessary in order to perform such precise dances and survive the scrutiny of the dance masters. However, the essence and beauty of the dance can be seen in much simpler presentations. I think of my own personal dance of joy when my son was born. The unrestrained energies fired through my soul like lightning bolts. I ran through the halls of the hospital hopping, skipping, singing, and dancing. It took no rehearsal or years of training. Simple joy made it happen. Later, I watched that same boy listening to music on the radio. Without coaching, his one year old body began to dance, up and down, then side to side. It was his baby dance. The music moved into that place inside his being and flipped the switch of dance and he has not stopped yet.

Another form of pure but powerful dance was the dance of anguish I saw embodied in a Sarejevo mother as she scrambled through the ruins of a bombed out building. She would dig, then she would run, then she would hop, then she screamed in agony, and then she would dig some more. The spirit of motherhood, the loss of a child lit the fires of the dance within her. Sometimes it is hard to recognize such moments as dance, but it is the energy and the movement that identifies it to me as something more than random action or reaction. All of these movements are the dances of life.

Indigenous people practice to perfection the dances of their existence. They refine the steps and open their potential. The Cook Islanders of the South Pacific have the unity dance, which signifies the importance of the group rather than the individual. The Apache sunrise dance and ceremony marks the transition of a young girl into womanhood. Some natives of Mozambique celebrate the birth of a child with the same dance as the passing of an elder. To them they are the same process, birth and rebirth. Every nation has been given the dance. Even more than language, dance is a unifying force of the earth.

On the buttes of South Dakota, along the shores of the Columbia River, knee deep in the swamps of the everglades, on the edge of a fiery volcano, you will find ceremony and the dance: The green corn dance of the Cherokee; the great serpent dance of the Kamarakoto natives; the silent and lost dances of the southwest Anasazi. A dance that rose up from the ashes of despair in the late 1800s was given to the Indian people by the Paiute prophet, Wovoka. By performing the mystical ghost dance, the participants sought to bring back the buffalo and reclaim their lands and lives. This dance, and the movement it inspired, was crushed by the U.S. Government, as evidenced by the assassination of Sitting Bull and the Wounded Knee massacre of 1890. Another dance of renewal which was banned by the same government in the 1880s was the sun dance. It was forced underground for many years, but it has seen a revival in the past fifty years. It is unquestionably one of the purest forms of religious expression known to man—an outward flow of sacrifice and an inward flow of enlightenment. The sun dancers do not merely dance for themselves but for a greater and more noble purpose: their families and their people.

The experience of the dance inspired me and forever changed me. I saw the visible expressions and movements of love through the dance. In the end, by the grace of God, I became absorbed into the spiritual aura of the invisible dance and for shimmering moments I saw those on the other side and they were dancing too!

It was along the sun dance trails of South Dakota that I made my very personal and emotional journey. It was there, amid the sacred sage, that the healing was sought, the fires of the dance were ignited, the people gathered, and the pipe bag came home.

Lionel Little Eagle

Prelude to BOOK I

I sat on the couch watching TV on a Sunday afternoon. The Yankees were losing to the Mariners for a change. Baby Trapper had just slipped off to slumberland beside me, so trusting and beautiful. The phone rang. I recognized the voice of Old Coyote.

"Whatcha doin'?"

"Watching the Mariners beat up on the Yankees."

"Yeah, sure!" he laughed disbelievingly. "When you get a chance, come by the house. I got something to talk to you about."

"Sure. I'll be by in about 15 minutes."

It was evident by his voice that whatever it was, it was important. I rearranged the baby on a blanket on the carpet and headed out the door. My wife was working happily in her flower garden.

"Who was that on the phone?"

"Old Coyote. He said he wanted to talk to me. It sounded like something important."

"Don't be too long," she said. "I'll have supper ready in an hour or so." She knew that sometimes my talks with Old Coyote can get a little long.

I pushed open the squeaky gate and strolled up the walkway past the usual items in his yard: An eight-foot totem, a canoe, and a number of small pieces of cedar cut into sections, later to be made into whistles. I knocked a couple times and entered. The children were there to greet me in their loving way. Old Coyote and his wife, Rita, were in the living room. I joined them.

"What's up?"

"A lot!" Old Coyote explained. "In a few weeks a once-in-a-lifetime event will be taking place in South Dakota. The kind of event that will draw people from all corners of the world... The Most Sacred Pipe will be brought out!"

BOOK I

LEARNING THE DANCE

"Hoka Hey! Follow Me! Follow Me!
Today is a good day to fight,
today is a good day to die!"
Crazy Horse, June 1876

"Today is a good day to live!"
Tamara Lynn, June 1989

1. RAIN BUGS IN PARADISE
Dance Back the Rain

The temperature continued to rise on the that mid July day as we drove the long, straight, forever roads of South Dakota. Distinctive buttes dotted the vast horizon and identified this mystic land as the place of the Wakan Chanunpa, the most holy pipe. With me was Steven Old Coyote, a long time friend and Cree medicine man. His life was filled with the unique and the unbelievable. He had come from the wild horse races in White Swan, Washington to shovelhead Harleys of the motorcycle gangs of Oakland, from the ranch lands in bitter cold Montana to the skid row of inner-city Portland, Oregon. His progression had now taken him to the highly honored position of spiritual leader of the Suquamish nation. Old Coyote had brought his son, James, and I was accompanied by my eldest son, Jody.

Over the years of our friendship, Old Coyote has honored me with his good counsel, as well as with his special knowledge of nature and his infectious sense of humor. The most important thing that he shared with me was his medicine. I call him a man of energy: energy of family, of spirit, and of love for his and all cultures. Now he has guided me to this place, at this time, to share in the mystery that dwells in this quiet land. We had left Washington State some one thousand miles earlier as good and trusted friends. Little did we know that during our stay at Greengrass we would become even closer in friendship and in spirit.

On our way to Greengrass we made a detour to visit some relatives of James in Wambli, South Dakota. It was an enjoyable stay. We got in some needed rest. It would be in this remote little town that I would realize that this was indeed a journey of mystery.

Close to noon the next day, Old Coyote and I sat under a tree watching the boys play basketball. The dust, from the lack of rain, filled the bumpy basketball court. The boys didn't seem to care or even notice. I looked down at my feet and spotted a bug, and I recalled a story I had once heard about a medicine man who had brought on a fierce rainstorm by drawing from the power of nature through a black beetle with a yellow stripe down its back. Old Coyote had also spotted the bug and gently picked it up in his large, callused hand. Upon closer examination, I found that this bug was identical to the one described in the story: black with a yellow stripe down its back! It seemed strange that it should be here. I relayed the story of the storm maker to Old Coyote. He smiled and noted that he too had heard of and even seen such an event. I informed him that I was not sure in what manner the process was conducted.

He explained, "It's actually rather simple, but it must be done in a sincere way." The bug was looking for a way off its unfamiliar perch on Old Coyote's hand. He stopped it, gently rolled the bug onto its back, and said, "Here is how you pull the energy from this small bug."

He began to rub the belly of the unsuspecting bug. The bug jumped back onto its legs. Old Coyote, just as quickly, turned it over and continued the stroking. A thought came to me that Old Coyote was, in effect, creating an energy through the bug. I instinctively glanced skyward, and, to my surprise, I spotted a line of clouds on the western horizon that I had not noticed before! The ground where we sat looked like it had not seen a raindrop in at least a couple of months, maybe longer. I joked to old Coyote, "Looks like we might be in for a little rain!"

Old Coyote did not acknowledge my statement. He seemed to be consumed with the bug and its actions. Each time the bug would right itself, he would flip it and rub its belly. The sweat rolled off his face as the intensity increased! I looked toward the clouds in the west and saw dramatic changes. They were closer, darker, and had spread from the southern to the northern skyline. They moved across the sky like an army formation. I realized that Old Coyote was doing just what we had spoken of; he was bringing rain! Thoughts of coincidence crossed my mind but quickly dispersed as I watched the Cree's energy becoming visible. By this time the bug seemed to have swollen. You could actually feel its anger. Radiant heat and energy seemed to be emanating from Old Coyote. The ominous clouds had passed overhead now, blocking out the hot rays of the noonday sun.

"Coyote," I said softly, "it's happening!"

With this, he raised his head. The bug appeared to be near submission. Old Coyote peered, not at the clouds overhead, but at the air around him, as if he was sensing something strange in the atmosphere. He laughed a little and then, gently pinching the bug between his fingers and thumb, carefully placed it at his feet. The bug scurried quickly away, but the clouds remained, and before long I felt one raindrop, then another splatter on my forearm. Looking toward the basketball court, I could see little puffs of dust explode as the large drops plopped onto the dry ground. Within moments, the clouds opened up and the cool wet rain filled the physical atmosphere and our spiritual senses.

I heard one of the local boys yell, "Hey, it's raining!" The ball he had been holding fell to the ground as he took off toward a house calling, "Grandma, Grandma, it's raining!" The door on the house opened, and a woman leaned out, looking skyward.

"I'll be damned!" she exclaimed. "We been needin' this for a long time."

The rain was falling heavily now and more people made their way outside. I looked over to Old Coyote and he began to laugh. I could not help but join in. Soon we were roaring with laughter, our faces soaked in the joy of rain!

That afternoon we were on our way again, heading north for Greengrass. It had rained on and off all day. I glanced toward Old Coyote who sat in the passenger seat, a familiar smile on his face. It was like he was reading my mind. I thought to myself, amazing, simply amazing, those rain bugs in paradise.

2. DOWNTOWN GREENGRASS
Dance Back the Pipe

When we made the turn at Eagle Butte, we knew we were only a few miles from Greengrass. We had purposely arrived a couple of days early in order to prepare ourselves for this most special ceremony. Soon the pipe of legend would be brought out: the White Buffalo Calf Maiden pipe of the Lakota nation, and in spirit, of all nations!

Seven years had passed since the last time the pipe was used in ceremony. The pipe keeper felt at the time that it was necessary to do so for the protection and respect of that holy instrument. During that ceremony the Lakota came together and solemnly put the pipe away. It was now determined that the time and atmosphere were in order and the Lakota were again called to release the good energies of the sacred bundle.

Greengrass is actually too small to be called a town. It is more like a typical middle-of-nowhere Indian community. We first noticed a couple of houses on our immediate left, and what appeared to be HUD government homes farther up the hill. Soon we noticed the International sun dance arbor on our right and it did not take long to spot the local church up ahead. It was here, near the church, that we would find the dusty road leading to the place where the pipe ceremony would take place. We fell in behind three other cars.

After turning in our cameras and recording devices at the security checkpoint, we were allowed to enter the sacred grounds. Our group was among the first to arrive. I counted eight camping tents and three large teepees. It was easy to see that the grounds for the ceremony had received many blessings in the past; it was the location of the second sun dance grounds, where the annual ceremony took place each summer. It was a magnificent site, covering about 250 square yards and set within the natural protection of a horseshoe-shaped butte. An occasional clump of trees lent its green to the field, but overall, dry grass predominated. I could see three log cabins; two were about a half mile away, and the third was on a nearby ridge. This was the home of the pipe keeper, Arval Looking Horse. I knew very little about this man. He had been selected and trained as a young boy to one day receive the trust of the holy pipe. His grandmother, Lucy Looking Horse, was the previous keeper. Arval Looking Horse being the ninetieth keeper was now entrusted with the obligation of protecting this most sacred instrument of the spirit.

This land, so barren and uninviting, seemed to be the last place that a person would want to live. That the Indian nations of the land were long ago driven from their true homelands and made to live and die here is an all-too-familiar story. With the Indian people came the Indian spirit, however, and even though that spirit was mistreated and made to suffer, it is alive in the land today! So within this unforgiving, natural, and visible place, the supernatural dwells invisibly and remains protected.

Our preparation would consist of prayer, counsel, and the Inipi sweatlodge ceremony. The pipe keeper had already let it be known that all who wished to share in the event would have to be properly prepared. This included at least one sweatlodge ceremony and daily participation in the noon pipe ceremony. No one should ever presume to seek spiritual knowledge or enlightenment without a clear and purified mind and body to receive it. This requires the process of cleansing: cleansing in a spiritual way with sincere prayers, and in a physical way with the Inipi ceremony. This ceremony is an ancient practice that was given to the Indian people for the purpose of purification. Among the Lakota, its existence is sacred and it is one of their seven sacred rites. All people wishing to enter this ceremony should put aside any materialistic thoughts that would interfere with their abilities to focus on what is truly important. In such a station of surrender, one will be surrounded by the old ones and blessed by the Mystery.

3. RICK BIG BEAR'S SWEAT
Dance Back the Sweat

When we arrived it was nearly dusk. The fires for the sweats were burning brightly. We quickly set up our tent and camp gear. I counted five men's and three women's sweatlodges ready to go with people gathered at each of them. After the long day and night of travel, our first thought was to head for the sweats. The leader of our first sweat was a Lakota man named Rick Big Bear. He was in his thirties, a mountain of a man, standing at least six foot four and weighing at least 300 pounds. He carried with him a big, inviting smile, and it was easy to tell that he enjoyed the lighter side of life. A jolly, roaring laugh was always just around the corner of his next story. As we prepared to enter the sweat, he told us the first of many humorous stories that we would hear during our stay at Greengrass:

"You know, when I was a small boy, the elders would only let me learn a bit at a time about the sweatlodge. First I learned how to gather firewood, then how to collect the proper rocks, and later they let me work on the construction of the lodge. Eventually I was allowed to tend the rocks, under close guidance. I had two uncles who always got a kick out of watching me bust my butt learning. Once they both decided to participate in a sweat along with six or seven other men. It was a night sweat, a very dark one. The moon was in hiding, and there wasn't a star in the sky. While they were inside, I decided to have a little fun. I gathered together all their boots and shuffled them around. It was the funniest thing I'd ever seen, but my uncles didn't think so. I was lucky to get away that night! Ha!"

Rick Big Bear jumped right into another story. "Then there was the time I was sitting in a sweat and someone accidentally kicked a whole bucket of water onto about twenty-one red hot rocks. I headed for the door and some guy grabbed me by my arm and said I couldn't leave without permission of the sweat leader. I jerked my arm away from him and said, "Hey, I am the sweat leader!" Rick Big Bear's sweat was powerful and memorable. Energy and mystery floated all around the ceremony and the Lakota sweat leader generated a lot of heat to go along with his stories. At the completion of the sweat we returned to our campsite, where old Coyote began to work on something diligently. I asked, "What are you working on, Coyote?"

He held up his project. It was a bundle of hoka sage which he had braided into a circle about eight inches in diameter. It reminded me of a crown of honor worn by the sun dancers during that holy ceremony. "Very nice," I noted, not really sure of its purpose.

Old Coyote explained, "This will have a special place in our camp. A place of honor and love, for it will be the physical symbol of our honor and love, our wives Rita and Tammy. It will be a visible reminder of those women. Should we become weak in spirit, it will give us strength. Should we become lonely or sad, it will comfort us and make us happy." It made sense to me. When Old Coyote finished, he hung the braided sage over the entrance of our tent.

Another long and spirit-filled day and night was coming to an end. As I climbed into my sleeping bag, a tingly feeling of happiness entered my being. A good day to remember.

4. EAGLE DREAM

Dance Back the Dreams

It was during the first night's sleep that I experienced an unusual dream or vision. A great eagle came to me. His flight seemed very far away and I seemed very unimportant compared to him. Around his head were stars, or perhaps they were dancing lights. As I gazed in his direction, I began to feel dizzy. My eyes slowly closed, but I did not want to lose sight of the great bird, so I forced them back open. At that moment, I felt a great surge of power, as if I was being lifted into the sky. When my eyes were completely open, I saw the eagle again. This time he was directly in front of my face, no more than a foot away! At first I was afraid, but soon this feeling gave way to sensations of comfort and safety. As I watched him and he watched me, I saw a tear appear in his left eye. As I peered into the teardrop, I began to see the image of my wife, Tammy.

Around her head, but not touching it, was Old Coyote's braided sage. It looked like a glowing halo. As I gazed closer, I found myself being absorbed into that calm and peaceful place. I felt as though I was in a blue bubble, floating gently through the endless universe, my darling wife beside me. She seemed at ease in our dreamlike environment. I had no sensation of physical form or who I was. Where I was seemed to be my purpose. My sight wandered aimlessly in the sphere of blue. It seemed like hours had gone by, but when I woke, I realized it had only been half an hour. I lay in my bed roll, looking up at the circle of sage, thinking of Tammy and contemplating my incredible vision for some time. Then I went back to sleep.

5. "HEY YOU!"
Dance Back the Power

The next morning I woke to the sound of moving hooves. Flipping open the door flap of our tent, I peered out. There to greet me were about seven horses. They mingled among the tents as if they belonged there, and of course they did. I could see that a few more vehicles had arrived during the night, and a couple more were driving up the road. I knew that as the pipe day drew closer, more people would be coming from the four directions of the four sacred colors of humankind.

It must have been around 7:00 AM when I made my way toward the makeshift kitchen. I could not help but notice a rumbling of laughter coming from one of the tents along the way. It seemed that one of the campers had decided to leave his shoes outside beneath the awning of his tent. The problem was that some horses had also decided to utilize the convenient awning; they had stood under it during the night to keep the flies off their backs, and of course they had to relieve themselves a couple of times. Well, as the young man banged his shoes against a rock, angrily cursing the horses, a few of the others, including Rick Big Bear, were getting a real good laugh out of his frustration.

The elders had long been up. I inhaled the aromas of fresh buffalo steaks, eggs, biscuits, and two large pots of coffee. As I neared the coffee, I heard a yell: "Hey you!" I turned quickly to see who was getting yelled at and discovered it was me! One of the women, apparently the kitchen boss, beckoned to me. She stood about five feet tall and was about half that in width. She wore a long, homemade dress, and her gray-black hair hung in braids below her abundant waist. Her stance suggested she was capable of wrestling a bear into submission. When I was within reach, she handed me an ax and told me she needed wood for the cook stove. The subject did not seem to be open for discussion, and I went right to work. After I had been busting logs for about an hour, she came over and informed me I had cut enough for now and should have some breakfast. The sweat was still rolling off my forehead as I stood beside the stove pouring that first cup of coffee. A young man walked up beside me, said good morning, and reached for the coffee pot. I heard the familiar yell: "Hey you!" This time, fortunately, it was directed toward the young fellow who had just arrived. I knew then that one would always have to put some time into the kitchen duties in order to partake of the kitchen goods.

6. MICMACS IN SOUTH DAKOTA
Dance Back the Elder

As noon approached, the temperature neared 90 degrees. The Moreau River that snaked through the reservation at Greengrass was only about a half mile from our camp, and our sons, Jody and James, had already made their way to the coolness of the river. Old Coyote and I mingled among the campers, found some old friends, and made a few new ones. The largest lodge in the camp was about twenty feet high. It appeared to be the home of two, maybe three, families. I determined by their auto tags that they were from New Brunswick and Nova Scotia, Canada. Excitement moved inside me, for I knew they might be of the Micmac nation, my father's people. In time, I announced myself at their door. From within I heard the words that told me I was indeed at the lodge of a Micmac: "Come to the front of our lodge and be welcomed!" These words are the traditional Micmac greeting.

In a respectful way I entered and introduced myself to the families. I was greeted warmly by all present and offered coffee and a place to sit. The interior of the lodge was set up in typical contemporary Indian style. Mats and rolled up sleeping bags lined the western side. On the northern side was a small cooking area. A two burner Coleman stove was set atop a rickety-legged fold-up card table. On the south side were some trunks and suitcases. Throughout the lodge were low, legless lounge chairs and sitting mats. Our conversation was light and pleasant. I observed a man sleeping near the back of the lodge whom I presumed was the family elder. Soon he woke and turned in my direction. I stood up to greet him, and his wife introduced us to each other. His name was Sam Bald Eagle. His eyes of many winters told of his wisdom. His deep baritone voice was strong and clear. He looked into my heart with a smile and spoke his first words to me: "I have been waiting for you. I am glad you have finally come!"

Sam Bald Eagle's aged face was familiar to me, as though we had met before. His leisurely style was highlighted by his loosely fitting jeans and gray flannel shirt. He wore a beautiful necklace of red, blue, and white stones. Strangely, his hair was cut short. Soon his son and grandson entered the lodge and joined in our conversation. They too were dressed leisurely, but their hair was very long and in braids. Bald Eagle spoke: "You know, a little less than two years ago my hair was very long. Last year in August my hair was completely gone! But that is not why I received my name, Bald Eagle!" That got a laugh out of us all. He continued, "I had cancer and was required to go through all kinds of Chemo and radiation treatments. It left me clean as a cue ball on top! After we were done the doctors told me that chances were not very good. I laughed in their faces! I knew I had another way to rid myself of this illness. That was through prayers and the sweatlodge!" He poured himself a cup of coffee and continued, "Those fancy doctors think in a very limited way. They make their decisions on what has actually been done, not on what can be done. They look one direction and we look four directions. The sweats have given me new life and I have never felt so good about life! The medicine was there, the doctors were there, the cancer was there. It's very easy to believe in those things because you can see them and touch them. The care of a family is also there, the power of the sweatlodge is there, and the love of God is there. These things you can't see or touch. You must simply believe in your heart and you will be healed! This I tell you Little Eagle, because it is true!"

I was not sure why the elder had decided to tell me his story; it was not for me to question, but to listen and remember. Over the remainder of my time at Greengrass I would become very close to this man and his family, my relations! It would be through our conversations and shared Inipi ceremonies that I would learn more about my Micmac heritage.

7. COUNCIL TREE
Dance Back the Counsel

There was a big cottonwood tree near the center of the camp. I could tell that the elders had already laid claim to its shade for a council area and gathering place. This tree would become the center for the old stories and legends that would fill the hot days and long nights of our stay. Thoughts ran through my mind as to what this old tree had seen and heard over the years in this sacred place: What stories could it tell of its mystic history, of the loves, the battles, the victories, the surrenders, and the resurrections that had taken place under its branches?

By noon, many people had gathered around the council tree. A number of elders and medicine men were speaking among themselves. Most of the conversations were in the Lakota language. I knew the pipe keeper was among the men, but which one was he? After a while, a tall, lanky man in his mid-thirties stood up. He looked at the ground for a moment, then pushed his black rimmed glasses off his nose and said in a mild voice, "Hello everyone. I am Arval Looking Horse. Please be welcome to this place and make yourselves at home."

At first, he did not fit my ideal image of the person who should have the great and honorable duty of being trusted to carry the most sacred pipe. But there he was with his black hair hanging loose on his wide shoulders and wearing western style clothes: a large-brimmed cowboy hat with a single eagle feather hanging off the left side, and a well-used pair of pointy black boots he used to kick the dirt around as he talked. Even though he appeared to be a simple man, he was of great importance to the Indian people. He was the one chosen to take care of the most sacred of pipes. That holy pipe has always been kept within families of the same bloodline. Each keeper has dedicated his or her life to its well-being, and at some point has been given a vision identifying the next pipe keeper. Before Arval Looking Horse, his grandmother, Lucy Looking Horse, was the keeper. It was her vision that selected a young twelve-year-old boy to be her successor. Arval Looking Horse was set aside from the other children in order to receive training in the many aspects of the pipe. He not only learned the history and legends of the pipe, but was taught the discipline and responsibilities of his exalted station. Along with his grandmother, many elders and medicine men taught the young man, including his father, Stanley Looking Horse, whose knowledge and wisdom were of the greatest importance to the new pipe keeper. Now, for the first time in his life, Arval Looking Horse was given complete responsibility for the pipe. It would be his decision when, where, and how the pipe would be presented. With that authority, he called for this great gathering to bring out the buffalo robe bundle that contained the sacred pipe.

On this particular day he instructed everyone to make a large circle. We moved into position, and more people began to show up. In all, about sixty people joined in. The purpose, Looking Horse explained, was to offer the noontime prayers and to smoke, not the Buffalo Calf pipe, but his personal pipe. A stillness settled over the grounds as the pipe keeper sat down in the center of the circle. He prepared and loaded his pipe in the old and proper way, then offered tobacco prayers to the four directions and to Father Sky and Mother Earth. Once he had lit the pipe, he wrapped it in sage and gave it to his assistant, who in turn delivered it to the person at the easternmost position in the circle. It was then passed clockwise, and each person accepted it in due form, said personal prayers, smoked, and passed it along. Once the pipe had returned to the pipe keeper, he carefully cleaned it and emptied the bowl of any remaining tobacco. When this was done, he once again said prayers and then separated the bowl from the stem. A collective "Hau!" sounded from the participants, completing this noontime prayer ceremony.

8. FIRST SWEAT

Dance Back My Son

The sweats had been going strong all morning and into the afternoon. Once again we participated, and again our sweat was powered by the Creator's breath. The leader of the sweat was a Lakota elder. As I prepared to enter, my son Jody joined me. His presence made the ceremony even more significant, for it was his first Inipi, a young boy's step into manhood. I initially had some concern as to the effect of the sweat on him. In most cases, a sweat is never hotter than the newest person can stand, but our sweat leader could only speak Lakota. I asked my son if he was truly prepared to take such a step. He confidently nodded his head. Once inside, he sat at my right. At least ten others joined us. The sweat leader called quickly for the rocks. The heat began to rise as the door was closed and the elder poured water again and again on the glowing red rocks. I prayed deeply for my son's protection. Occasionally I would pat his knee, and he would in turn acknowledge me by resting his hand on mine. The heat continued to increase. Hotter and hotter it became until I felt close to giving up! I prayed for strength and stamina to help us both through the powerful sweat. It was during the intense heat that I felt my son's hand rest on my knee, there to comfort my concerns. I realized there were no more rocks or water to be brought to this sweat. It was as if the sweat leader knew of the new one in his presence. He ordered the door opened and in the steam and semi-darkness, I saw my son sitting tall and straight. He had succeeded and taken a step into manhood. I would look upon him as more than a son; he was now a brother as well.

Outside the lodge, our bodies and spirits settled down, and I asked Jody how he felt. He said he felt fine, was impressed by the ceremony, and was glad I was with him. He then looked across toward Sam Bald Eagle and their eyes met and they smiled. It was not until then that I realized Bald Eagle had been in the lodge with us sitting to Jody's right. It was as if he had been sent to help the young Micmac in his first sweat. I approached the elder and offered my hand in thanks. He readily accepted and noted that Jody had done very well for such a young man. I then invited him to our campsite for something to drink. The invitation pleased him and we all started in that direction. Sam Bald Eagle's pace was easygoing.

9. SAM BALD EAGLE'S COUNSEL

Dance Back the Micmac

Once settled at the camp, Jody opened our iceless ice-chest and produced a couple of sodas. Bald Eagle declined and asked for water instead. Jody obliged and poured us each a cup.

As we relaxed I respectfully asked Bald Eagle if I might ask him a question. He nodded in the affirmative. "I have heard much," I said, "of the Micmac hero, or should I say legend, who was known as Glouscap." Bald Eagle seemed a little shocked by my opening statement. He raised his head and his smile seemed to fade away. It was as if I had mentioned a long lost relative. I continued, "Could you tell me a bit about him?"

"Maybe...," he said in a protective way. "First I'd like to know what you know about Glouscap."

"Sure," I replied, "but it won't take long. All I know is the little bit I've read and the few stories my grandmother, Lucy Charles, told me as a child." Sam Bald Eagle listened attentively as I continued. "From that information I would call him a trickster. He possessed many powers, such as the power to change his appearance. He was very much like the coyote trickster of the Plains Indians." Jody filled Bald Eagle's cup with more water. "My beloved grandmother would gather her grandchildren around in the evenings and tell us stories about the adventures and antics of Glouscap. She would tell us about the difficult times the Micmacs had in their dealings with the trickster. Sometimes he would be very mean, and at other times he would be very kind." I paused for a moment, trying to group together my next thought. "My grandmother told me stories of his magical powers. I remember some of them, but unfortunately not in proper detail."

"Uh huh," Bald Eagle answered. "That's to be expected. As children we are told children's stories, not so much to remember them in absolute detail, but just for the fun of it. In youth we are taught the lessons and histories of the stories. In addition, we are also expected to learn and remember these stories. As adults we are taught more than the stories. We are expected to learn the pure essence and spirit of our heritage." Bald Eagle tapped his chest with his finger and continued, "We are required to absorb and keep them here." He then slowly pointed his finger to his head, "and here too!"

Bald Eagle sat quietly for a moment, then continued. "As elders, we are obligated to teach those who wish to learn. Whether it be a children's story or an adult's, the traditions and stories must go on!" Bald Eagle looked directly at me. "Do you understand?"

"Yes," I replied and nodded. Bald Eagle seemed happy with my answer. He looked toward Jody. "How about you young man?"

"I think so," Jody replied, "but I don't quite understand why elders of today are so often mistreated. Most people avoid them or don't let them speak. Why is this, Mr. Bald Eagle?"

"Call me Sam, young fella." Jody acknowledged his instruction and Sam Bald Eagle continued. "It is because of this modern society that the elders are treated this way. The ones who are the perpetrators of this wrongdoing will one day become the victims themselves. The ones who help, listen, and are kind to the elders are the ones that will be blessed." Pointing to the sky, Bald Eagle finished his statement, "Blessed by the Creator himself."

Jody sat quietly Bald Eagle continued his lesson to ensure that the young man had understood. "It is like this." Bald Eagle held up his dark, well-callused hand, fingers wide and extended. Then with the other hand he pointed at the first. "This represents the story of man." Pointing out the four fingers he continued, "and these are the four stages of a man's life." Then starting with the fourth, pinkie finger, he began his counsel. "This first one is infancy and early childhood. In this stage, we are completely helpless and totally dependent upon our parents. Now," he said, selecting the next finger in line, "this finger represents the next stage in life, that is, adolescence or young adulthood. Now we are more responsible, able to distinguish harm from what benefits, good from bad, right from wrong. We can think for ourselves, and protect ourselves." Looking at Jody more intensely, Bald Eagle noted, "This is your present level in life. If we do our work as good as we can at this level, then we will move on to the next level." He then pointed to the large middle finger. "Here we come to the next stage, manhood, a most important and fulfilling stage. We become the protectors of the little ones, the leaders of our families. We become the eagle that builds the nest!" Directing his attention to the next finger, he continued, "This is the elders' stage of life. We are no longer tall and strong as before. Our years on this earth have taken their toll on our bodies. It is only natural. It is our time to rest and reap the seeds we have planted in our lives. We become the guiding lights of wisdom in our families. And if things are in proper order and we have lived a good life, done the best we can, we then move on to the greatest stage." He now spoke with more intensity in his voice. "Listen closely!" He held his thumb in an upward direction. "This, my son, represents God, our Creator!" He hesitated momentarily then continued. "This is the ultimate and supreme level that all men strive to grow closer to!" He touched the thumb to the fourth finger, making an O shape. "As you can see, the elder is closest to the holy realm. It is he to whom the Creator has given the most power." Bald Eagle moved his thumb down the rest of the fingers: "God can touch and assist us at all our growing levels, but it is close to the elders that he makes his home." Smiling at Jody, he asked, "Do you know why our elders are so important?"

"Yes," Jody said confidently, "I do. I understand what you mean."

I, too, understood the elder's message. This was one of those adult lessons to learn and remember, not only for my son, but for myself as well. I pointed out, "Sam, I was taken away from my family stories as a very young boy and, unfortunately, I was never taught those more important family lessons."

"Uh huh, I know what you mean. You must always remember that those childhood stories are important also. Our Micmac hero was much more than a mere trickster." Bald Eagle hesitated, looked cautiously over his shoulder, and said, "This is not the proper time or place to tell you the complete story of Glouscap. It is something that would take a very long time to properly explain. I will tell you this...Glouscap was also known as a prophet of the Micmac!"

I was stunned and amazed at his statement. A prophet! Bald Eagle continued, "That is the adult story. Glouscap came to the Micmac people in a holy way. He walked among our ancestors in the same fashion that the white man's prophet did with their ancestors. It is believed that the two were one in spirit."

"When I was old enough," Bald Eagle continued, "my father taught me the proper way to set and prepare a trap. In time, he gave me my first knife, and with that gift he also gave instructions on how to use it without harming myself or anyone else. As I grew older and more mature, he gave me his prized rifle and allowed me to hunt on my own. As I progressed in life, I was taught more and given more of the tools of life that would be of use to me. At some point he began to take me to the ceremonies, and eventually he gifted me with the counsel of spirit. That is when I truly felt I had moved beyond childhood. He spoke to me of God and the spirit world." Bald Eagle handed his emptied cup back to Jody and smiled at him, then at me. "So I say to you, when the child is ready to learn, the teacher will come."

It was during the late afternoon of the second day that I discovered work going on near the pipe keeper's cabin. I found out that they were in the process of building a new pipe house for the most great pipe. It was to be a six-sided cabin made completely of logs and having one main entrance. Six carpenters were hard at work completing the base. I could not imagine them finishing the project in time for the final ceremony, but something told me not to worry. This was a spiritual undertaking and the Spirit would ensure that the work would be done.

10. OLD COYOTE AND THE KITCHEN BOSS
Dance Back the Heat

Later that day I was lounging around our campsite when I caught a view of Old Coyote making his way toward me. He was returning from the kitchen. As he drew closer I could see his face with a half smile on it. His shirt was completely soaked through with sweat. He finally sort of rolled to the ground beside me. I asked, "Coyot', what in the world you been doing?"

"We got any water around here?" he asked. I poured him a big cup of nearly cool water and he quickly drank it down. He then answered my question: "You won't believe it. I ran into the toughest elder lady I've ever met in my life!"

Now it began to dawn on me. He must have met the kitchen boss.

"I just finished cutting up two cows and a buffalo!"

"Holy mackerel!" I exclaimed. "No wonder you were gone most of the day!" I looked at his hands and saw them bleeding. I asked, "By yourself, with no one to help?"

Old Coyote sat for a moment then gave out a good laugh. "No, actually the elder did ask me if I needed some help."

"Oh yeah!?" I acknowledged.

"Yeah, she came over to me when I was about half way through with the second cow and took my knife. A few minutes later she brought it back to me and said, 'There I sharpened it up for you, that should help you! Now get back to work!'"

I laughed with Old Coyote as I realized what help she had provided.

11. THE CHANGING PIPE
Dance Back the Legends

That evening the elders called for all who wished to hear the old stories to gather at the council tree. These wonderful stories and legends went on for most of the night. Such fire and excitement as I had never experienced flowed from these storytellers as they sang their legends and relived their histories.

Of the many stories I can recall, there was one concerning the changing pipe. The elder spoke broken English but easily conveyed his message. He talked of the pipe as seen by his grandfather.

"It was very, very large." He gestured with his arms, indicating at least five feet in length. "The bowl of the pipe was as large as this child's head." He pointed to a small baby in his mother's arms. "Over many years the pipe has been the spirit of our people. When we are in a good spirit, the pipe is also in a good spirit." He stopped for a moment as if to listen to our thoughts. "Now, these are bad years. Man is pitted against man, brother against brother. This has brought a sadness into our lives. The alcohol has drained us of spiritual life. We are a dying people! The sacred pipe has also felt these bad times and is suffering too. The abuse of Indian by Indian is having a terrible effect on the pipe. Today, the pipe is much smaller in its physical size." He gestured with his arms, making a shrinking motion. "In time, it could simply disappear!" He stopped once again, and then pointed up the hill in the direction of the sacred pipe. He spoke passionately: "The pipe is our life, our hope! The outside world cannot understand why it's our life, but it is! We must do whatever is necessary to save it, and it will thereby save us."

"I have traveled to Rapid City and have seen the pipes, our sacred pipes, for sale in the drug stores, gas stations, and even the saloons. This is wrong! You cannot sell the air because the air is a gift from the Creator. You cannot sell the pipe for the same reason. It is against God!"

An anger rose in his voice and showed in his eyes as he continued: "The federal government lays claim to the pipe quarries of Minnesota, but they do not properly take care of this spiritual place. They allow people from foreign lands to buy the pipestone, people who don't understand its spiritual purpose! The pipe is not a wall ornament to show off to your friends. When placed in the proper hands and used in a proper way, it is a giving power. It's a power of guidance, a power of love, a power of peace, and, yes, a power of war, if necessary. But the most important power the pipe possesses is the power of healing! You must spread the word to your people that these pipes are Indian in spirit and should not be abused! You should not buy the pipe." He paused briefly, looking through the silent crowd. "No one should buy the pipe! In time, when you are ready, the pipe will find its way to you in the form of a gift. Be patient!"

"The Indian people were given the responsibility of the pipe and that also means the place where we obtain our sacred red stone. It is now called Pipestone National Park. The grounds are treated like all national parks. Anyone who pays the entry fee can roam freely through the sacred quarries. This is not a national park, my brothers and sisters. This holy ground was given to us by the Creator himself! Use of this land should be restricted and approached only when necessary and only by Indian people as it was in the past! This place has forever been the sacred grounds of Indian people for as long as our traditions are old. That is, until about one hundred years ago, when our people were manipulated into giving up this sacred ground. This is a trick familiar to Indian people. Now that the injustice has been legally and publicly recognized, it is our sacred obligation to do whatever is needed to bring this holy land back to our people."

The elder then pointed to another man sitting on the ground near him. "My brother, my friend, Billy Yellow Hawk, is a Yankton Sioux, and it was his people who were victimized by the greedy railroad companies, local and national politicians, as well as the so-called Supreme Court. He has a story to tell you, so pay attention."

12. LAND OF EYANSKA

Dance Back the Quarries

When Billy Yellow Hawk rose I could see that he was a young man in his mid-twenties. A red flannel shirt covered his large chest. His braids hung down his front. A small, well-used, beaded leather pouch hung from around his neck. When he spoke it was with a unique gentleness. I listened carefully.

"Hello, my friends. I have come here to this special ceremony for the same reason as most everyone else. I have also come here to share a sacred secret of our land, the Land of Eyanska, the red stone! Too often people look at this place as a political arena or a mere campground for the tourist to visit. The spirit being that brought the first Indian to this sacred ground still lives in that place today! This spirit is known to us as Wa-Root-Ka, or Spirit Woman. This spirit and others are the guardians of the sacred quarry and are still on the guard. This powerful and blessed land has served as a refuge to Indian people from all over the great Turtle Island, also known as North America. When Indian people came to this place, they considered their journey a sacred pilgrimage in the same way that the Christian goes to Israel, their holy land. In our tradition, the quarry is the place where Wakan Tanka created the first Indian people! It was here that their ceremony was performed. The medicine man would prepare an offering of tobacco. No man dared to bring any form of weapon to this place! All knives, arrows, and clubs were actually buried at a distance from the quarries. A divine and strict peace was always in order at this place. Even your worst enemy would share, in peace, this place with you. The waters that ran through the quarry were also a source of energy and spirit. The men would cleanse themselves before proceeding. The medicine man, who was always in the lead, would make his offerings along the trail and at predetermined locations. He would also make other offerings of valuable items. He would then offer up his most solemn and sincere prayers. At the completion of this portion of the ceremony, they would make camp on the prairie in hopes that the offerings were pleasantly accepted by the guardian spirits. A reverent silence was observed through the night. This was done in respect for the ceremony and in hopes of hearing Wa-Root-Ka doing her sacred engraving on the red stones. Sparks were often seen dancing upward into the dark, starry skies.

"At sunrise the men once again approached the quarry trails to find their offerings gone and a sign or sacred symbol engraved at that location. If found, the group then understood that they had been given permission to enter. The medicine man would once again lead the party into the quarries. With sacred song and prayer, he would designate the exact point where the men should dig. The men would quickly and respectfully go to work. Word would go back to the camp, and the women and children were then allowed to join the men and watch the dig. Once the proper amount of red rock was collected, the medicine man would lead the party back to the camp and eventually back to their homeland. Oftentimes great celebrations and feasts were held in honor of the groups when they returned.

"This is the story of how the pipestone was collected and the reverence with which this process was conducted. I will now tell you how the sacred pipestone quarries were introduced to the Indian people.

"Many thousands of years ago, Wakan Tanka took the form of a spirit bird to see how his creation was doing. The sacred bird flew across this Turtle Island and observed many things. Some things he observed were good, but unfortunately most were bad. War and hate had come to his people. Everywhere that the holy bird flew he witnessed battles and conflicts. Nowhere could he find a place where peace and harmony prevailed. At the end of his journey, Wanka Tanka returned to his unknown but holy place to contemplate the things he had seen.

"He was very sad that so much hate poisoned the land. He decided to return to the earth in his spirit form. He then called all the Indian nations together. He stood high on the great plains and reached down into the Earth Mother and broke off a piece of red rock and said to the nations, 'Behold what you see in my hand!' The many people were very surprised at the strange looking rock that the Creator had produced. 'This red rock is sacred.' With that, he began to roll it in his powerful hands until it became a very large pipe bowl. 'The color of the pipe was made from the blood that you have spilled upon my land!' An uneasiness began to rattle through the people. Even fear! The Creator continued, 'It is through your hate and war that you see this object. It is now time to end these bad ways! The Creator waved his powerful hand over the bowl and then a pipe stem appeared from the bowl forming the first pipe of the people, and from it came the first whiffs of smoke. He blew the smoke over and through the people. Then to the north, the east, the south, and the west. The spirit smoke penetrated their very beings, seeping deep into their souls. A gentle peace had been made. The Creator continued, 'This red stone is your flesh and blood. It is your family. It shall be known to all nations far and near to this place that this land is a land of sacred peace!' With this the Holy One waved his arms over the land and all the weapons that had been brought on the land that day were gone! He spoke again: 'This is my instruction to you and to all your families now and forever.' At last the Creator took a final puff from the pipe, and he disappeared into a great white cloud. The entire surface where he'd been standing had melted and glazed for several miles. A great opening appeared and from it approached a holy woman. She too then melted into the great prairie. It is this spirit woman whose counsel is sought by our medicine men, even today. The voice of the spirits can be heard from the silver waters of the falls gushing from the center of the quarries. It is by them, in a spiritual way, that the quarry is protected, and it is by you, in a physical way, that the quarry is protected. It is our responsibility to respect and protect this place. The pipestone quarries must be returned to the hands of the Indian people. Take this message back to your families and peoples. No one else will do it for you! Thank you."

13. PIPE BAG VISITS

Dance Back the Pipe Bag

The third day began with the sound of a voice outside our tent. "We need help with the rocks. Can you come?" We all decided to help. Those morning sweats were very powerful; the rocks were especially hot! After working two sweats as a rock man, I felt it was time to partake in my third sweat since arriving at Greengrass. I made my way to the next available lodge and joined the others who were awaiting the arrival of the sweat leader. During my wait, I began to realize that this was a very special group I was with. They were mostly sun dancers; scars of sacrifice adorned their chests and backs. Their arms were covered with signs of the many flesh offerings they had made. Things began to stir as a 1967 Ford pickup pulled up and the man who would lead our sweat stepped out.

It was none other than the pipe keeper, Arval Looking Horse. A rush of excitement moved through my body. I wondered if I was worthy. Was I strong enough for this most honored ceremony? I did not have the answers but soon found myself wrapped in the darkness of the sweatlodge.

The pipe keeper was in deep prayer and the others were chanting or singing softly. Invisible energies were moving around me. I could feel the heat as Arval Looking Horse began to pour the water onto the rocks. On and on he poured. Hotter and hotter it became. I was near to breakdown when I decided to say my prayers. I placed a small piece of sage under my tongue to help with the heat. By this time, others within the lodge were also feeling the heat. Cries of sacrifice filled the lodge. It was during this intense moment that the image of Crazy Horse's pipe bag suddenly appeared in my thoughts. My eyes and nose were burning with the heat, the sweat rolled off my body, and still the pipe keeper poured on more water. As the rocks sizzled, I became consumed by the powerful ritual. The pipe bag was still in my thoughts, in my hands! I prayed. Suddenly, the heat was gone! I could still hear the voices of the other participants, but they seemed far away. I felt my spirit floating freely within the lodge, the sacred pipe bag firmly in my hands. From above, I could see the sweat, the rocks, the water, and Arval Looking Horse. I felt as though I was leaving this place for the spirit world and that it was proper. The next moment I felt the presence of many others around me. They were from the other side, the spirit world. I could feel what I thought was my mother and the presence of a little girl playing joyfully around me, touching my head, my back. It seemed as though words were floating around me, but I could not understand them. The words were in Lakota, Micmac, and English but unintelligible. Young voices, old voices, male and female voices. After awhile the voices all seemed to blend together. I became at ease with my environment. I felt I was ready for whatever was to happen. Just as I was at what seemed to be the point of no return, the strong voice of Arval Looking Horse reached in and brought me back to the lodge and the physical world. "Mitakuye Oyasin! Open the door!" he exclaimed, and the cool air of the morning entered the lodge.

The ceremony was over, and we all sat outside taking in the morning's coolness. The pipe keeper approached me. I started to stand, and he waved at me to remain seated. He then sat next to me and, not looking at me, said, "The sweat, it was powerful! I felt the presence of many." I just nodded in affirmation and he continued, "It is good!" He then got back to his feet and walked away. I felt again the special purpose of the sweatlodge and especially of this one.

Later on that morning I spoke to my friend and counselor, Steven Old Coyote, about my Inipi vision. Once I finished, he sat deep in thought for a moment, then startled me with the revelation that the pipe bag of the vision would soon be coming to me, and that it would bring a healing strength to my life. I asked him what kind of healing I would need. He did not know, but said the need would be there, and I would know it when the time came. He believed that the sacred pipe bag would be brought to this place, and here it would be united with the most holy pipe. When the pipe bag had completed its purpose outside the Lakota nation, it would find its way to this place and, in sacred ceremony, would be placed in the good and proper hands of the pipe keeper. These words concerned me for a number of reasons: my worthiness, my readiness, and primarily because the pipe bag of my vision was in the safe keeping of my father-in-law, Vinson Brown, and I had no reason to believe that it would not remain so for many years to come.

14. WAMBLI COMES TO GREENGRASS

Dance Back the Eagle

By the time of the noon pipe ceremony, many more people had arrived, and I could see that they were not limited to Indian people. All the sacred colors of humankind were represented, and still more cars were coming. The word went out that more sweatlodges were needed to accommodate the ever increasing number of people: more wood for the fires, more rocks for the sweats, more blankets and tarps for the coverings. There was work to be done! Different groups went in different directions to do what was needed. Jody and James went with the rock collectors. Old Coyote and I hopped aboard the firewood truck. Firewood was a rarity in these parts. You had to look long and hard to find that precious commodity. There were about six of us in the back of an old pickup, rumbling and tumbling over the roadless hills and buttes of Greengrass.

We had driven about five miles into the wilderness of the prairie before we made our first stop. Two large cottonwood trees were lying on the ground. The chainsaw made quick work of both of them. After loading them up, we were once again on our way. The jerking motion of the truck made me think about the land once again and the first natives to move here. If hearts could cry, I am sure they would have then. There were a couple more firewood stops along the route, but we eventually made it back to the camp, unloaded our bounty, and were off again.

It was during the third trip out that we went to the cabin of the pipe keeper's parents, Stanley and Celia Looking Horse. The elder, Stanley, waved us to stop and then in his native language instructed us to take a load from his winter stock of firewood. We began to load up. As I tossed the wood into the truck, Old Coyote was right beside me. He gave out a yip, and I thought he had come across a rattler. I looked at what he was seeing and discovered it was a yellow striped beetle! My thoughts quickly jumped back to the rainy day in Wambli. Old Coyote and I stood for a moment, then slowly looked at each other and almost in harmony said, "Naaa!" We both laughed at our thoughts.

After returning to the camp area with our third load of wood, we stopped for a break and a drink of cool water. Old Coyote headed over to where the lodges were being built. I sat and relaxed for a while. It was during this relaxing time that the Great Spirit, in the form of a Wambli eagle, visited our gathering place. It was magnificent! With at least an eight foot wing span, its white crown and distinctive tail feathers showed brightly against the clear blue sky. I was stunned! Never before had I seen such a powerful creature. I pointed but could not speak. The great bird circled low over the new sweatlodges where Old Coyote and other men were hard at work. Then it circled over a group of playing children that included Jody and James. All the kids stopped and looked in amazement in the direction of the eagle. After viewing the area, the great bird gave one mighty flap of its wings and disappeared over a butte. I stood gazing into the sky where it had departed, and I gestured in honor. Then I looked toward the council tree to see if anyone else had noticed the eagle's visitation. They had indeed! I saw elders on their knees, arms raised in supplication. Others had tears flowing down their faces. One elder woman held a small child up to the sky as she sang a soft prayer. The child had received a powerful blessing, as did we all.

In my dreams I had seen this great bird of power and peace! Such an eagle would be able to see a fly on a lodgepole from the highest cloud; yet it had come to be seen, not just to see. It had come to bless this special gathering. The stars were the human beings that had come to dance in rhythm with the sacred pipe.

During the evening of that third night, a drum was brought out and singers gathered to offer their prayers in true and ancient form. Some of the Indian nations' most famous singers and drummers had come to this place, and they had brought their magic. The mystical heartbeat of all Indian people moved through the cool night air, bringing with it a peace that was soothing to the soul.

15. GATHERING SONGS

Dance Back the People

The fourth morning began with familiar sounds and sights. Fires were burning brightly for the sweats, horses shuffled about awaiting morning snacks, and the kitchen boss was giving instructions to all within hearing range. As I made my way into the beautiful day, I discovered that still more autos had come into the camp overnight. They came from Florida, North Dakota, Minnesota, Oregon, Utah, California, and Ontario and New Brunswick, Canada. People even came from Mexico and Europe! The importance of this event was evident in the growing number of participants and in the atmosphere of each new sunrise. You could look into the faces of the people and see that this ceremony was of much greater importance that an ordinary pow-wow. The reason for their incredible interest was simple: Wakan Chanunpa, the most holy and mystic pipe, was calling. Having been brought out for the first time in seven years for this sacred ceremony, the pipe was very much alive and filled with the overwhelming beauty and majesty of the Creator. It is a symbol that holds the hearts and souls of the Indian people, especially those of the Lakota nation, for the Lakota were given the task of its safekeeping, and thereby they are blessed by its presence. It is, without doubt, the most holy object held by the Indian people on this good earth, a pure and beautiful symbol of a pure and beautiful religion. It is said that the pipe has given the gift of sunrise to the blind, the song of birds to the deaf, wisdom to the ignorant, and life to the lifeless. Such a precious heritage links our troubled present to the spirit of a time past when we lived in harmony with the earth and in tune with the Creator. Through this holy instrument a spirit flows that we all can share, helping us to gain wisdom and leading to an enlightened time in the future. A peace is yet to be.

16. GIVE AWAY

Dance Back the Dead

The morning hours went by quickly, and on this day we were all honored by participating in a special ceremony called the "give-away." One of the elders who was very important to the local community had passed on to the other side, and in the tradition of the Indian people, a give-away was conducted by his family. During this ceremony, as an exhibition of love and respect, all the person's earthly belongings are given away. Among the elder's many articles were some clothes, furniture, a television, a camera, a radio, blankets, farm tools, two milk cows, three horses, and an old Chevy pickup. Everything went! It is believed that to hold on to the material possessions of a departed one is to hold on to the person's spirit. To release these things is to release that special person from the bonds of the earthly realm. This brings solace to his or her family. It is an expression of genuine generosity, but even more an expression of love and respect for the departed one. In addition, the traveling one's earthly name is never used again within the household. He or she is given a new and holy name known only by the family.

17. OLD COYOTE'S VISION
Dance Back the Vision

In the late afternoon I went for a walk along the Moreau River's muddy twists and turns. Along the river were campsites, sweatlodges, and another kitchen area. I realized that there must be close to a thousand people here!

When I returned I saw Old Coyote sitting pensively at our campsite. I could tell he had something on his mind. I sat down also and after a little while, I asked him if he would like to share his thoughts. He told me that he had just received a vision of special significance. He spoke of a hole appearing between the sun dance arbor and the council tree. From this mystic hole emerged a flock of beautiful white birds that flew to the north, then a flock of red birds that flew to the east, followed by a flock of yellow birds that flew to the south, and lastly a flock of black birds that flew to the west. Later he spoke to one of the Lakota medicine men about his vision. He was told that the birds were a sign of the returning of White Buffalo Calf Maiden as prophesied by the holy woman herself when she first brought the pipe to the Lakota.

18. MINGLING SPIRITS
Dance Back the Chiefs

There was an especially large gathering at the council tree that evening. One of the elders spoke through a translator. He said that this was the twentieth such pipe ceremony over the past fifty years that he could recall. He also spoke with reverence of the many medicine men and tribal leaders who had come to these sacred grounds for nearly 200 years for this ceremony: "Just as we have done today, so did leaders such as Fools Crow, Black Elk, Horn Chips, Hump, Gall,

Sitting Bull, and Crazy Horse." He mentioned many more names, some of which I recognized and some I did not.

Once he motioned with his arm across the crowd, saying that there were many medicine people here now. "The spirits of the living are mingled with the spirits of the ancestors."

The elder spoke of how easy it is to see the kind and good hearts of true medicine people as well as to see the ones who are untrue, or "backwards," whose desires and hopes are for themselves, not for their people or even their own families. They use their "little medicine" to line their own pockets and this, he said, is wrong and frowned upon by the Creator. The backward ones see medicine as a part-time job that is done whenever they feel like doing it. He pointed out that "medicine is a full-time job that must be done every minute of every day. It is not easy work, but it is good work." The backward ones will fall away "like snake skins and the good ones will grow stronger and more powerful like the council tree we stand beneath." He went on to speak of the understanding that would come from this gathering. He spoke of the many old friends he had seen again and the many new ones he had come to know over the past week. He was elated, and created an excitement in us all. Stories of the pipe went on all night. I listened to them all, as did many others.

19. CALF PIPE STORY
Dance Back the Holy Woman

Before the next person stepped up to tell the most important story of the evening, another man addressed the gathering. There was great pride in his voice as he began to introduce the next speaker and his subject: "The stories of the holy pipe have been passed down through the voices of our elders. Some of the unknowing ones called the story a mere myth; others have recognized it for what it is, a miracle, and a miracle of the same degree as the Ten Commandments or the turning of water into wine. The pipe and its existence have, without doubt, remained a most secret subject. Even the location of the pipe was for many years kept quiet. Only a chosen few have known. These precautions were necessary not only to protect its physical being but its spiritual essence as well. In recent years, with the Freedom of Religion Act and a general acceptance and respect by more people toward Indian beliefs and customs, we have become more open about the sacred pipe.

However, great care is still necessary, and the pipe's security should never be taken for granted.

"The story of the pipe has been passed from father to son for as long as it has existed. The way in which the story is given will vary somewhat depending on who is telling it. The important thing is that the overall history and the lessons of the pipe have always remained clear. We are fortunate this evening to have an elder with us who carries this story for our people, not in a book, but rather in his heart and soul. You must listen with your heart and soul in order to receive and understand. He is our storyteller."

With this, he pointed into the crowd. An old man slowly made his way to the council tree, his cane in hand. This would be the first and the last time I would see him. His body was slumped from the years of a hard and long life. His eyes squinted in an attempt to search the attentive faces. His assistant, a younger man, set up a wooden folding chair, and the elder eased his way into it. The assistant took the elder's cane and hung it on the back of the chair. The elder then removed his well-used straw hat and handed it to the younger man. I looked into the crowd and found many medicine men and elders there. Among them was the pipe keeper, Arval Looking Horse. A respectful silence pervaded the crowd as the storyteller began.

"I will tell you about the pipe and how it was brought to the people many winters ago by the holy woman sent to us by the Creator. She was the White Buffalo Calf Maiden.

"Two young Lakota warriors were out one day hunting for game. During their travels they saw something on a distant butte coming toward them that was very strange. When the mysterious thing had drawn near to them, they recognized it to be a very beautiful maiden. Her flowing, black hair laid across the shoulders of her white buckskin gown that was decorated with quill and bead work. On her back she carried a bundle. It is said that her beauty was so powerful that one young man began to think impure thoughts about her. He wanted her in a physical way. The other warrior knew that she was 'Wakan,' of great power and mystery. He avoided any impure thoughts."

The elder stopped momentarily to pull a pack of Camels from his red-flanneled shirt pocket. His young assistant quickly struck a match and held it to the elder's cigarette. After a couple of light draws, he continued.

"The holy woman removed the bundle from her back and summoned the young warrior with lustful thoughts to come over to her. She told him he would receive that which he desired. As he approached her, they were both covered in a dust cloud. Soon the cloud faded away, and the mysterious woman stood alone. At her feet were the bones of the young warrior and they were covered with terrible snakes. This is why we have a snake problem around these parts now."

Ashes fell from his cigarette as he gestured with his hands. "The mysterious woman pointed to the remains and spoke to the pure-hearted warrior: 'Behold what you see! I am coming to your people, and I wish to have a council with them and your chief. Go back now to your people and tell then to prepare a large teepee. There your chief should gather together all his people. I have an important gift to present to them.

"The young warrior returned to his chief as told and informed him of the mysterious woman and what had happened. The chief, whose name was Standing Hollow Horn, was a great and wise man, and he ordered that the work be done. A great lodge was constructed. He then told all his people to wear their most beautiful clothes and to gather at the great lodge as soon as possible. Everyone was filled with excitement as they waited for the holy woman's arrival. No one knew what to expect or what gift she would be bringing.

"Soon the maiden arrived. She entered the lodge and walked around it four times in a sacred manner. Then she stopped in front of the chief. She removed her bundle and held it out with both hands and spoke: 'Behold! What you see is love. It is a very sacred thing and you must protect it. No one with impure thoughts should ever touch it or even see it, for within this bundle is the sacred pipe. I give it to you for the good of the people. You must pray with it, seek guidance from it, and love it.'

"After saying this, she removed the pipe from the bundle and also a small, round red rock, which she laid at the center of the lodge. She then held the pipe up toward the sky and said, 'With this sacred pipe you will walk in a humble way upon the Earth Mother, for she is holy and sacred to all the people. Each step you take should be a prayer. The bowl of the pipe is made of the red stone of Mother Earth. It represents the blood of all Indian people. Carved into the stone is a buffalo calf, who represents all the four legged beings who dwell on this sacred earth. The stem of the pipe is made of wood, and it represents the backbone of all Indian people and all things grown from the earth. Here you see twelve spotted eagle feathers attached to the stem of the bowl. These represent the winged ones of the air. All these beings of the earth and beyond are made one and holy when the pipe is smoked. When the pipe is smoked you speak to the Creator. When you pray with the pipe, you pray to all creation."

"The holy woman then touched the bowl of the pipe to the round red stone at the center of the lodge and said, 'With this pipe you are bound together with all your relatives, past, present, and future. This round stone is made of the same stone that the pipe bowl is made of. It has also been given to you by the Great Spirit. The Great Spirit has also given you the good red road to follow. This is a road of truth and goodness. All these things are sacred to us. Every new day is a blessing. The Great Spirit has created us all in a holy way. We must show honor and respect to all that He has created. The sacred pipe that has dwelled with the Creator will now remain on the red earth.' She then turned to the chief and said to him, 'You are the keeper of the sacred pipe and it is yours to protect. Treat it in a proper way. Through it you will receive knowledge and wisdom to help your people. This is a gift from the Creator, and you should always be grateful!'"

The elder's excitement was contagious as he shuffled around in his chair. He caught his breath and then continued. "The sacred woman then prepared to depart. She looked at the chief once again and said, 'Behold this pipe! Always remember to keep it safe and away from the unclean. This pipe will take you to the end and then to the beginning. Remember, in me there are four ages. I will leave now, but I will return to see you at every new time, and at the end I shall return again with a new message. Listen carefully!'

"The holy woman left as she had come, in a sacred manner. All the people followed her outside the lodge. After walking a short distance she fell to the earth and rolled on the ground. Then she sprang up in the form of a red buffalo and galloped a short distance away. She then rolled again in the dust, and this time she became a black buffalo. Once again she rolled and took the form of a yellow buffalo. Finally, she rose again from the dust in the form of the sacred white buffalo, and with great speed, she ran off into the distance, snorting and moving her head from side to side."

The elder looked at the crowd and then finished up his story. "Now, that is the story of White Buffalo Calf Maiden. I will go now, but you must remember what you have heard and let it sink into your hearts." With this the elder slowly returned to his feet, gathered his cane and straw hat, and departed.

20. OLD COYOTE'S MESSAGE
Dance Back the Elders and Children

It was late in the evening when Old Coyote made his way to the speaking area. His son accompanied him, carrying a bag of tobacco ties and beads from the Suquamish people. His talk was brief, but familiar to me. I had heard these words before, and, as always, I was touched by their power.

"Hau! Greetings, my friends! I have come from west of the Rocky Mountains, and I am very glad to be here. I have not come alone; I have brought many people with me. My beautiful wife, Rita, and our daughters, are back in Suquamish, Washington, but in spirit they are with me now. The elders of our tribe have asked me to come and represent them here, so they are with me also. I hurt inside so badly when I think of the many years of neglect and suffering they have had to endure, the years of abuse and disrespect forced upon them by their own people. It brings tears to my soul. Their wisdom is so important to us, so vital to our survival, yet we have been wrong to think that this special knowledge can simply be taken from them. We must ask them to share their gifts, for they would be glad to take that knowledge with them to the other side. I am here for these elders! I have also come for the children. Not just for the children of Suquamish, but for all the children who exist on the good earth. The cruelty and suffering that they have known is truly evil! Some of our children have seen more in their short years than most of us have ever seen! There are little ones tonight who are alone and hungry on our big city streets. There are some who fear the evil that might come into their own bedrooms! Those children have been born into this world by the grace of our Creator. He has made no mistake. They have a right to be here, a right to be happy! We are the guardians of these children. It is our responsibility to take care of these precious ones. I am here for the children! I ask you to pray for them and keep them in your hearts during these ceremonies. I thank you. Hau!"

The hour was late. One more sunrise and the great day would be upon us. The men working on the new pipe house were still busy, and its form was well developed. Its completion, however, looked at least three days away. But I knew it would be ready tomorrow; somehow, some way, the work would be done.

21. TIME TO DANCE
Dance Back the Energy

I woke before dawn on the last day and went out alone to say my prayers. The stars were bright, and the half moon high in the sky. As always, I spoke of my family members and their sacrifice for me. My beloved wife, Tammy, had, in the short two years we had been married, become very important to my life. She was always there to help with good advice, to guide me when I might go astray, to cheer me up when I might be sad, but most of all to simply love me like no other had before. I have never been an easy person to be with and I can blame no one but myself, but here she was with her sparkling eyes and warm spirit. A description of her as merely my wife would be incomplete. Her place with me was like green in the evergreens, like the smoke in the pipe. She was a sacred friend, a soul mate, one that I knew would never be limited to this brief plane of existence. My sons were also with me in spirit, as were my family elders, present and past. I reflected on my stay here, the many wonderful people, and the events of which I was a part. I thought about my dream of the great eagle and the elders' stories. They were the teachers and the guides for us to follow. I saw the four colors of humankind rising like a rainbow over these holy grounds. I thought of the good words written by my father-in-law, Vinson Brown. In his book, *Warriors of the Rainbow*, an elder woman speaks to her young grandchild of the significance of the rainbow:

The rainbow is a sign from Him who is in all things....It is a sign of the union of all peoples like one big family. Go to the mountaintop, child of my flesh, and learn to be a Warrior of the Rainbow, for it is only by spreading love and joy to others that hate in this world can be changed to understanding and kindness, and war and destruction shall end!

Thoughts moved through my mind like the shadowy clouds of the early morning hour, and I once again found myself thinking of the sacred pipe bag of Crazy Horse. There it was across my arms. The bead work was bright and beautiful; the soft antelope hide was gentle to the touch; its energy was powerful and uplifting. I recalled the many years that my elder and teacher, Vinson Brown, had carried that bag. I also thought of the ceremony that was to take place later this day when the pipe would be brought out for the enlightenment of the Lakota and others. My heart pounded with excitement and anticipation. I loaded my pipe in sacred fashion and watched as the glorious sun made its approach from the eastern horizon. I lit and smoked my pipe, and tears rolled down my face. The pipe day had come!

When I returned to the camp, people were already milling about in and around the arbor area where the pipe ceremony would be taking place. Many people were in quiet prayer, others in soft conversation. The women were busy laying a path of sage three feet wide and nearly a quarter mile long which ran from the pipe keeper's cabin to the center point of the arbor. A large lodge had been erected at that center and four chokecherry saplings had been placed near it. Red, white, yellow, and black flags were attached to the saplings. A buffalo robe was in place with a painted buffalo skull at the southeastern side of the altar.

The pipe keeper made many trips between the altar and his cabin, checking on arrangements, ensuring that everything was in order, inspecting the smallest details. With him were two highly respected medicine men, seating people and directing other details of the ceremony. Their work was diligent and purposeful and performed in a spiritual manner.

When the pipe keeper finally completed his arrangements, he stood still, and a hush came over the crowd. With a quiet but clear voice he announced that all pipe carriers should make their way to the arbor now for blessings. By this time there were at least 500 people gathered in the area. Among them were pipe carriers from all over Turtle Island. They had come to represent their tribes, their families, and themselves. About 150 men and women holding pipes made their way slowly to the arbor to take their place for the sacred ceremony. There were three drum groups set at different points along the perimeter of the arbor. As the songs began those who carried pipes, (the Greengrass pipe dancers), began to dance the holy dance of the pipe. After a few minutes, nine horsemen in full Indian regalia rode up the ridge of the surrounding butte and spaced themselves across its length. Excitement filled the air! Looks of awe appeared on the faces of all present. The drums continued their compelling beat. A vibration moved into the arbor, movement within movement!

From the top of the ridge a horseman waved his eagle staff. All eyes were focused on the place from which the pipe would come. A Lakota elder with another eagle staff commenced the procession of the pipe. He was followed by four young girls.

Behind them came the pipe keeper, in whose arms was the sacred Buffalo Calf pipe wrapped in a buffalo robe. It looked very large and heavy in his arms. He held it as a mother holds her baby. Behind him came ten Lakota elders and medicine men. People lined both sides of the path, and as the pipe passed, they raised their arms and saluted to the most sacred of sacreds. As the pipe keeper passed by, I saw tears flowing heavily down his face. Tears were also evident on many of the elders' faces as they followed.

While the pipe keeper placed the pipe bundle on the altar, a strange new silence filled the hot South Dakota air, a silence so filled with anticipation and excitement that it seemed to live and breathe. I forced myself to take a deep breath, and the pipe was at last in place. In the far distance I heard an eagle call. We were blessed once again. Once the pipe keeper finished setting up, he took his place, cross-legged, beside the sacred pipe. By this time, it looked as though a full thousand people were present. The other medicine men instructed us this time, for the pipe keeper was at his station. The drummers had stopped momentarily as the pipe was put in place but quickly built back up to a rhythmic pulse. Then the medicine men directed all pipe carriers to prepare their pipes. As we filled our own pipes, they called on the elders and disabled ones to come to the front, for they would be the first to pray with the pipe. After them a long line of people formed. At first one, then two, and eventually three at a time paid their respects and said their prayers with the sacred pipe.

Once we had filled our pipes, the pipe carriers began to dance again. The good earth absorbed our steps and blessed our efforts. The drums and the dancing went on and on, giving us strength in our ceremony. After nearly three hours of continuous visitation by the other participants, it was finally time for the pipe dancers to pay respect and visit with the pipe bundle. I had already seen my son Jody pass by in prayer, and this made me very proud to be his father. It was now my turn to pass through the chokecherry saplings and pray beside the Pipe of Life. Holding my pipe, I placed my hands against the bundle. Instantly I felt a surge of power move from the pipe bundle into my arms, then into my body, and finally into the deepest parts of my soul. I prayed, wept, gave thanks, and asked for guidance and understanding in my life. I felt my family around me once again with their love and honor. My darling wife's beautiful face flashed into my head, smiling as though she knew the sacred power of this moment. Her gentle blue eyes told of a silent prophecy and a healing to come. It was during this moment that I, for the first time in my life, felt the true essence of everlasting life! The spirit never dies; it simply changes worlds!

I prayed: Wakan Tanka, Niskaminu, Tunkasila! I pray at this sacred place in the presence of this most holy pipe. Bring peace and love to the hearts of the people who have come to this place. I pray in humbleness for you to bring understanding to my heart so that I may be better prepared to assist my family and fellow human beings on this sacred Mother Earth. I pledge my life to the service of your most great cause. I will do your will gladly and thereby abide by the same. All my relations, Mitakuye Oyasin.

With this I rose to my feet and departed. I had touched spirit and was touched by spirit.

After everyone had visited the pipe, Arval Looking Horse gathered the pipe bundle, and with his escort, departed the arbor. Each person he passed fell in behind the procession until almost all present were following the path of sage which led to the newly completed pipe house. At least a thousand good spirits helped place the pipe in its new home. The pipe keeper entered the well-built pipe house, along with elders and medicine men. The pipe was placed on a tripod altar and left there to rest until needed again. When the pipe keeper left the pipe house, he spoke very few words. He simply said that we should take this experience with us. The memories will last forever. He noted that we should share this time with our families and friends and that we should pray to better understand our visions, their meanings, and their purpose. With this he turned and padlocked the door. An instinctive "Hau!" sounded among those present.

I eventually returned to my position with the other pipe carriers, and as I was settling in to contemplate the events of this very special, one-of-a-kind ceremony, I was distracted by a sudden movement on a distant butte. It seemed like a flash of light, as from a mirror reflecting the sun's rays, but when I turned I saw no sign of any reflector or light. However, I immediately felt a deep, almost spiritual, movement in the air. I concluded it was the general atmosphere of the event.

The great ceremony was finished. The most holy pipe was placed at rest, out of sight of mortals, but forever leaving its influence upon our souls. As the people shared in a potluck style meal in the kitchen area, I realized that we had been made spiritually one with and around the pipe. We were all bonded by this ceremony, bonded by the drum, bonded by the dance.

As we broke camp, little was spoken. We knew without words what was going on in each other's minds. We had found old friends and discovered new ones. We were bettered by the experience. I asked the boys and my friend Old Coyote if they had noticed any lights on the distant buttes. They had not noticed anything. That light was a spiritual communication, sent down as a prophecy or maybe even a warning. What was evident is that the message was for me alone.

We had come to Greengrass to share time together, to share a power together in a rare event. We had accomplished this but more than that we were now departing as Greengrass pipe dancers. Hau!

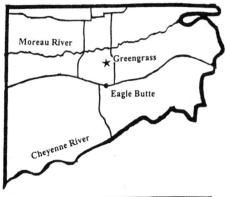

CHEYENNE RIVER RESERVATION

Moreau River

★ Greengrass

Eagle Butte

Cheyenne River

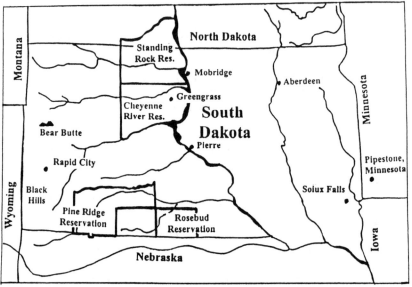

Montana

North Dakota

Standing Rock Res.

Mobridge

Aberdeen

Cheyenne River Res.

Greengrass

South Dakota

Bear Butte

Pierre

Minnesota

Rapid City

Pipestone, Minnesota

Wyoming

Black Hills

Pine Ridge Reservation

Rosebud Reservation

Sioux Falls

Iowa

Nebraska

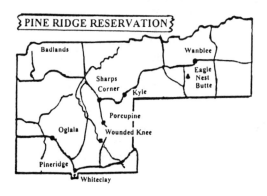

PINE RIDGE RESERVATION

Badlands

Wanblee

Sharps Corner

Kyle

Eagle Nest Butte

Oglala

Porcupine

Wounded Knee

Pineridge

Whiteclay

BOOK II

RETURNING THE DANCE

"Love her and she will be healed!"
Fools Crow, July 1988

"Love is my healing."
Tamara Lynn, July 1988

22. Returning the Dance
Dance Back the Spirit

One year later, as we wended our way down the dirt roads along the now-familiar buttes of Greengrass, I recognized a stark difference in its surroundings, although not in the layout of the terrain, for it has appeared the same for centuries. The change was in the lack of people. There were no hoards of adventurers or spirit seekers. All that was present were two small dome tents and a large teepee near the council tree. We had come back to Greengrass at a time of tranquillity. Thoughts flooded my head from my first trip, thoughts of the many spectacular events. The old council tree and the buttes had witnessed the voices of many medicine men and other orators but now they were witnessing an even more powerful experience, a deep silence. Most people today focus so much on the audible and visual aspects of life, that they neglect life's necessary and beautiful quietness.

Accompanying me on this journey of healing were my sons, Jeremiah, age thirteen, and Trapper, who was not quite two. Also with me was the source of my inspiration, my wife, Tammy. It was for all of us to be deepened and blessed by this spirit, place, and time, but more so for her. An illness called cancer had exploded into her life like a clap of lightning in a clear blue sky. It had struck our lives with its fiery reality and crumbled a gentle and beautiful lady and her family to their knees. It was now time to stand up again. The wide-eyed fear of this unexpected and unwanted lightning bolt had become quiet and hidden away, and now we sat, ever so gingerly, on the bubble of life. Our time now was a time of healing, both in a physical way and in a spiritual way.

Drawing closer I could see the pipe house and other surrounding structures. They all looked the same. But where a horse corral once stood, a strongly-built cabin had been erected. I got out of the car and proceeded to the pipe keeper's cabin. My knock on the door was answered by a lady with a baby in her arms. Other children scurried all around. She informed me that the pipe keeper was not home but at the Rapid City Powwow. She expected him back sometime that night or the next day. She invited us to set up camp down by the council tree. I thanked her and left.

As I was pulling the car out of gear, I could see that the people who had set up the other tents and teepee were not home. I was a bit concerned that we might be intruding. Jeremiah was working hard with the unloading and set-up, a process that he had mastered by this point of our journey. I looked for Tammy and Trapper and found them walking toward the massive butte which had become so significant during my last visit. This was a very special time, a time of memories to make, of love to hold. I had spoken to her for countless hours about this place, and now she was living it. She stood silhouetted against the buttes, welcoming the cleansing winds. Our entire trip had been filled with nature's spectacular beauty, yet this simple and quiet land seemed more spectacular than any place we had witnessed.

After we had set up, I settled into my favorite lounge chair and Tammy started our evening meal; Jeremiah had gone off exploring, and Trapper had found a new friend, the council tree. It was drawing him near. Some other children had rigged a rope swing from one of its branches and he swung it back and forth a few times, but, amazingly, he spent more time sitting snugly at its base between two large roots; if he was missing, you could more than likely find him, quiet and smiling, with his new tree friend.

23. TOM CALFROBE
Dance Back the Environment

It was nearly dusk when I first heard, then saw, a rumbling brown Chevrolet Impala approaching. The dust kicked up behind it like a headless snake; the passenger side was damaged; only two of the four hubcaps were on, and the dust was so thick on the windows I could not see in. When it had come to a stop near the larger of the two tents, the dust rolled on by as though someone had forgotten to tell it to stop. Our neighbors had returned.

There was no activity for a moment. I suspected the occupants were checking us out, or perhaps they were waiting for the dust to settle. Eventually, both doors opened and two people got out. The driver was an older man, maybe mid-sixties, with long gray braids, flannel shirt, and jeans. He did not look in our direction, but went around to the trunk of the car and began unloading grocery sacks. The second person was an older lady, also in her sixties, with long braids, wearing a colorful, flowered dress, which covered her abundant body from the neck to ankle. She did stop for a moment and looked sternly in our direction. Something about her seemed familiar.

I finally decided that it was the proper time to introduce ourselves to our neighbors. As I started walking toward their camp, I saw the man walking toward me. When we were close enough to each other I extended my hand. "Hello, my name is Lionel Little Eagle."

He hesitated for a moment, then accepted my hand. With a smile he answered, "Hello, I'm Tom Calfrobe. Where are you folks from?"

His inviting smile put me at ease. "We'll, it's sort of a long story." I went on to explain our journey. He listened with interest, occasionally nodding his head. His gray-black braids were wrapped in the traditional way of a medicine man, intertwined with red cloth. His face was etched with the years and a hard life, but through the rough exterior I could feel the gentleness of a man who was at peace with himself. After a bit, I invited him to our camp for coffee, which he gladly accepted by turning and heading that way. "Sounds good."

ELDER CALFROBE

As I focused in on our camp, I realized that Tammy had company too. It was Tom Calfrobe's wife, Shirley, to whom I was later introduced. She was sitting in a chair sipping a cup of coffee. They both looked up and smiled as we reached camp. "How's the coffee?" I asked as I lifted the pot. Shirley hummed a sign of satisfaction and said, "Good. Nice and hot!"

The dusk gave way to darkness and we all sat contentedly around the campfire, breathing in the gentle relaxation of this sacred place. I soon found out through our conversation that Shirley Calfrobe was from the Cheyenne River Sioux reservation and Tom Calfrobe was from Standing Rock. Just as it was for us, it was for them, a mission and a purpose for being here at Greengrass. As Calfrobe stated, "The others left here seven days ago on the march to Pipestone. I figure about thirty or so." He looked over at Shirley, who was nodding in agreement, and continued, "We are unable to make such a journey. It must be 200 miles or more, so Arval asked us to stay and watch the camp."

"Arval went with them?" I asked.

"Oh no! He's in Rapid City for the powwow. He's planning on driving to meet the marchers when he gets back, whenever that happens."

Concern appeared on our faces. "You mean he might not come back here. The lady I spoke with at the house told us he'd be in tonight or tomorrow morning."

The two looked at each other and began to laugh. Shirley Calfrobe spoke. Her voice was strong and deliberate.

"No one, not even Arval, knows when he'll be back. He's always on the road. He visits many people, our elders, the children, the sick ones." With a faint smile she lowered her voice and with reverence said, "He's the pipe keeper!"

Tom Calfrobe added, "He'll make it in due time."

I found myself once again watching Shirley Calfrobe, the way she carried herself, her voice, her general appearance. Something about her was familiar, but what? Redirecting my attention to Tom Calfrobe, I asked, "Do you come here often?"

"Oh, yes. This has been a place for me and my family for many years. This will be my eighth year to dance at the sun dance."

I was not sure what I had heard. Did he say his eighth year? Now I knew why he wore a red cloth braided in his hair. He was one of the sacred ones. I reached into my bag and pulled out a small leather bag of tobacco. Standing and removing my cap, I offered it to Calfrobe. He seemed a bit surprised but quickly stood and, shaking my hand, accepted it.

"Thank you," he said as he bowed his head.

Respectfully, I asked if I might talk about the sun dance with him.

"Sure," he said in a joyful manner. "What would you like to know?"

I had associated with sun dancers before, but the subject was never raised. I was sure this place, this time, and this man would make such things easier to talk about. "You've actually danced seven years," I began.

"Oh, yes."

"What is it that makes you return?"

He raised his bushy eyebrows slightly. "The dance, son. Why does one eat, why does one sleep?"

I said, "To live."

Now a smile appeared on his face. "Yes, to live. I dance to live because the food of the dance fills me up with something even more important than the food of the earth. Our sleep at night is needed to survive on this earth. The food of the dance is needed to survive in the spirit land."

"Do all people need the nourishment of the dance to survive in the spirit world?"

Finishing his coffee, he answered, "Oh, no. What is good for me might be wrong for you. The dance is a religion. Not all people belong to the same church yet all people have the same rights to the one true God. There are many paths to the Creator's good lodge; no one path is better than the other. I chose the sun dance."

I hesitated for a moment and then continued, "I have not participated in the sun dance."

"I know," he noted.

"But I am going into a very important period in my life and the sun dance has been in my mind. What are some of the requirements?"

"The desire to dance the sun dance that you have in your mind must find its way to your heart." He pulled a couple of small sticks from his shirt pocket as well as his knife and began whittling on them. "You must also have an earthly reason for such a step. There must be a cause in your life for which you are willing to make that sacred sacrifice."

"I'm not sure I know what you mean by a 'cause', Tom?"

He paused for a moment, then turned his face in Tammy's direction, "There is your cause." Then he found Trapper near the council tree. "And over there is another cause."

Tammy and Shirley Calfrobe had been carrying on their own conversation until that point. Tammy raised her head and glanced at Tom Calfrobe, then turned toward me. The gentle glow of the fire shone on her face. I recalled her earlier conversation with me about an elder who appeared in her dreams, a strong, wise face that held answers to our questions. Could this be the man? I told Tom Calfrobe, "My wife and I have traveled many miles to come to this place, and her cause is my cause."

Tom Calfrobe looked skyward. "Yes, I know."

"How do you know?" I asked.

A fleeting, familiar smile appeared on his face. He pointed upward. "The clouds have told me. I am what is known as a cloud watcher. Most of our young ones have not learned the secret language of the clouds. They do not believe that the patterns formed are questions answered; they want to read it in the newspaper or see it on TV. The answers are right there in the clouds. That is another reason why I am here. The clouds have told me to come." He turned toward the sun dance arbor. "It's very much like the sun dance."

"In what way?" I asked.

"Every year, beginning with the first full moon of August, we have our sun dance, and every year I see the young ones come to make their pledges. Some only dance and do not pierce. Some just watch, but the young men and women are always here. I talk to them, help them in their preparations. But when all is done, they leave their Indian ways here and take home something I don't understand. When you pledge yourself to Can-Wakan, the Mystery Tree, it's not to be temporary, or for mere status. It is for life that you pledge. This is done in the spirit of the Creator. But the young ones, they come one year, maybe two. But then I never see them again. I often wonder if they are dead!"

I sat quietly for a moment, questioning my own sincerity, wondering whether my reasons and purpose were worthy enough. My thoughts were abruptly shaken by the strong voice of Shirley Calfrobe.

24. HEY YOU! PART TWO

Dance Back the Laughter

"Hey you! What's a person supposed to do to get more coffee around here?"

Both Tammy and I reached for the pot at the same time, and as Tammy poured the hot, black coffee into her cup, I felt a spark of excitement. It was coming back to me. I looked over at Shirley and said, "I remember you now."

Looking at me speculatively, she said, "Do you, now?"

"Yes," I said. "You were here for the pipe ceremony last year. You spent most of your time in the kitchen area."

Laughing, she replied, "Most of the time, hell, I spent all my time there. I ran that kitchen." She continued more sternly, "The young women are so lazy. They don't want to help. Next year," she said, with a touch of longing, "I will let them run the kitchen themselves and I will sit on a blanket under the arbor and watch the dancers." She crossed her arms across her chest.

The kitchen boss! I could scarcely believe it. The toughest little lady who ever shook a gravy spoon. "I knew I had met you before," I said, smiling reminiscently.

"Yes," she announced. "I remember you, too. Have you gotten any better with the ax?"

She, Tom Calfrobe, and Tammy burst into laughter. After this, we talked for a little longer. Then Tom and Shirley Calfrobe headed for their camp. It had been a wonderful evening for us all.

Later that night, as we lay in our sleeping bags, and the cottonwood trees rustled outside our tents, I mentioned to Tammy that I would like to show Tom the pipe bag and seek his counsel.

"Yes," she softly concurred. "I had been thinking about that also."

She snuggled up in the crook of my arm as I lay content, feeling the power and inspiration of this place, and the peace of my darling Tammy's presence. I breathed in deep the fragrance of her love and knew that there was no place I would rather be in the world. Outside, the winds began to pick up slightly in intensity. I listened, then slept.

25. GREENGRASS MORNINGS
Dance Back the Sunrise

We woke fairly late the next morning. Something seemed especially fresh and clean about that day as our camp began to come alive. Jeremiah had been up for a while and was gathering some scarce firewood. He seemed to be growing up right in front of my eyes. His long black hair was still a bit mussed from sleep, and at six feet, he was taller than most boys two years older. I found myself sometimes mistaking him for my brother, Kenny. When I called him my brother's name, he would just laugh and tease me for my mistake.

Tom and Shirley Calfrobe had long since eaten their breakfast and were relaxing over their morning coffee. I looked up toward Arval Looking Horse's cabin for any indication that he might have returned during the night. All was quiet and serene. The home stood as it might have stood for fifty years, although those years had left their mark on its structure. It was a small dwelling, yet I knew at least four adults and six children called it home. It had no electricity or running water. An outhouse stood about thirty yards behind it. On the south side of the house, nearest the butte, was strung a clothesline full of laundry, damp from the morning dew. In the front, four or five dogs of undetermined parentage rested in the dust, their eyes intently focused on the front door of the cabin. These were the simplest of living conditions, yet I knew that even in this apparent poverty, a richness of culture existed. Parked on the roadside near the cabin was one car that had been there the day before. No new arrivals. Maybe later, I hoped.

26. TOP OF THE WORLD
Dance Back the Peace

After we had finished breakfast, Tammy decided it was time we explored the butte, so off we went, Trapper on Jeremiah's shoulders, Tammy in the lead. I followed behind. As I worked my way up the steep hillside, I recalled the pipe ceremony and the horsemen who had traveled this same ridge.

Tammy, Jeremiah, and Trapper were waiting for me when I arrived at the top of the butte. It and the rolling hills beyond were quite a contrast to the more serene area below. I was first startled by the gusty winds that swirled unobstructed for as far as the eye could see. It was actually difficult to stand at some points. And through the wind, an astounding unseen energy could be felt, a movement stronger than the wind itself. The energy that lived here was something I had rarely experienced. It was as though the Great Spirit had picked this place as a personal sanctuary. It was so moving in spirit that I found myself stilled with wonderment. I looked around and found Jeremiah and Trapper exploring the terrain, oblivious to anything but their physical surroundings. I turned my gaze to Tammy and found her deep in contemplation. She was looking in a southerly direction, the wind blowing her hair and clothing, yet she seemed at ease. As I watched her, she slowly turned toward me and smiled, her eyes sparkling with happiness. She reached across to me. In her silent way, she communicated to me a feeling of joy, a perception of life eternal.

Scattered on many of the surrounding hills were vision pits, five in all. These places were very special. Each pit was constructed in a traditional way. Four flags: red, black, white, and yellow were tied to chokecherry saplings and positioned on the four corners. Tobacco ties, also in the four sacred colors, were placed in a circle within the chokecherry saplings. Inside this circle, the person seeking his or her vision would sit. The seeker was allowed the simplest of possessions: a wooden cup, pipe, and tobacco. In most ceremonies, the seeker would only have a loincloth on for the stay. In some places, a blanket would be provided for protection against the never-ceasing winds.

From our vantage point I could see more homes in the distance. The muddy Moreau River rambled through the scene. Clumps of short, stumpy trees dotted the landscape, and waves of flowing grass moved purposely in the wind. Just below us were the familiar sights that had become so much a part of my life. Dominating these was the sun dance arbor with its new addition, a sleeping area to the western side. During the evenings the sun dancers would use this brush-covered room as a place to rest and prepare for the next day's ceremony. To the left of the arbor stood the age-old council tree, and beyond it, the mounds of our tents and the cone of the one large teepee.

Something was so appealing about this place. It seemed easy to draw upon the influence of nature. The sky was in balance with the earth. Even in the face of the strong wind, peace prevailed. Jeremiah moved about like a young deer, Trapper toddling not far behind, both excited about life's majesty. Tammy still stood quietly, lost in thought, prayer, or conversation. I walked to her, drew her into my arms, and asked, "What do you think?"

She turned her gentle blue eyes toward me and looked into my heart. "I love it! It is the way you described it and more." She turned toward the vision quest sites. "There is something else here. I can feel it." She hesitated for a moment. "This is a special place, Lionel. Up here I feel closer to God." She took a slow, deep breath. "It's like standing on top of the world and it feels good." She was silent for a moment and then added, "I feel like I have always been here and I'll always be here."

I looked back toward the road, hoping to see a car, maybe Looking Horse's coming in. There were no vehicles, no people. Nothing seemed to be moving. It was as though the earth had brought movement to a standstill. It was as though time stood still in a land that time had passed by.

27. GOD'S BIG TOE

Dance Back the Ants

I found the boys kneeling down, congregated around an ant hill. The wind had kept its height down, but it was at least three feet in diameter. The entrance hole was the size of a dime. Occasionally, a rather large red ant would enter or depart. Neither of the boys moved to disturb the ant hill. Jeremiah looked at me and humorously asked, "Dad, what would happen if I were to accidentally mess up this ant hill?"

Patting him on his back, I knelt down. "First of all, Son, it would not be an accident. When an ant hill is disturbed, it should be the proper time for it to be disturbed. When that happens, the ants will just go to work to repair the damage."

Jeremiah picked up a long stick and pointed it at the ant hill. "How do we know when it's the right time?"

"We don't. It's like life itself. If I took my big toe and pushed the sand into the hole, the ants would know that something had disturbed their environment. It is very unlikely that they would know what caused such a drastic change in their previously comfortable living conditions. You and I, however, would know what caused that change, my big toe."

A look of confusion appeared on Jeremiah's face. "Yeah, Dad, but what does that have to do with life?"

Carefully wording my answer, I continued. "Well, those ants have to deal with big, sometimes drastic changes. You can see that we are bigger, more knowledgeable beings. We are superior to them in a lot of ways. One way is that we understand what caused their disturbance. For the ants to deny that we changed their world would, in our eyes, be crazy, right?"

Jeremiah agreed by nodding his head.

I continued, "So in life we have our own changes, which are sometimes drastic, too. One minute we can be happy, without a care in the world, then the next minute everything crumbles around us."

Jeremiah replied, "I see what you mean. We're like the ants in the world of life."

I smiled. "Yes, in a way that is true. When those changes happen, we cannot regard them as mere chance, coincidence, or an accident. Just like those ants in the hill, we, too, have a Superior Being watching over us."

Jeremiah became quiet for a moment and then noted, "You mean like God?"

"Exactly, Son. For us to deny the existence of the Superior Being, the Great Mystery, is crazy!"

We both laughed, and as we were leaving, Jeremiah tossed his stick off to the side.

28. LISTENING TO THE CLOUDS
Dance Back the Wolf and the Bowl

I felt good as we made our way down the slope of the butte. A quick look toward Looking Horse's cabin let me know that he still had not arrived. I looked in the direction of the Calfrobe camp. Shirley Calfrobe was busy with her chores; there were a couple of children playing about her, probably from the cabin. Occasionally, I could hear her voice raised in frustration toward her young companions. Tom Calfrobe was sitting in his lounge chair at the rear of his car. The trunk was open. After a short visit to our camp, I proceeded to Tom Calfrobe's location.

"Hi Tom."

"Good morning, Little Eagle. How did you all sleep last night?"

I noticed he was again carving on the two pieces of wood with his pocketknife. "We slept well. How about you and Shirley?"

"Just fine." Then pointing with his eyebrows to the butte, he went on, "I see you and the family made a trip up the butte. Nice up there, huh!"

Tom Calfrobe went back to gently flicking wood. I answered, "It seemed even better than nice. That place is very powerful. I can see why so many vision pits are there."

The elder nodded his head and added, "Yes, that place is used quite often. Almost every weekend someone will be up there."

I had noticed that Tom had his dance outfit along with many other relics in the trunk of his car. His peculiar carving interested me.

"Whatcha carving there, Tom?"

He smiled without looking up. "Oh, it's a gift for a friend."

He closed up his knife and placed the two pencil-like wood carvings in his pocket. Standing up, he took a deep breath, stretched his arms over his head, and spoke, "It's going to be a nice day. I think I'm going to take a walk." He then glanced at me and asked, "Want to come along?"

There was no way I could refuse his request. "Yes, that sounds good to me."

Our walk was a long one. After about an hour, he stopped, looked skyward, and said, "This is a good spot!"

At that point any spot was a good one as far as I was concerned. There really was not anything of interest to me here, but I knew that my eyes could not see the same way as this man's.

Tom Calfrobe spoke again. "Watch out for the little cactus. If they get you in the butt, you're goin' to hurt for a while."

Being careful to find a spot without cactus, I gladly sat down. I was just about to speak when Tom Calfrobe raised his hand.

"Listen! Do you hear that?"

I quickly looked around to see if anything or anybody was approaching. There was no one in sight. I became very still and began to listen carefully. I closed my eyes. For a moment, there was nothing, then there was something, a gentle whoosh, like something gliding by, perhaps a large bird. I could feel more with my eyes closed than with them open. Even though the day was getting warmer, a coolness seemed to be settling over me. But I had not seen any clouds earlier, so what could it be?

When I finally opened my eyes, I found Tom Calfrobe lying flat on his back looking upward. When I followed his line of sight, I saw that clouds were present, large, fluffy white clouds. An hour before there had been none. I thought of Tom Calfrobe's earlier words when he described himself as a cloud watcher. Could he be a cloud caller also?

As I looked over toward him, he spoke to me, "You can see better from this position." So I joined him, lying on the brown grass of Greengrass, facing to the east. He then announced that it was time to listen to the clouds. I felt as though I was not supposed to be here, but that thinking was soon over. As I listened attentively to the elder's voice, I knew he had planned for me to share this very special ritual with him. His voice seemed softer, but very clear. "Watch the clouds, boy."

The puffy, white clouds dominated the sky so it was easy to watch them. I could not help but think about my childhood years, watching the clouds, looking for animal forms, or cars, or even a flying dragon.

Now, as I focused on one cluster of clouds, another would roll in. I would watch the center of one mass and the edge of another would ease into my line of sight. All of a sudden I saw a wolf's head, mouth open as if it were howling. I wondered if this could be a message. Concentrating on the head, I observed it turning in my direction. The mouth began to close. Protruding from its left eye I could see what appeared to be a stick or arrow. As I focused more intently on its eye, I realized it was in pain. The wolf's head then floated away. I watched it until I could no longer recognize its form.

Looking back to the area where I first saw the wolf's head appear, I now saw a massive bowl with a large chip missing. It appeared very old and its position precarious. Smaller clouds were beginning to blend into its sides, as if to destroy it. Large cracks were appearing, and the bowl was fragmented into many pieces as it spread across the sky.

As my eyes danced from cloud to cloud, a new formation soon developed. It appeared to be an old style cabin with windows and even a chimney. It looked as though smoke was rising from the chimney. The scene seemed noteworthy but quickly dispersed into the never-ending Dakota sky.

I was suddenly aware of Tom Calfrobe's chanting. It seemed to be a prayer or song of some sort. I wanted to ask him if he had seen the last formation, but realized that this was not the proper time.

I lay motionless, watching the thick rolling clouds. It seemed to be about half an hour before the chanting ceased and he became very quiet. After another half hour, I looked in his direction and he was gone. I was startled and got to my feet hastily. From directly behind me, I heard his voice, "Time to go."

I tried to hide my initial shock at not seeing Tom Calfrobe, but the slight smile on his face told me I had not been successful.

On our way back, I asked if he could help me understand what I had seen in the clouds. He said he would try. I told him about the wolf's head, the stick, and the howling. He said, "The wolf's head is a symbol of nature's strength; the stick in the eye shows that the wolf is suffering from a terrible wound and the damage caused is irreparable. The wolf was searching for help. He needs the kind of help that one man cannot give; the help has to come from all men."

Calfrobe was silent for a moment, so I asked him about the second form I had seen in the clouds, the broken bowl. He explained, "The bowl represents knowledge and wisdom. It is very old and time has made it very fragile. It will be destroyed in time. The crack in the bowl allows the release of the sacred knowledge and wisdom. That was the scattering you saw."

I asked, "Shouldn't this concern me? Shouldn't I be doing something to save the bowl?"

"There are things that cannot be changed right now," Tom Calfrobe replied solemnly. "These things happen because that is the way it is supposed to be."

My concern was evident. "What has caused this deterioration?"

Calfrobe smiled for a moment and then answered. "Man has done this. The things that should be important have been replaced with those that are not: fancy cars, excess commodities, greed for material possessions. The pollution in the air is killing our good earth. The worst thing is that so many don't even care! These aerosols, plastics, and Styrofoam do not dissolve as they should. They destroy the environment in a way that you cannot see. As time passes we will feel the changes even more, in the water we drink, in the air we breathe. Only if human beings wake up and begin to truly care, the bowl of life and knowledge will live on."

Desperately I asked, "What can we do?"

Calfrobe answered quickly. "We have to remove that which is doing the most harm: the pollution, gases, plastics, and Styrofoam." We were entering our campsite and we saw Tammy changing Trapper's diaper. Calfrobe commented, "Like those diapers, they are made of plastics. You will be done with them in a matter of hours, but the earth will be dealing with them for many years to come, long after you son's son has grown out of them. They call them disposable diapers, but they do not go away."

I waved to Tammy and Trapper and they waved back, but before I joined them I was curious to know what Tom Calfrobe had seen in the clouds, so I asked him.

He smiled and said, "I saw a wolf in pain and a bowl in shame."

My reading of the clouds was the same as his! As we separated, I mentioned that I had also seen a cabin in the clouds. Calfrobe reacted with obvious shock. He stopped in his tracks. So I asked, "Did you see the cabin?"

"No!" he said. "We will talk more later." He turned and entered his camp area. His strange reaction bothered me a bit, but I wasn't about to intrude on him. We would talk later.

29. MOTHER'S WISDOM
Dance Back Eternity

As I expected, Tammy showed great interest in my cloud experience. No matter what, when, or where things happened to me, she cared. Her love was so evident, so real, that I was constantly amazed by it. What did she find in me that made her care so deeply, be so devoted and loyal to me? I knew her life in the deepest ways, her dearest joys, and almost unbearable heartbreaks. She was so intelligent that, oftentimes, I was unable to touch her depths. Some things are private, even in marriage. But I had never felt inadequate beside her greater intellect. "You have more wisdom," she would tell me. "It keeps us in balance, Love."

Both of us had traveled down the familiar road of unsuccessful marriage, and the experience had matured us. We were each blessed with two fine sons from each of those prior marriages. Now we had a fifth son, Trapper. His, hers, and ours, I would often joke.

After the collapse of my first marriage, I began to rebuild the hopes of finding that special person who would be a true and everlasting love. I never lost hope. I knew she existed somewhere on this good earth. I just was not sure where or when I would find her until the wisdom of a mother brought us together. That mother was Tammy's mother, Barbara. She took a quick and certain look into my heart. She was able to determine that I was that person, one who sought a simple and good love. She believed in me and she brought her daughter to see my heart. Her wisdom went beyond her own vision. The glorious journey that lay ahead of all of us was yet to be manifested. I knew that some might view such a love as an unrealistic fantasy, but the Great Mystery had made it real. He had blessed us with a love and companionship that went deeper than the physical world. This union was for eternity, and, we both knew it!

30. LIVING PIPE BAG

Dance Back the Happiness

Tammy suggested that we invite Tom and Shirley Calfrobe over for a viewing of the pipe bag. After a short rest, they joined us at our campsite. I prepared for the viewing of the pipe bag as I had been instructed by the previous keeper of the bag. I first gathered sage for the ceremony. After smudging myself, I smudged the area where the bag would be placed. I laid sage down for the placing of the bag. I began prayers—prayers that would continue until I felt the time was proper. I had been taught that prayers and good sense would tell me whether the time and environment was right for the pipe bag to be displayed. After these prayers, I would smudge the area and the people who would be present. I would then ask an elder for his permission to continue with the ceremony. Then I would get the cherrywood case that contained the pipe bag. This was always done with sage in both hands. In a prayerful way I would bring it to the circle of people and place it on its altar of sage. After smudging the case and saying more prayers, I would open the case. The pipe bag was then revealed to all present. In some cases, as with this ceremony, I would remove the bag from the case, and lay it, in the same manner as I would a baby, upon its own bed of sage.

Once everyone had ample time to view the bag, I would tell the stories of the pipe bag and how it had come into my care. This was only the second time that I had ceremonially displayed the bag since it had been given into my protection, and this was the first time the bag had been displayed in its mother land, Lakota territory, since 1967. I felt a strange surge when I first opened the bag's case, as if it were taking a deep and loving breath.

Calfrobe was silent for a while. Then he spoke with slow and deliberate words. "There is life here!" He held his hands outstretched toward the bag. "This bag has power and it is gathering more as we watch."

I was surprised at the effect it had on him. I did feel the difference myself. At this point, Calfrobe raised his hands upward and began praying in a Lakota tongue that I could not understand, but I was certain that the bag would.

After a time I asked Calfrobe for guidance and thoughts regarding my duties as the pipe bag keeper. Without taking his eyes from the bag, he spoke, "This bag is very powerful and it is also happy."

"Happy?" I questioned.

"Yes, it is evident that your family has taken good care of it." He pointed to the bead patterns on the pipe bag. "This style of beading is an Oglala style that is quite common. It has existed for hundreds of years."

He then surprised me by noting that the hide was antelope and not deer skin as we had thought. "It's easy to make the mistake. They are very similar in appearance, but the deer skin would not be as soft at this age."

I told him about the bag and its connection to the holy man, Crazy Horse. His eyes brightened and he looked deeply into me as if I had touched something very sacred. He then said, "I hesitated in saying this, but when you first opened the case, Crazy Horse came in my mind. His band used this design or one very similar to it." Calfrobe went into his thoughts for a moment and then continued. "So many stories have been told of Crazy Horse's life, and his belongings, too. A lot of people refer to him as a chief. He was not a chief in the bloodline way. He acquired his chief's position on the field of battle. There never was a more skillful warrior or a more compassionate leader. His life has been an inspiration to all Indian people."

Looking up toward me, he added, "Most believe that all his possessions were destroyed by the cavalry when he was captured and later killed. But I have heard of other objects existing that escaped the fires."

I agreed. "Yes, I, too, have heard that his belongings were destroyed. I cannot say this pipe bag belonged to Crazy Horse. I was not there. Only the ones who lived there at that time would know." Hesitatingly, I asked, "How should I hold this pipe bag?"

Calfrobe quickly answered, "Just as you are now, in a sacred manner. Hold it as though you were holding it for Crazy Horse. You can't go wrong that way. " I understood what he meant.

I then explained, "Back in 1966, my father-in-law, the previous keeper of the pipe bag, gave it to Frank Fools Crow to keep for one year so that he could determine its origins. After that year passed, Fools Crow announced at his sun dance in Kyle that the pipe bag did indeed belong to Crazy Horse. He made the statement based upon his conversations with the elders at the time and also from the counsel of his own prayers." Calfrobe nodded and I continued, "Are there any of the old ones who could help me with this question of Crazy Horse?"

Calfrobe answered with a slight chuckle, "No. There are no old ones that old who can help you. In fact, Fools Crow is said to be nearly 100 years old now and his mind is not all together any more. He sometimes travels away from us. However, his powerful spirit still inspires the people of Indian nations." A thought came to him. "This is something he could do for you, because even though the bag is in a physical form, it also has a spiritual essence."

I asked, "Is Fools Crow still at Pine Ridge?"

"Yes, I believe in Kyle, maybe at Sharp's Corner."

I observed, "In fact, there is no one alive now who could verify the authenticity of the pipe bag!"

Calfrobe smiled while shaking his head, "Authenticity? I don't believe I know that word. But I don't believe you should concern yourself about it. Do not keep that bag merely for the reason that it might have once belonged to a great man. Keep it in your heart and soul," he said, tapping his chest with his fingers, "and it might make you a great man."

Calfrobe looked at the bag again. "I feel there is something else important about this bag. There's a healing force about it."

I agreed. "Yes, our family has also felt that."

31. CABINS IN THE CLOUDS
Dance Back the Smoke

Calfrobe was quiet for a short time. "I must tell you about the third part of your cloud readings earlier today. When you spoke of seeing a cabin, it made me wonder." He looked at me sternly. "Tell me more about what you saw."

A knot of fear rose in my chest. "It was a simple cabin with a couple of windows. There was smoke coming from the chimney."

I noticed that Shirley Calfrobe had directed her attention toward her husband. He nodded wisely. "Was it an old cabin?"

"I really didn't notice the age," I replied.

Calfrobe pointed his finger at me. "Yes, you did notice. You must go into your feeling now. Listen to your heart." He then asked, "Was there anyone home?"

I must have presented a look of confusion, for he repeated, "Listen to your heart."

I closed my eyes and a vision of my beloved wife eased from my heart to my mind. "Yes," I said with a smile. "My wife is there!"

Shirley Calfrobe appeared shocked and stirred in her seat. Tom Calfrobe did not speak. He finally replied, "I must tell you the truth as I see it. Certain types of dwellings represent a bad thing in the watcher's eyes. They tell of misfortune, illness, and maybe even death for that person or someone close to that person."

Now I began to understand the fear that had rolled in my body. I knew what he was getting around to. I had seen my wife's illness in the clouds. But in spite of what he had said, I felt the tightness in my chest begin to dissipate. I glanced toward Tammy and she touched my hand; her face was typically serene. I could tell that she had resolved the same feelings as I had.

Calfrobe seemed burdened as he spoke again. "I'm not sure why this thing has come along at this time, but it has. You are here and I am here. The readings of the clouds are created by the forces that exist here with us and our families."

I wanted to interrupt him to tell him that we already knew of the illness and of the foreboding possibilities, but instead I went ahead and listened to his view.

Calfrobe continued, "Because it was your wife in that cabin, I must conclude that she may be the one affected. I feel that she will be sick or is sick now with a very dangerous illness. You also spoke of seeing smoke coming from the chimney. This is good! It means that she has a good chance of overcoming that misfortune. A cold cabin is a dead cabin. Yours is a warm one, warmed with love and life."

Both Tammy and I knew exactly what he was referring to, and I felt now I should let Tom Calfrobe know. "Tom, your analysis of the clouds is truly an extraordinary gift and very accurate. We do have an illness that has entered our lives. My wife has cancer. She had her surgery back in September of last year, and since then has gone through chemotherapy and radiation treatments. Because the illness has recurred a second time, the doctors say she has very little chance of living for more than a few years. This has been one of the driving forces for our move back to the northwest and that is why I was given the keeping of the pipe bag."

"Uh huh," Calfrobe nodded, "this is what I saw in your cloud picture. It is not the first time I have been forced to read the cabin in the sky. You are fortunate people."

"In what way?" I asked.

Calfrobe smiled. "You have the smoke rising from your cabin. This is a sign of strength and life." I reached over and held Tammy's hand and he continued. "You also have a beautiful love that is very evident to me. You must keep that fire glowing. You must keep it stoked up with love and prayer." Calfrobe looked deep into my heart. "Be in constant prayer."

He then looked over at Tammy. "You have a great battle ahead of you. Strengthen yourself with your children, your husband, your family. There are no physical means on this good earth that can give you the strength to overcome such a battle; only the unseen, untouched, and unheard can do that. Things like prayer and love, the strength in the Creator's hands."

We were all quiet for an extended time. I put away the pipe bag in the proper way. During that process, Tom Calfrobe commented, "I come to this place every year during this time to seek guidance and prepare for the upcoming sun dance. I rarely know what might happen, but I do know that something will happen. This year I have been given a new family, your family. I will be dancing for the eighth year and this dance I will dedicate to you." He looked toward Tammy. "Your name, face, and spirit will be my strength. I will dance for your battle, my sister."

Tammy, in her quiet way, thanked Tom Calfrobe for this most sacred vow.

As the afternoon faded into evening, the Calfrobes returned to their tent. We knew that our lives had been enriched by the experiences of the day. It was obvious to both of us that the Calfrobes were the reason for our time in Greengrass. We decided that we would push on the next morning, with or without visiting Arval Looking Horse. Our evening was a quiet one, with only a little conversation around the campfire. Soon we went off to our sleeping bags for an early bedtime. The long days of driving and the early morning risings must have caught up with me. I tried to contemplate the many amazing events of that day, but I fell quickly asleep.

32. PIPE KEEPER'S VISIT
Dance Back the Breath

I was awakened around 8:00 AM by Trapper's desire for his morning bottle. He was, as usual, impatient, and he did not seem to mind that the bottle was cold. He enjoyed it completely. I felt well rested and built our morning fire. In the process, I looked toward the Looking Horse cabin in the hopes of seeing something that would indicate that Arval was there. There were two additional autos. They must have arrived during the late night hours. Tom and Shirley Calfrobe were also up for the day. I could smell the familiar aroma of bacon cooking.

The thought of Looking Horse being here excited me, invoking butterflies as well. I was not sure if he'd remember me, and more importantly, feel comfortable speaking with me. I had written him about two months earlier, letting him know that I would be traveling through Greengrass with my family, but I was not sure if he had gotten the letter. I never really expected him to write back.

Tammy cooked us an excellent breakfast and we sat drinking our coffee afterwards, mostly talking amongst ourselves hopeful about a visit from Looking Horse. After about an hour Jeremiah walked out from behind the car with two baseball mitts and a ball. "Let's go Dad!" he said, as he tossed a glove in my direction. It must be the ultimate highlight in a father's life to throw a baseball with his son. I bent the old "uncle charley" in to him. He zipped back his fast ball.

"The kid's a natural!" I yelled out to Tammy, who was watching from the campsite. All fathers must feel their sons are naturals.

Trapper had climbed into his comfortable seat among the roots of the council tree. He was drawn to that place.

I had, by this time, worked up a good sweat. My big curve ball had ceased to curve and more often than not would put Jeremiah into action trying to catch it. Unfortunately, Jeremiah's fast ball had not slowed in velocity and was beginning to take its toll on my hand. "How about a break, Son!"

Jeremiah smiled. "Yeah, sure Dad!"

I found my way to the limited shade of the campsite and sat down. No sooner did I get comfortable than Tammy informed me, "You need to start packing up. We've got a long ways to travel!"

Pulling my cap down over my eyes, I replied, "Okay honey, give me a minute and I'll get hopping."

Tammy smiled her knowing smile. My minute turned into thirty minutes before I began the task of packing up. I had carefully arranged our supplies for the process. The first item to go in was the pipe bag, so I decided to take one more look toward the cabin in hopes of seeing Arval Looking Horse. From just beyond the small hill I spotted a rather large cowboy hat. As the wearer drew nearer, I could tell that he was indeed Looking Horse. His steps seemed easy yet purposeful. He glanced in our direction, and then back toward the ground.

I really was not sure how I would be received, but it did not matter at this point. Looking Horse extended his big hand toward me and I accepted it. It was a gentle handshake.

"How you doin'?" Looking Horse said with a smile.

"Real good. How about you?"

"Busy, real busy!" Looking Horse remarked.

I thought we might miss you," I told him.

"Yes, I've been spending a lot of time on the road. Just got back from Rapid City Powwow. Didn't think it was going to be as long as it was."

I asked, "Did you receive my letter?"

"Oh yes," he replied. "Sorry about not writing back."

"Oh, that's okay," I said. Placing my hand on Tammy's back, I introduced her. "This is my wife, Tammy. I mentioned her in the letter."

He removed his hat. I noticed that he had let his hair grow since last summer and it now hung down to his shoulders. He extended his hand and Tammy accepted it. "Nice to meet you."

Tammy smiled shyly as she took a quick look up at him. "Nice to meet you, also. Little Eagle has told me a lot about you, the pipe ceremony, and about this beautiful place."

Looking Horse nodded, "Uh huh."

Tammy continued, "Do you know, it's even more beautiful than I expected."

Looking Horse spoke, "Hmm. That's interesting. Most people don't really care for it that much and rarely does anyone find beauty here." A slight smile parted his lips. "It does my heart good to find the ones who see the beauty. I love this land, and I have lived here my whole life."

I then introduced Jeremiah and Trapper.

"Fine looking boys," Looking Horse stated.

I offered Looking Horse a cup of coffee. We all moved to the shade. I broke the temporary silence. "We have been here for a couple of days now. During that time we did some exploring along the butte. That's a wonderful place."

Looking Horse nodded, "Oh, yes. Did you see the vision pits?"

"Yes," I answered.

"It seems there is someone up there every weekend, sometimes three or four people." Looking Horse looked up toward the butte. "There are answers up there for anything you want to know."

Again, a silence followed his statement. Eventually, I asked, "How was the Powwow in Rapid City?"

This question seemed to rouse him from his apparent reverie. "Oh, very good. A lot of people. They always have a good one out there."

Looking Horse looked over my shoulder and waved to Shirley. She returned his wave. He then asked, "Did you get a chance to visit with the Calfrobes?"

"Oh yes," I replied. "We were able to get to know them a little bit."

"They are very good people. Tom is one of our respected elders at the sun dance and Shirley is always ready to help with whatever she can."

I added, "Tom is also a cloud watcher."

Looking Horse looked quickly in my direction. "Oh yes, he's one of the very few from around these parts. He received his ability to read cloud messages while he was on the sun dance pole as a young man." He paused and glanced over toward the Calfrobe camp. "They are good people, a good family!" He then asked, "How long will you be staying?"

I replied, "Well to tell you the truth, we were just about to start our packing when we saw you coming."

"Uh huh. Where's your next stop?"

"From here we're heading south to Pine Ridge. We hope to visit with a number of the elders and medicine people."

Looking Horse halfway smiled and pointed out, "You shouldn't have any problem finding them."

I then said, "As I mentioned in my letter we are on a dual mission now. One is to bring the pipe bag out for viewing and hopefully receive counsel as to what we should do with it. Our second and primary reason for this journey is my wife. We are looking for guidance and good counsel to help her find wellness."

Looking Horse's face reflected a deeper concentration. "I'm sure you'll find that guidance."

"If you like, Arval, we can stay on a couple more days."

He answered, "Oh no, that will not be necessary. I'm going to be leaving for Pipestone, Minnesota real soon. I'll be trying to catch up with the marchers."

"Oh yes," I responded. "Tom told us about the march earlier. I wish we had time to join you."

Looking Horse nodded his head. "Yes, that would be nice, but your own journey is just as important. You see, this is my job as the pipe keeper. This is the thing I do. It seems like I'm always on the road. It's not unusual for me to arrive one day and leave the same."

"It seems like a lot for one person to do!"

Looking Horse beamed his familiar smile. "Maybe, but it's my job. For the rest of my life I will do these things."

I then asked, "Since you will be leaving so soon, I wonder if I might show you the pipe bag?"

Looking Horse was silent for a moment and then replied, "I'd be honored."

We all gathered around the council tree. I prepared for the ceremony in the way that I had been taught. Looking Horse became even more quiet than usual. He seemed to drop off into a meditative state. His eyes became fixed upon the cherrywood pipe bag case. I opened with a prayer.

"Grandfather, Niskaminu, Wakan Tanka, I am Indian, my soul is Indian; I pray that what I am about to do is proper and in your order. I am thankful to be here and to be with these very special friends and family at this displaying of the pipe bag. Mitakuye Oyasin!"

At this point, I looked over at Arval Looking Horse. "With your permission I will continue on with this work." Looking Horse quickly nodded. I then filled an abalone shell with sage, lit it, and with my redtail hawk feather fan, began to smudge all present. After finishing this, I smudged the pipe bag case and offered the smoke to the four directions. I noticed that Looking Horse was whispering a low and quiet song. I opened the case and after a short period I prepared to remove the glass cover that protected the bag. Looking Horse raised his hands as if to say stop. I looked toward him and he slowly lowered his hand.

"This bag is alive and breathing!" He then pointed to a spot on the glass at the center of the bag. "Look there, do you see that?"

I looked back at the bag and amazingly saw exactly what he was referring to. A steamy area, such as you would see if you blew on a window, showed on the glass about three inches in diameter. I was startled and was not sure if I should continue on with the ceremony.

Looking Horse spoke with his almost hypnotic voice. "This bag was dying and now it is living." Glancing at the bead and quill work he continued, "I have seen this bead and quill pattern all through my life. It is Oglala; very typical of the patterns of the old ones. I am not sure what particular band or individual used this pattern, but it is Oglala. Can you tell me how it came to you?"

I was glad to relay the story. After I had finished, Looking Horse added, "It's obvious that this bag has been taken good care of over those years it's been with your family. You and your family should be thanked."

"Yes, it's been a sacred obligation of ours since we received it. I have now returned to this place to seek counsel as to what my next step should be with this bag. I have come to you in hopes that you will give me direction."

"Uh huh!" Looking Horse seemed to understand. "What I advise you is this: I offer to keep the pipe bag for you here, in the pipe house next to the holy pipe. This bag possesses a power, a good power. But your decision concerning the fate of this bag should not be answered by any one person or event. You should seek counsel from others as well. It will be welcome in the pipe house when you feel it is the proper time; maybe next year during our sun dance in August. That is the most important time of the year for the Lakota. But you should take the bag with you now. Show it to those elders and medicine people on Pine Ridge. They will help you with your decision."

Looking Horse redirected his thoughts and words toward Tammy. "Concerning your illness, I feel that this bag has a healing force about it, and it should be used for your healing. But you will need more than that in order to receive a full and complete healing." He hesitated for a moment. "I'm not sure what other types of healing you will need. Remember, the healing may not be just for you but for your husband, your children, and your whole family also."

Then looking back to me, he went on, "You might keep in mind that healing can come from the sun dance. I know people who have claimed miracles with the sun dance."

"Yes," I responded, "the thought of the sun dance has been with me for a long time. I know it requires a lot of preparation, but I'm not sure what specific things I would need to do."

Looking Horse interjected, "I just said it is a possible direction, not a required direction. It's not for everyone. As for what preparation you would need to make, your sponsor would help you with that."

"Sponsor? I think Tom Calfrobe would help me."

Looking Horse said, "If he is unable, please feel free to ask me. I would be glad to help."

I was truly amazed. The pipe keeper had given his personal offer of assistance. "Thank you, Arval. You honor me greatly!"

He smiled. "Ho! But let us not forget our other options."

"Like what," I asked.

"I know of two medicine men who have cured cancer. One of them lives on Standing Rock. His name is John Stands-In-Timber. The other is Fools Crow, who lives in Kyle. Another route you have is the vision quest." Pointing up toward the butte, he went on. "Up there are our vision pits. Many have used them for various reasons, including healing. This might be the best way. Most sun dancers seek guidance up there before they decide to dance."

I smiled at Tammy and said, "We have a lot to think about and decide."

Looking Horse had not finished. "Yes, but there are still two other things that you can do which require no thought or decision making." He paused to gather our complete attention. "Love each other and pray all the time!" Sometimes that may be all that is required. I feel your love for each other is strong." He pointed at me. "You should direct that strong love to her healing. And you," he directed his attention to Tammy, "should direct your love to your healing! Do this for your husband." He was typically quiet and then spoke, "Love is the most powerful healing source that is known to man. It brings the red sky in the evening to the vision seekers; it takes away the pain from the sun dancers. Love is first and most important. Without it, nothing will help! You should also pray often. In the morning, afternoon, and at night, pray together when you can."

I reached for Tammy's hand, and when our hands met she squeezed mine gently, for we knew that our lives were filled with a strong love and powerful prayer. I felt very good.

As I put away the bag, Looking Horse spoke. "Thank you for allowing me to see the bag."

I said, "I must thank you for your good counsel. I will keep your words in my heart always. I will also consider your kind offer to keep the pipe bag with the sacred pipe."

Looking Horse said, "That's up to you. In your travels you might discover other options that seem better. Whatever you decide, I wish you'd let me know. I'd like to see you and your family again next year, so come on back."

Smiling, I accepted. "You have honored us deeply, Arval, with your good and kind heart. We will try our best to return next year."

A car horn blared from near Looking Horse's cabin. I could see a couple of men looking in our direction. Looking Horse waved to them and said, "Well, I must go now. Got to catch up to the Pipestone marchers."

I shook his hand. "Thank you again for your time. Our prayers will be with you on the march."

Looking Horse nodded and looked toward Tammy. "When I am at the sun dance this year I will pray for your good health and long life."

Tammy smiled. "Thank you!"

As I went back to finish packing, Looking Horse and his friends drove off down the road. The dust kicked up heavily behind them. The windows of their car were so covered with dust, I could not see anyone in it, but I knew a friend was there. I waved good-bye.

33. GREENGRASS FAREWELL

Dance Back the Heart

Our packing was completed and we stood silently, looking out toward the council tree and the arbor. Jeremiah was doing his usual good job of keeping Trapper amused. Tammy broke the silence. "We should say good-byes to Tom and Shirley." I agreed.

As we turned toward their camp, we saw them both approaching. When they drew closer, I spoke. "Well, we've packed and are fixin' to get on our horse."

Tom Calfrobe smiled. "I hope the rest of your journey is safe and fulfilling."

I told him, "If we were to head directly home now, we would both feel that our journey had been fulfilling because of the time we've spent here with you and Shirley."

They both smiled. Shirley went over to Tammy and gave her a hug. "You take care of yourself, and don't worry. You're going to be fine."

I turned my attention to Tom Calfrobe but quickly realized that Shirley was not done with me. "Hey you!" she startled me. "You better take care of her or you'll have me to answer to!"

"Yes ma'am," I quickly answered.

From my pocket I pulled out a white seashell and held it out to Tom Calfrobe. "For your words and for allowing me to share your cloud ceremony, I wish you to have this."

"Hau!" he answered. "I thank you." He extended his hand for me to shake. I did so and felt something in my hand. When our hands separated, I discovered that Tom Calfrobe had placed two finely carved, smooth sticks, about the thickness of a pencil and three inches long, in my hands. They were partially wrapped with red cloth and tied with a red cotton string. I recognized them as the same sticks he had been carving since the first time we met. They were sun dancer piercing sticks. I stood speechless and motionless, my mind racing for something to say.

Tom Calfrobe spoke instead. "Keep these sticks in a special place. You might have a need for them some day. And for you," he turned to Tammy, "I will say prayers at the sun dance this year and I will look forward to seeing you and your family next year."

Our good-byes were now completed, but our journey was only beginning. This special place called Greengrass had woven its magic again. As we drove away I thought of the many good words and the counsel we had received. I slowed the car as we passed Looking Horse's cabin. Kids were playing outside as kids do, and a lady was hanging out the eternal laundry. The pipe house stood like a memorial to the Indian way, to a way that was unseen by most people, but was alive and enduring in the hearts of the believers. Hau!

34. PINE RIDGE
Dance Back the Mystery

We drove for a day and part of a night before we reached the outskirts of the Pine Ridge Reservation. I had traveled through here the previous year and Tammy had been here in her teens. I could not help but be amazed by the awesome landscape of the Badlands. So barren a place, I wondered how anyone could survive here without going crazy. It was obvious what the oppressive government was thinking when it banished the native people to the confines of this reservation.

I was a bit uncertain regarding whom or what I might see during our stay. We had made arrangements with a lady who lived and worked on the reservation to assist us with introductions and suggestions during our stay. Her name was Marie Not-Help-Him and we hoped that she would help us.

As we left the Badlands and drove through the colorful buttes, I could not help but think about Crazy Horse. It was here that he was born and grew up. It was here that he achieved his well-deserved leadership position among the Lakota. It was here that his body disappeared forever, its whereabouts known to no one save God. I said a prayer in his honor and to ask him for guidance in this country of his.

Our first task was to find Marie Not-Help-Him. We knew she lived outside Porcupine, that she worked for the schools, and also part time as a talk-show hostess for the local Lakota-speaking radio station, KILI. The first town we entered was Kyle. I remembered Tom Calfrobe saying that Fools Crow lived somewhere near here. I hoped that I might have the honor of a visit with him.

Kyle was a small reservation town. Its buildings were old and worn except for the newer school with strange art work in front. A lady walked along the road, two small children at her side and one in her arms. Tammy suggested that we stop at a store and ask for assistance. We had passed the only store, so I turned around and drove back. I walked in to find a jovial group of locals. They became silent once they recognized me as a stranger. I first strolled down an aisle until I found the chewing gum. I laid a pack of gum on the counter.

The man at the cash register looked at me from under his Busch beer cap. "Will that be all for you?"

"Yea, that's it," I answered.

He rang it up on his rather primitive cash register. "That'll be 55 cents."

I handed him a dollar bill. "I'm looking for a lady who lives in this area. Her name is Marie Not-Help-Him. Can you give me any idea where I might find her?"

He laid my change on the counter. "Yeah, I've heard that name, but I couldn't tell you where you could find her. You might ask Truman. He's at the back of the store. He pretty much knows everyone in these parts."

I thanked him and headed for the rear of the store. In an attached room I found two pool tables and a few chairs here and there. Lined up along the walls were numerous 50 cent pull tab machines. There was only one man in the room. He wore old Levis and a plaid shirt with the sleeves rolled up. He pushed his well-worn John Deere cap back exposing his middle aged, pockmarked face.

"Are you Truman?" I asked.

"Maybe, who wants to know?" he asked with a rough but quiet voice.

"My name is Lionel Little Eagle and I'm traveling through these parts looking for a ..." Before I could complete the sentence he interrupted me. "I know who you are. Been hearing about you for a couple of weeks now. I bet you're lookin' for Marie, aren't you?"

He surprised me, but I quickly answered, "Yep, could you tell me where I might find her."

"Oh yeah," he answered, as he straightened up from his leaning position against a pool table. "I know Marie. She works up at the school and lives near Porcupine."

Truman pulled a rack from under the table and began to rack up the pool balls. I continued, "I guess my best bet would be to head on up to the school and try to catch her there."

"Nope!" Truman replied while shaking his head.

"Well then, maybe she'll be home," I said, waiting cautiously.

"Nope. You won't find her there either."

I was becoming a bit frustrated. "Where might I find her?"

Truman smiled. "Don't really know." He paused. "She drives some kind of blue car. I guess you'll just have to look for her."

By this time I figured I had exhausted all the leads Truman had for me, so I thanked him and left.

"Good luck," I heard him holler, followed by the distinctive crack of the balls being broken. "She'll probably find you first."

"Any luck?" Jeremiah asked as I climbed into the car.

Sitting back in the seat I answered, "I don't know if I would call it luck, but I found out where she's not."

35. FOOLS CROW'S EYES
Dance Back the Waiting Man

We decided to take a couple of loops around Kyle in the hopes of spotting her blue car. I drove by the Post

Office and what appeared to be the community center. An elderly man was sitting on the edge of the sidewalk. He was very striking, for he sat upright in spite of his apparent years and there was a dignity about his pose.

"Perhaps someone will know something at the community center," Tammy suggested.

"Maybe, but let's take a look around first," I replied. As I continued on, once again the elder caught my attention, this time from afar. He looked familiar, but I didn't know anyone around these parts.

It didn't take long to drive the length of Kyle, twice. There were only a few buildings and houses, all covered with dust. Just as with the rest of the Midwest, Kyle was suffering from a terrible drought.

As we drove up to the community center, I was drawn by the elder's eyes. "You're right," I told Tammy as I turned into the dusty gravel parking lot. "We have to stop here."

As I drove closer I could not help staring. The elder, who had not changed position since our first drive by, was focused on me and in me. The gravel crackled under the wheels as I brought the car to a complete stop. I was still for a moment, then spoke. "That elder...it's Fools Crow."

"Fools Crow?" Tammy looked closer. "It might be. I'm not sure. It's been twenty years since I met him. What makes you think that's him?"

The elder's eyes and mine were locked. "He told me." I opened the car door and climbed out. "I'll go inside and see what I can find out."

I closed the door and looked over the top of the car. The elder seemed to have released me, but only after he had acquired my attention. I removed my cap and respectfully nodded in his direction. His right hand shot up and he enthusiastically waved to me, a wisp of a smile across his lips.

I went into the Post Office which was attached to the large community center. There was no one at the window, so I rang the bell. A young Indian woman appeared at the window.

"May I help you?" she asked politely.

"I hope so. I'm looking for Marie Not-Help-Him."

She smiled. "Oh yes. I know Marie." She hesitated and her quick smile disappeared. "You must be the guy...the guy with the pipe bag."

My shock must have been obvious. How could she know that? I was lost for a moment, and then asked, "Do you know where I can find Marie?"

She pointed through the teller-like bars toward the community center. "You might try in there."

I turned and saw another door which was the entrance to the community center, then I turned back toward the young lady.

"Does Fools Crow still live in this area?"

"Oh yes. They can help you with that in the center also." As I headed toward the door I wondered how she knew about the pipe bag. I turned to look at her once again, but she was gone. So was the bell.

As I opened the door, the first thing I noticed was a loud radio over which came the voice of a female DJ speaking entirely in Lakota. I stood for a moment in the doorway and found about forty elders enjoying conversation and their noon meal. There were a couple of couches and a number of long tables in use. To my right, as I walked in, was a rather large kitchen with four ladies hard at work. Once I entered the room, everyone became silent. No one looked directly at me and the conversation soon resumed. Finally, I spotted one of the kitchen ladies taking a breather.

I quickly made my way to her. She appeared to be in her middle to late forties with long black hair and a pockmarked face. I removed my cap. "Hello, I wonder if you might be able to help me out. I'm trying to find someone."

Not looking at me directly, she answered, "Maybe. Who is it you're looking for?"

"Marie Not-Help-Him."

Another lady giggled and we both looked in her direction. The lady I was talking to began to giggle. "That's easy. Just close your eyes and listen." This really got the nearby elders laughing.

"I'm sorry, but I don't understand."

Pointing up to the rather large speakers of the rather loud radio, she exclaimed, "That's her right there!"

I looked up, fully expecting to see her in the rafters and then I finally figured out what she was talking about. "You mean that's her on the radio?"

"You got it!" she said smiling.

"Well," I began to laugh as well, "I'd really like to see her in person. I've got to ...."

She interrupted me. "I know who you are. You're the man who's bringing the pipe bag to us!"

Nodding my head, I replied , "Yes, that's me."

"What's your name?" she demanded.

"I'm called Lionel Little Eagle. Who might you be?"

"They call me Margaret Lives-In-Sky. You want some coffee?" She led me to the kitchen area. By this time the elders' Lakota conversation was in full swing once again. I did feel that the primary topic of conversation was me.

As I filled my Styrofoam cup from the coffee maker, I asked Margaret, "How is it that you know about me and the pipe bag?"

"Oh, that's easy. Marie told us on the radio."

I took a cautious sip of the hot coffee and thought about what Margaret had said. It bothered me somewhat that she had made our visit so public, but I did not really feel threatened by it. In due time, many would have become aware of it anyway.

"This is some good coffee. Thanks," I told Margaret.

"You're welcome. How long do you plan to be here in Pine Ridge?"

"Well, I'm not really sure. Do you know how I can get in touch with Marie?"

Margaret reached for the nearby wall phone. "I'll just give her a call."

I gestured to thank her. As she was making the call I noticed that the DJ on the radio was a man now. I looked out the kitchen doorway. The many elders were still enjoying their lunch. It was good to see them being well taken care of. I felt Margaret's hand tapping me on the shoulder. "She's on her way here."

I smiled. "Great! Thanks for the help."

Margaret turned back to the kitchen and began filling coffee cups and setting them on a serving tray. Once again I interrupted her. "Excuse me, but is Fools Crow still living in the area?"

She did not slow her pace while working. "Oh, yes. He's sitting outside on the curb where he always sits."

Now I knew my feelings had been right. The old one who had drawn me with his eyes to this place was Fools Crow. I slowly began working my way toward the rear exit. I knew I would see Fools Crow from there. As I looked through the screen door, I could see Tammy and Trapper sitting in the front seat of the car. Jeremiah was standing outside the car. The elder was sitting with his back to me. He seemed to be looking in the direction of my family. I felt I needed to introduce myself to him. I had a great urge to simply shake his hand, but I knew that in the traditional way, it was not proper to just go up and disturb him. As I stood there unsure of what I should do next, I silently said his name in my own thoughts.

His head jerked up as if he heard me and he slowly turned in my direction and looked into my eyes and then into my soul. Without using the spoken word, he answered, "Yes!" I was surprised and must have acted that way. He smiled a knowing, almost mischievous smile.

Margaret walked up and retrieved me from my daze, saying, "We got a lot of flies around these parts. You might close your mouth before one gets in there."

I heard her snicker. She put her hand on the screen door and continued, "The old man doesn't speak much English. If you'd like to talk to him, I can translate for you."

I hesitated, then asked, "Do you think it would be proper for me to talk with him?"

"Oh yes. He likes visitors and he gets his share of them. He'd be glad to meet you."

The screen door squeaked loudly as Margaret opened it. Fools Crow did not move a muscle. I made eye contact with Tammy from afar and pointed with my head to Fools Crow. I then mouthed the words, "Bring my bag." She understood and reached for my bag from under the front seat.

Margaret and I circled around to the front of the renowned and legendary Lakota medicine man. She leaned toward him and spoke quickly and loudly in Lakota. He watched and listened intently to her, then answered. His voice was soft, and his words seemed short and to the point. His dark, thin face was thick with lines of age. He was wearing a faded, red, long sleeve plaid shirt and jeans, a well-used pair of cowboy boots, a wide-brimmed black cowboy hat with a small eagle plume feather dangling to one side, and a turquoise bracelet on his left arm. Out of his aged face shone two magnificent eyes that reminded me of planets deep in the universe.

He turned and looked over my shoulder at Tammy approaching with my bag, then turned his eyes directly at me.

"What's your name," Margaret translated his first words to me.

"Lionel Little Eagle," I answered. Tammy handed me my bag. I pulled a small pouch of Prince Albert tobacco from it.

Margaret told him my name and he nodded. I held out the tobacco toward him and said, "Fools Crow, I am honored to meet you. I have some tobacco for you."

Margaret was closer to Fools Crow now and still speaking loudly. He reached over and took the tobacco from my hand, squeezed it with both hands and then shoved it into his shirt pocket.

Margaret looked at me. "He says he's glad to meet you too and he wants to know your wife's name."

I smiled with pride. "This is Tammy." By this time Jeremiah had arrived with Trapper in tow. "And these are two of my sons, Jeremiah and Trapper."

More words were exchanged between Margaret and Fools Crow and she relayed them to me. "He wants to know why you have come here."

"Tell him we have come for counsel and guidance. Tell him that I am the keeper of a pipe bag and I have it here with me."

While Margaret translated, I reflected on the story my father-in-law, the previous keeper, had told me about how Fools Crow had kept this same bag for an entire year, from 1966 to 1967. That was twenty-one years ago and I was not sure he would remember.

Margaret said, "He wants to know if you are the owner of the bag."

"No," I answered, "I am just keeping it for the rightful owners, the Lakota people."

Margaret had to ask him to repeat his next question, and it was directed to Tammy. "How old is your baby?"

She answered, "He'll be two in September."

He smiled and Margaret translated, "He's a big boy!"

We both nodded in agreement. I heard the loud squeak of the screen door again. I looked back and saw four ladies standing at the door. One of them was holding a plastic dish with food in it. In her other hand was a cup of red juice. She, too, spoke loudly and handed the food and drink to Fools Crow. He accepted the food, but he did not start to eat. I asked Margaret, "Are we interrupting his meal time?"

"Oh, no. He always waits until he gets home to eat."

"Will he be leaving soon?"

"Yes," she replied, "as soon as he can find a ride home."

I looked at Tammy and she nodded her head, understanding what I was thinking. Then I directed my attention to Margaret. "I would be glad to take him home, if it's okay with him."

Margaret turned to Fools Crow and translated my offer. He seemed pleased and began to rise, with help from Margaret.

It seemed so strange to me that all this was happening, yet I felt comfortable with the situation. I just hoped Fools Crow felt the same way. Tammy and the boys stayed with Margaret at the center.

36. FOOLS CROW SWEAT

Dance Back the Dancing Bag

The dust billowed from under the car as we pulled away. When I reached the first stop sign, it finally dawned upon me that I did not know where Fools Crow lived, and worst of all, I could not ask. I turned in my seat and looked back toward the center in hopes of seeing someone who might be there to help. It was as if they had all disappeared. I suddenly felt a nudge on my shoulder. Fools Crow pointed to the left. Then I knew that he would just guide me with gestures, so off we went.

The old man held his dish and cup up above his knees as we bounced over the rugged Pine Ridge roads. I began to feel a bit lost in our non-verbal situation. I could sense him looking around in the car, but I did not want to place him in the awkward position of not being able to understand my English. So I just drove silently and watched the never-changing scenery.

After about three or four miles and a half dozen or so intersections, I became uncomfortable about whether or not I was going in the right direction. I turned toward Fools Crow, and before I could gesture or ask, he pointed straight ahead. Another mile or so passed in silence. I continued to feel uneasy about our lack of communication. I was hoping that Fools Crow was not having the same problem.

For just a moment I heard a very quiet song come from his gravelly voice; it reminded me of a Lakota prayer song. Then suddenly he asked, "Where you from?" His voice filled up the entire car. I was stunned. The last thing I expected to hear from him was the English language.

"Seattle!" I said, loud and clear.

"Where you going?" was his next question.

"Back to Seattle," I answered. I could see that he was smiling, like the cat who got the bird.

"It rains a lot there I hear."

"Certain times of the year we do get a lot of rain, but other times it's really nice."

Nodding, he answered, "Uh huh!" He gazed out the window and continued, "We need some of that rain around here."

After a short pause Fools Crow spoke again, "In one week we sun dance here!" Looking at me, he asked, "Will you be coming?"

I answered, "I'm not sure. We hope to be here, but we'll probably have to leave before then."

"You are welcome to come," he assured me.

"Thank you," I replied. I felt very good that he would invite me even though he had just met me. The elder had his way of reading people and I must have read well to him.

"Turn up here; my house is not far." He pointed with a gnarled finger. "It's a pink house. My sun dance arbor is right beside it."

I turned to the right off the main road onto a dusty driveway. I could see an old, pink framed house up ahead. There were three junk cars on rims and blocks in the front yard, and a woman was hanging out laundry. She gave us a quick look and returned to her work. I saw the sun dance arbor to the left of the house and about a hundred yards away three shirtless young men were working. As I came to a stop, I saw a middle-aged man on the front porch. With him was a tiny girl, maybe four years old.

Fools Crow fumbled unsuccessfully for the door handle. I hustled around to let him out of the car. When I opened the door, he handed me his dish and juice, then after standing and gaining his balance, he retrieved his lunch back from me. The man from the porch arrived at this point and escorted Fools Crow to the house.

I stood where I was for a moment, not sure what I should do. As he reached the porch, Fools Crow turned and beckoned to me. Then he and his assistant continued on into the house. I walked up to the door and was welcomed by the man who had assisted the elder.

"Hello," he said. "My name is John Pawnee Leggings." He extended a hand. "Please come in. Grandpa Fools Crow wants to talk to you."

As I entered and removed my cap, the first thing I noticed was the scarcity of furnishings. I guess I was expecting a museum-like atmosphere with eagle feathers and old Indian relics hanging on the walls. But the walls were barren with the exception of a photo collage in a single frame. Fools Crow sat in the only chair in the room, which was situated next to the furnace. To his right was a coffee table with an ashtray half-filled with well-smoked Pall Malls and his lunch and drink from the community center. Fools Crow was in the process of lighting a cigarette. The little girl approached him and began to fumble with the dish of food. Fools Crow assisted her and she quickly began to eat. After a few mouthfuls, she looked up and gave me a big smile. Then she returned to the lunch, which was obviously hers now.

John Pawnee Leggings came up beside me. He was holding two cups of black coffee. He handed one to me and set the other next to Fools Crow on the coffee table. I thanked him and he nodded.

Speaking in Lakota, John Pawnee Leggings and Fools Crow conversed for a couple of minutes. Neither looked in my direction, but I knew I was their topic. Pawnee Leggings eventually turned to me and said, "I am his stepson and he has asked me to translate for him."

"Thank you," I replied. "He spoke pretty good English coming over from the center."

"Yes," John Pawnee Leggings explained, " he does speak good English, but Lakota is his spirit tongue and he much more comfortable with that language."

I understood and then commented, "I'm not sure why he wants to talk to me."

"He does," affirmed Pawnee Leggings. "You have the pipe bag that we've heard about on the radio."

"Yes, I do. Please tell Fools Crow that I would be honored if he would take a look at it."

Pawnee Leggings relayed the message and the elder replied with a nod.

I went out to the car and procured my medicine bag and the pipe bag in its case. When I returned to the house, I placed the case at the center of the room in front of Fools Crow. I filled an abalone shell with sage for smudging purposes. Waving his hands around, he smudged himself. I held the smoke toward John and he, too, waved his hands through the smoke and then brushed them along his arms, legs, and through his hair. I then set the abalone on the coffee table and smudged myself.

Prior to opening the cherrywood case I said my prayers. I could feel both Pawnee Leggings and Fools Crow watching me. I prayed that my work would be good and in proper order. I prayed that I would bring no shame to the pipe bag or to this ceremony. After I had finished, I opened the case.

For a moment everyone was silent. Then I heard the elder's voice. Pawnee Leggings relayed, "I have seen this bag before!"

I explained, "Yes, about twenty years ago the previous pipe bag keeper brought it to you. You kept it for a year and showed it to others. He hoped to find out more about the bag and its origins."

John used his hands as much as his voice to translate. Fools Crow listened carefully, looking at the bag. It appeared he had finished, so I continued, "You used the bag in the sun dance of 1967. Vinson Brown was the keeper at that time. He said that the bag was hung on the sacred tree at the center of the arbor."

Fools Crow seemed to perk up during the translation. He said, "Yes! Vinson Brown. I remember him. A tall man with a pleasant smile. He was driving a green car and had a number of others with him: children, girls and boys both. My wife, Kate, really liked him and cooked a big pot of wajapi soup. We walked together a lot. He was quite a traveler and, oh, yes...he was a writer, he wrote books. I remember he sent me some books to read. I lost them in the fire. He was a good man. Is he still alive?"

I was dumbfounded. John picked up my astonishment and spoke. "You can believe him. He's off on the year sometimes, but he's always doing that. It's funny. He'll forget where he lays his cigarettes ten times a day." Fools Crow repeated his question, "Is Mr. Brown still alive?"

"Oh, yes," I responded quickly. He is doing very well. He lives in Northern California. He asked me to bring his personal greetings to you."

After a slight smile and a nod from Fools Crow, I continued, "He has also given me the task of keeping and protecting the pipe bag. He told me to bring it here to you for counsel. I have done so, and I respectfully ask for that counsel regarding my duties and responsibilities as its keeper."

Fools Crow spoke for a long time back and forth with Pawnee Leggings. It seemed as though Pawnee Leggings was having a problem with the translation. Finally, Fools Crow leaned back in his chair and gestured with both hands toward the bag. He wanted to hold it. Pawnee Leggings confirmed this. I immediately started the process. Again Pawnee Leggings and Fools Crow were talking, more easily this time. Pawnee Leggings reached over to my extra sage and gave some to Fools Crow. He vigorously rubbed it on his hands, front and back, and up and down his arms. He gave the remaining sage back to John and placed his hands, palms up, on his lap. As I reached over to hand him the bag, he first reached out, then quickly pulled his hands back! This caught me off guard. I looked up at him and again he began to reach out for the bag but once again he withdrew his hands. I was beginning to feel I was doing something wrong. I looked quickly to Pawnee Leggings and he held out four fingers and said "four" first in Lakota, then in English. "Four times; he'll take it on the fourth time."

I understood then. On the fourth time, he accepted the bag. For a moment he was very still, head slightly tilted, as if he were listening. Then a quiet prayer eased from his lips. I looked toward Pawnee Leggings, but he never moved his focus from the bag. There was no need for translation. The elder was talking to God.

As time went by I began to feel a strange warmth. Sweat began to roll down my face. I thought it might be anxiety, or perhaps the sun was hitting the house just right. I looked at Pawnee Leggings again. He, too, was drenched with sweat and his eyes were closed tightly. I looked back at Fools Crow. The bag was still in his unmoving hands. He was obviously not perspiring, but I could perceive now that the heat was emanating from him. It was all around him. His gentle prayers seemed to be coming more rhythmic and the heat intensified. My ears began to ring and I felt faint. I felt myself slumping to the floor with absorbed intensity. I finally found the strength to raise my head and I looked at Fools Crow again. What I saw was magical! His demeanor had not changed. His lips were still, but his voice was filling my entire being! In front of him was the pipe bag, floating! His hands were in the same position, palms up. However, the bag was levitated about a foot above his hands. Upon closer observation I could see that the bag was moving or vibrating slowly. As I focused in on this supernatural event, the heat that had been encircling me diminished. I felt comfort now. Fools Crow began to slowly move his hands, left, then right, along the length of the bag. His voice was still in my head, a strong Lakota voice. He then moved his hands upward, above the bag. As they moved past the bag, it began to move with him until it had completely turned over exposing the rarely observed green side of the bag. Once it was revealed, I realized that the bag seemed different on this side. It was still vibrating with Fools Crow's power, but the bag was presenting itself in a new way. The predominately green beads on the white background seemed to be stirring individually. They were sparkling with a newness I had not seen before. The bag was over a hundred years old, yet it had become a brand new bag. The red and blue beads were vibrant. The porcupine quill work was flawless and seemed crisp and fresh. I was truly astounded by this obvious display of power.

Somehow time rolled by without my noticing. The next thing I felt was Pawnee Leggings' hand on my shoulder. I raised my head as if I'd been sleeping, but I knew I had not been. What had happened? I looked at Fools Crow. He was sitting quietly in his chair, puffing on a cigarette. The pipe bag was no longer in his hands.

I looked toward the case and found it lying peacefully in place. I noticed Pawnee Leggings heading for the kitchen. I was confused. Had I dreamed this, I wondered to myself. "No," Fools Crow's voice jumped into my head. As Pawnee Leggings rustled about the kitchen, I sat in pure wonderment of the events I had witnessed.

37. SMOKING WITH THE POPE
Dance Back the Magic

"It's time we smoked." I once again heard the elder's voice in my head. When I looked at him, he was holding his hands in a semi-closed fashion, as if to represent a pipe. With one hand he pointed to the opening at the top of his other hand, the symbol of the bowl. I knew exactly what he meant. I reached for my bag and removed my personal pipe and kinnikinick tobacco. I had some concerns about my personal pipe ceremony but continued without hesitation. After all, this was Fools Crow.

I asked, in prayer, for guidance in this ceremony, an ancient ceremony, as sacred as communion or baptism to Christians, as time-honored as the lighting of the Hanukkah candles in the Jewish Faith, as spiritually eloquent and powerful as a Buddhist chant. I was to share this unique rite with one who has been called the Pope of the Indian world.

I laid out a large piece of soft deer hide. Sitting cross-legged on the floor, I placed the stem, bowl, tobacco, and the abalone shell with sage on the deer hide. After relighting the sage, I passed the stem, then the bowl, through the purifying smoke. I then held the stem in my right hand and the bowl in my left hand. I prayed, "Grandfather, Tunkasila, Wakan Tanka. This pipe is a non-pipe as it now stands. This stem is merely wood and this bowl is a simple red stone." I placed the bowl and stem in conjunction and pushed them together. I continued my prayer. "Together, Grandfather, it is of great power. The bowl is alive with the blood of our ancestors. This is the woman's side. The stem represents the backbone of our traditions and customs. I recognize the man's side here. Grandfather, I pray that I do this work in a good way and that I bring no shame to myself or to this ceremony and pipe. Hau!"

My prayers completed, I pinched a small amount of tobacco between my first finger and thumb and held it up in an easterly direction. "Wakan Tanka, I offer this tobacco to the east, from where the new day comes, reminding us of new life." I then placed this tobacco into the bowl, being careful not to drop any. Once again, I pulled some tobacco from the pouch, this time holding it in a southerly direction. "Grandfathers, Sacred Ones, I offer this tobacco to the south from where growth comes, reminding us of our need to let our spirits grow and be renewed." I repeated the same process, this time to the west. "Sacred being, Tunkasila. I humbly offer this tobacco to the west, the place where the sun hides and sleeps, reminding us to be awake and ready for the Promised One's message!" Then to the north I held up the next pinch of tobacco. "Wakan Tanka, God! I offer this tobacco in a clean way to the north, the way of purity. This is to remind us to keep a pure and clean heart." Once again, with great care, I took more tobacco. Holding it skyward, I prayed, "Niskaminu, Creator of all, Taker of all. I offer this humble token to your power. This is to remind us that we are forever watched over and protected." A final time, I pinched a bit of tobacco and leaned forward, holding the herb to the floor. "Mother Earth, I offer this tobacco to you in honor of your sacrifice and love for us. This is to remind us to protect and love the earth and all her creatures, large and small." I then placed a small portion of sage, as a cap, on top of the tobacco filled bowl.

With the process of loading the pipe completed, I stood, holding the bowl in my left hand, and rotated the stem in a clockwise direction four times. I then offered the prepared pipe to Fools Crow. Three times I offered it to him, and on the fourth attempt, he accepted it. The elder struggled to the edge of his chair and, in a rather abbreviated fashion, offered his personal prayers to the four directions, to Mother Earth, and to Father Sky. He held it in a downward position. John, who had returned, unobserved, to the room, struck a match and held it to the tobacco. The elder drew deeply and swiftly. The smoke rolled from the pipe and his mouth until his head practically vanished within it. He then blew smoke in the four directions, up, and then down. After this he rotated the pipe clockwise, then handed it to me in four distinctive motions. I humbly accepted, and in a similar manner smoked the pipe, the same pipe that I had held reverently against the sacred bundle at Greengrass, the pipe that for many years had served honorably as a medium between my prayers and God. Now this pipe was blessed with even more power and wisdom. The holy man of the Oglala had taken it to his lips, to his spirit. I thanked God for this moment.

After I had smoked, I offered the pipe to Pawnee Leggings, who accepted and smoked. He finished and passed it on to Fools Crow, who looked carefully into the bowl. Pointing with his finger at the bowl, he looked up at Pawnee Leggings, who quickly lit another match. As he once again drew strongly on the pipe, I could hear the crackling sound from the bowl indicating it was nearly empty. He held the pipe out to me, and I accepted it with great respect. Fools Crow then smiled his big toothless smile and said, "Pilamiyah! Thank you!" I nodded and smiled in return. I then made sure that the bowl was completely empty and separated the bowl from the stem. "Hau!" The ceremony of the smoke was now done.

38. THE ELDER'S MESSAGE
Dance Back the Wisdom

We sat for a moment. I asked Fools Crow, "Can you give me any counsel as to what I should do with this pipe bag?" Pawnee Leggings translated my question.

Fools Crow answered, "The pipe bag will soon be returned to the Lakota people."

This statement caught me off guard. I felt it would be with me until Tammy's healing was completed, a process that could take an extended period time. I asked him about it.

He matter-of-factly agreed with me. "That is correct. Your wife's healing will be completed soon."

Instead of an elated feeling of happiness, a strange, uncomfortable feeling eased into my gut. I would not pursue the meaning of her healing being close to completion. The answers seemed too obvious. Instead I asked, "But to whom will the bag go?"

"I do not know, but you will know when the time comes."

I asked him about my duties and responsibilities to the pipe bag. He counseled, "Be very cautious of whom you allow to see this bag. There are those who would gladly take it from you, for its power or for its worth. You will see those ones and recognize them." He hesitated for a moment, lighting his fifth or sixth cigarette. "Your ceremony is good. It is obvious that your heart and spirit are dedicated to its keeping. You should keep it until that healing day comes, and then it will be time to return it."

I said, "The previous keeper told me that the bag once belonged to the Lakota holy man, Crazy Horse. He said that he was told this by you. Do you recall this?"

"Yes," he quickly replied. "The pipe bag was once the pipe bag of Crazy Horse. It was hidden by his family after he was killed."

It seemed the elder was becoming weary of the questions. I visited for a short time more and was then escorted to the front door by Pawnee Leggings. I stood at the door and said to Fools Crow, "Thank you for taking the time to help me. I won't be able to stay for the sun dance but I'll see you at another time."

Fools Crow's response was strange because Pawnee Leggings had to have him repeat it a couple of times. He then relayed it to me. "You won't be seeing me again. I will see your wife first."

My gut twisted again. It was too obvious what he meant. I did not want to believe him. I was still upset as John Pawnee Leggings escorted me to the car. To calm myself, I changed the subject and asked John if he was a Pawnee.

"No, I'm not Pawnee," he said, smiling. "A lot of people think that. My name comes from an ancestor who raided a Pawnee camp and stole a pair of leggings. We have been known by that name ever since."

I shook his hand, thanked him for his assistance, and started to leave. I looked back once more and asked him to thank Fools Crow for me again.

As I secured my medicine bag and the pipe bag in the car, I briefly reflected on the mystery of the moment: being drawn into the holy man's life by him, being allowed the honor of a pipe ceremony, and receiving his wise counsel. I looked over the top of the car. On the porch stood the little girl, who had disappeared during the previous events. She beamed back, waving her little hand energetically in the air as I drove away.

39. NOT-HELP-HIM, HELPING
"Dance Back the Sisters

Upon returning to the community center, I was met by Tammy and another woman. She was in her mid-thirties with short, waving brown hair and a pair of black-rimmed glasses. She wore a long skirt with a white blouse. Tammy introduced us. "Lionel, this is Marie Not-Help-Him."

I shook her hand. She smiled shyly with a slight glance toward my face.

"It's my pleasure to meet you, Marie."

"Thank you. I'm glad to meet you, too."

We spoke for a moment and then Marie suggested that we follow her home. I bid the women at the center farewell, thanking them for their assistance. I placed a bill in the donation can and departed. We drove through rolling hills of tall grass and clumps of sage. Marie Not-Help-Him's house was about fifteen miles from Kyle in the village of Porcupine. The first thing I noticed was the outhouse. It brought back memories of my childhood, visiting my grandparents. Their outhouse was a unique experience for me. Other homes in Porcupine also had outhouses.

We brought our car to a stop in the dusty driveway in front of her house. The next thing I noticed was that Marie's home was special in appearance. Although the house itself, like many others in the neighborhood, was little more than a shack, the grass and weeds around it were neatly cut. Along the pathway to the front door and along the borders of the yard were planted flowers and plants, each carefully watered. An old-fashioned pump-handled well stood near the entrance to the house. There were no hoses or sprinklers to water this yard in the wilting summer heat.

"Please, come in," Marie Not-Help-Him invited. Upon entering her two room house, I was even more impressed. It was simple and very neat. It was easy to see that she took pride in her home. The first room was the kitchen and dining area. Marie began to make a fresh pot of coffee. The house had electricity, but no running water. She dipped the water from a large plastic bucket for the coffee maker.

"Would anyone care for a cola instead of coffee?" she asked.

Jeremiah promptly accepted. She opened the door of the rather old refrigerator, saying, "I just bought this refrigerator. It is really nice to have." Tammy and I sat down at her kitchen table. Trapper sat strangely quiet on my knee, as if he was waiting for something.

"Please excuse me," Marie said. "I've got to make a couple of phone calls."

On the phone she spoke Lakota with an occasional English word interjected every now and then. The phone was in the kitchen with an extra long cord. She took it into her bedroom. The coffee maker hissed to completion, and I filled the cups that she had left near the pot. I sat down and had a hot sip. Tammy was also enjoying her usual half a cup. Trapper took off after Jeremiah and the red Coke can. They were both outside now.

Marie hung up the phone and joined us at the table. She recommended that we set up camp in her yard, saying it was a good general location, and accessible to a number of other areas. She also offered the use of her kitchen and phone. We accepted and thanked her for her kind invitation.

As Tammy and Marie talked, I glanced into the bedroom, which like the kitchen area presented a very neat appearance. The furnishings were not fancy, but they served their purpose. A dresser stood on one side of the room with a hairbrush, perfumes, and powder on top. Her queen-size bed took up most of the rest of the room. It had a frilly white spread with stuffed animals on the pillows. Another, taller dresser with knickknacks on top stood at the other side of the room. A steel bar had been nailed up across the corner to serve as her closet. Next to her bed on the nightstand, I spotted a familiar book, *Warriors of the Rainbow*, by Vinson Brown and Willy Willoya. Seeing it reminded me of the circumstance of our journey. It was this book and the communication between Vinson Brown and Marie Not-Help-Him that had allowed us a point of contact. Because of this, we had found a friend. I returned my attention to Tammy and Marie. They were smiling. It was curious, but I found them similar in demeanor.

Tammy spoke, "Marie has arranged a council with some of the medicine people and elders in the area."

"Wonderful!" I exclaimed.

"One of the first people I'd like you to meet," Marie said, "is my mother, Celane Not-Help-Him." The pride and love in Marie's voice as she spoke was a beautiful tribute from a daughter to a mother. "She's expecting us later today. She lives in the projects in Oglala. That's about twenty miles from here."

"I'm looking forward to meeting her," I offered.

We finished our coffee and I decided to see what the boys were doing. Excusing myself, I pushed open the screen door. I found them wandering about. The Coke was long gone.

"Where's the tent going to be, Dad?" Jeremiah asked.

"Well, I'm not really sure. There's not much in the way of shade anywhere." Looking around, I located a flat spot not far from the side of the house. "This looks like a good place."

Marie and Tammy came outside, and I asked for Marie's approval of the spot I had selected for the tent. She agreed upon the location.

Jeremiah and I began the well-practiced process of setting up camp. We were done in half an hour while Tammy made a quick lunch of hot dogs and beans. We sat around our camp for the rest of the afternoon, relaxing as best as we could in the hot Dakota sun. Trapper had fallen asleep with his bottle. Despite the heat, it was good to take a break. All the traveling and visiting was beginning to take its toll. We had been on the road for two and a half weeks and had a lot of traveling and visiting left ahead of us.

The sun was making a majestic departure over the nearby buttes when Marie reappeared. It looked as though she had also enjoyed an afternoon nap. "I just got off the phone with Mother," she said. "She's home now and has asked us to come over."

I finished off the cold coffee I had been working on; Tammy changed Trapper, and we all climbed into the car. "Will everything be okay here?" I asked Marie.

"I think so; maybe you shouldn't leave any valuables."

We could not think of any valuables we had left behind. The pipe bag was in a special place in the car.

Our trip consisted of familiar scenery. The road changed from blacktop to gravel a couple times. We were all very quiet. I asked Marie how long she had lived here.

"All my life. Just like my parents and their parents."

"You and your family must have seen a lot changes over the years," I observed. I mentioned the more recent history-making events: the American Indian Movement and the battles with the Federal Bureau of Investigation, the goon squads, and other governmental groups. "I imagine it must have been something to remember in the late sixties and early seventies. Did you see much of the conflict?"

"Oh yes," she answered. "More than I wanted to see." I noticed a bit of hesitancy in her voice, so I did not pursue the subject.

"You mentioned earlier others who might be able to share some guidance with me regarding the pipe bag."

"Uh huh," she nodded. "There are a number of people I think could help with the pipe bag, including some of our medicine people."

I replied, "As far as our time is concerned, we really don't have an actual date to leave. Both of us have decided that this is an important part of our journey, so we don't want to complicate this part with time restrictions."

She smiled. "That's what I was hoping for. I will do my best to keep things simple. Among the people I hope we will have a chance to visit with are Pete Catches, Severt Young Bear, and probably the most important family, the Chips up at Eagle Nest Butte."

I had heard of this family before, but asked Marie Not-Help-Him, "Why would this family be so important to us?"

She took a rare glance in my direction. "This family is very wakan. The great medicine man, Horn Chips, was a teacher of Crazy Horse. They will be able to determine whether or not the bag belonged to Crazy Horse."

"But how?" I wondered out loud.

"It is said that Crazy Horse appears to the family and communicates through them, especially through Godfrey Chips, who has a special relationship to him. Crazy Horse will tell him directly if that bag is his."

A chill moved up my back and into my neck. I knew that soon I would witness a mysterious force, something not experienced by many, something so powerful that it was not for everyone. I questioned my own purpose, my own reason for placing myself at the mercy of this mystery force. My purpose became very clear once again. I needed guidance and counsel as to my duties with the pipe bag. Beyond that I needed guidance and counsel for the wellness of my other wing, my wife.

I had known for many years about the power of healing that existed in this quiet land. The doctors at the Washington hospitals had done all they could to help Tammy with her cancer, but they had admittedly exhausted all their avenues for curing her. It would be easy to feel anger at the medical system, but I could not because I knew the best that modern medicine had to offer had already been utilized. Now we both agreed that we should try the best of spiritual medicine to make her well: daily and constant prayer, the sweat lodge, and other ceremonies were our new avenues. There is no more powerful a place to talk to God and to receive His blessing than this barren land. It would be here that we would surrender to the mystery force.

40. CELANE'S SMILE
Dance Back the Little Bear

Even though we had put well over 2,000 miles on the car since leaving Washington State, this trip to Oglala seemed a very long one. Finally, we arrived at a HUD housing complex. It was a familiar sight. The red brick duplexes appeared to be about five years old. Except for a few of the units, the yards were made up of rocks and dusty dirt. There were more cars on blocks than there were on all four tires. I estimated there were about fifty units. Vandals had taken their toll on the facility. Spray-painted graffiti decorated some of the red brick buildings. There were broken windows, doors off their hinges; taking a look around, most units were in need of some type of repair. The underlying problem was the usual one: the United States government's lack of attention to the real needs of Native American peoples.

However, within the cactus a flower bloomed, both in physical appearance and spiritual essence. As we turned into the driveway of Marie Not-Help-Him's mother's home, the first thing that caught my eye was a middle-aged man watering a well-groomed yard. The split-rail fence was lined with beautiful flowers. Plush green grass flourished in the yard. A couple of cars were already in the driveway as well as a motorcycle, which gleamed from a recent wax job.

Tammy and the boys remained in the car. Marie Not-Help-Him and I climbed out. She quickly entered the house. The man carefully watering the yard never looked up. From the looks of the yard, I could see that he took his work very seriously. I eased up toward him, keeping my eye on both him and the house. As I got within speaking range, I complimented him on his handiwork. He cut his eyes slightly in my direction and nodded his head.

I saw the front door open. Marie Not-Help-Him came out, followed by an elder woman. "Please come in," Marie Not-Help-Him said.

I looked over toward Tammy and motioned for her to come. She and the boys joined me. At the top of the steps going into the house, Marie Not-Help-Him stood with the older woman.

"This is my mother, Celane Not-Help-him." Marie Not-Help-Him turned to her mother, "Mom, this is Little Eagle, Tammy, Jeremiah, and Trapper."

Celane Not-Help-Him was a striking woman, about five-foot-five and 150 pounds. She wore her long graying hair in a single braid extending the length of her back. When she looked at Trapper, a big smile lit up her face; an unmistakable sparkle flashed in her eyes.

"It's a pleasure to meet you," I said. She gave me a quick look, then turned her attention back to Trapper, who was clinging to Tammy's leg.

"Nice to meet you, too. My daughter told me you'd be coming." She seemed to stop in midsentence and a distinct giggle emerged. She looked at me a little longer and then returned to Trapper. Once again she giggled, this time a bit more enthusiastically. She said something to Marie Not-Help-Him in Lakota, and they both began to laugh.

"That's one kid that couldn't get lost in a crowd!" Celane Not-Help-Him exclaimed.

It was then that I realized what struck her as so funny, something that I had seen and heard before.

"Trapper," she said. "You look like your dad all shrunk up!" She laughed some more. Trapper looked on with a curious look. "Let me see that boy!" Celane Not-Help-Him said with her arms extended in his direction.

I thought to myself, oh no! He's not going to go for that. But to my surprise, and Tammy's too, he immediately leaned forward and reached for her.

"Boy you're a cute one!" She looked over to Tammy. "He gets his cuteness from his mom, but he's a dead ringer for his Dad. Does he have an Indian name?"

"Yes," Tammy replied. "He's called Little Bear."

"Uh huh!" She looked at Trapper. "Mato Cikala, Little Bear. How old are you, Little Bear?"

Tammy answered for him. "He'll be two in September."

"Oh! He's a big one, too!"

"Want something to drink?" Marie Not-Help-Him interrupted.

"Sure," I answered.

"Would you like some coffee or something cold to drink instead?"

"I'll stick with the coffee," I replied. Tammy and the boys opted for some fresh squeezed lemonade.

The coffee was good. We all sat around the dining room table. Jeremiah and Trapper went to play with some other children.

"Have you met with anyone since you've been here?" Celane Not-Help-Him asked.

"Yes. I had the great honor of visiting with Frank Fools Crow earlier this morning."

"Uh huh. How's he doing?"

"He seemed to be doing real good."

Suddenly, I heard a crash down the hallway and saw Trapper on the floor. Celane Not-Help-Him, for all her size and age, ran to him like a fox. "You okay, little one?" she asked him.

"He's not real good at walking yet; seems to fall a lot," I told her.

Celane Not-Help-Him stood him up. "Maybe we should call him Falling Bear!" We all got a good laugh out of that. The name seemed to fit him.

As the small talk continued, I found it peculiar that neither Marie nor Celane Not-Help-Him mentioned the pipe bag. I was certain that both had thought of it, but not a word was mentioned.

Celane Not-Help-Him accompanied us when we left. We had agreed to call it a day and get some needed rest. As we drove back along the well-used roads, I paid closer attention to the historical markers that were quite common along the road. We passed the Wounded Knee Massacre marker, which had been erected close to the actual sight of the holocaust. Celane Not-Help-Him mentioned the unusual memorial march from northern South Dakota to these sacred grounds.

"I helped with the cooking and sun dance preparations," she announced. "There are only a handful who can guide marchers through the badlands."

I thought to myself that the journey must be a very difficult one, especially during that time of the year. I asked Celane Not-Help-Him, "Does everyone walk?"

"A lot do, but a lot ride horses, wagons, or even ride in cars." She let her eyes wander out across the unforgiving land and said solemnly, "Big Foot's band all walked. It was walk or die." She paused for a moment and said even more softly, "Then they killed them anyway."

She was quiet and Marie Not-Help-Him interjected, "We had a relative who died at Sand Creek."

41. THE LANCE SOCIETY
Dance Back the Warrior

I asked in a respectful way if they would share the history of the Not-Help-Him name. Marie smiled and looked in her mother's direction. Celane nodded in assent.

"The name is very powerful and important," Marie Not-Help-Him began." As you might guess, we get some peculiar looks and questions. But the way the story goes is that at one time there were a number of different warrior societies within the Lakotas. There aren't so many now. One of the most prestigious and honored groups was the Lance Society. If you were found to be brave enough, you could be asked to be a member. Our ancestor was asked and he accepted. The task required for his acceptance was the origin of our name. He was taken into enemy territory where he was tied at his waist to a large lance, which had been stuck into the ground. At this point, the others in his party retreated to the tree line. In time the enemy came and, as expected, began to attack our relative. He fought bravely, and at some point was close to being killed, but he did not quit or cry out for help. There were friends and family among the others at the tree line, and they wanted to help him, but the leader of the Lance Society said, 'No! you cannot help him. He must help himself.' So came our name, Not-Help-Him."

Did he survive?" I asked, not thinking first.

"Oh, yes!" Celane Not-Help-Him answered with a laugh. "I am living proof!"

Her daughter added, "Our ancestor eventually became the leader among the Lance Society."

"Does the Lance Society still exist?" I asked.

"No, not to my knowledge," Marie Not-Help-Him answered.

42. XAT MEDICINE SOCIETY
Dance Back the Medicine

"Do you know of a medicine society called Xat?" I asked.

"I have heard of the group, but I don't know anyone associated with it," Marie Not-Help-Him replied.

Celane added, "I have not heard of them. How do you spell that word."

I answered, "X.A.T. You pronounce it cat."

"Who are they?" she wondered.

"Well, the Xat Medicine Society is a medicine group that has been together since the mid-seventies. It was formed by a handful of medicine men living in the Northwest, among them Steven Old Coyote and the elder, Frank Chilcote."

Celane Not-Help-Him said that she knew of an Old Coyote family from Montana. I continued, "The guiding principle of this society is the path of acquiring wisdom. It is believed that all men of all races have those who are the medicine people. In some ways, they are very traditional medicine people. In other ways, they are quite unique. They originated from this country but have traveled to all parts of the world. Now they are returning and they are bringing their medicine to share with the people. They have also been called Rainbow Warriors. The Xat Medicine Society has become prominent throughout the world and especially here in the North American continent.

Marie Not-Help-Him asked, "Are you Xat?"

"I am," I answered proudly. "Since 1979 I have walked the Path. I have had many wonderful things come to my life because of my association with Xat and the people who are a part of it."

"Tell us more," requested Celane Not-Help-Him.

"Xat believes in a single Creator. He is known by many names, but He is the same. Xat is also devoted to the earth, Mother of us as well as all of nature. Xat gives great emphasis to the education of the children, both in an intellectual sense and a spiritual sense. It is our children who will be the torch carriers in the future. There is also a great deal of focus on traditional values, culture, and human rights. All people have a God-given right to be who they are. We are all the children of the same Creator."

"What of the women?" Celane Not-Help-Him asked, looking sternly out the front window.

"The women are sacred. They are the givers of life. They are the first teachers. It was a woman of the great Buffalo nation who brought the most sacred pipe! The women are wakan, holy, and they share the same medicine path as the men. The women are our balance. They are the other wing of the eagle, the ying of our yang."

"Huh!" Celane uttered surprise at the last part of my statement.

"Oh, it's just another way of saying that women are equal to men," I said.

That seemed to cause her some concern, but she did not say anything, so I expounded, "Not so much in the physical sense, because men are unable to do some of the physical things that women do, such as bring new life to this earth."

I noticed a slight nod and smile from Celane Not-Help-Him. She noted, "You know it would be hard to convince certain ones on this reservation that women and men are equal!"

"Yes," I answered. "I know what you are talking about, and I'm not here to convince anyone about anything. I am here to receive guidance. You asked me about my feelings and I expressed them to you. There are even members among the Xat Medicine Society who would be hard to convince, but that's the beauty of it! Every man and woman has his or her own feelings and ways of living and walking the Path."

I could see Marie Not-Help-Him's house ahead. Since the previous conversation, we had been quiet for a number of miles. I hoped that I had not offended Celane or Marie with my statements or opinions. Trapper had gone to sleep in his mother's arms. Once home, mother and daughter spoke to each other in Lakota as we unloaded the remaining things in the car and prepared to turn in. Later, from the house, we could hear the radio playing and an occasional giggle.

That evening after returning from the outhouse, I spotted Celane Not-Help-Him standing in the shadows of the front porch.

"Good night, Celane."

She smiled. "Good night, Little Eagle. Maybe, before you leave, we can talk some more about this Xat group."

I felt relieved. She had extended a feeling of ease to me with her statement.

43. TEARS FROM NOWHERE
Dance Back the Tears

It was nice to lie down. The day had been a full one with many memorable events to sleep by. Tammy and I said our evening prayers, after which the tent was quiet except for Trapper's baby snores. Jeremiah was asleep under the stars. I lay quietly, thinking of the beauty in my life. A tear rolled down the side of my face, finally coming to rest on my ear. I was not sure why it was there. It just happened sometimes. I would never bother Tammy with them. How could I explain tears from nowhere and for no apparent reason. She would just worry. I felt her familiar snuggling and heard her tender, "I love you."

"I love you, too," I answered as my ear filled with more tears.

44. *THE RAVEN'S TRAILER*
Dance Back the Fear

The next morning I was awakened by the ovenlike heat that filled our tent. It is nature's way of telling you it is time to get up. Once outside, it was not as bad. A gentle breeze wafted through our camp. Marie Not-Help-Him's car was gone. She was at work no doubt. We used her key to enter the house. Celane was gone as well. Tammy quickly got breakfast started, and I worked on the coffee. We enjoyed the morning crispness. Even the dust seemed fresh.

After breakfast Tammy filled the #10 washtub with water from the pump and proceeded to give Trapper a much needed bath. He was reluctant at first, but once he felt the cool water, he began to enjoy himself. I sat in a chair on the front porch drinking my coffee.

"I guess we're pretty much on our own today, Honey," I said.

"Yes. I imagine Marie will be at work until this afternoon. What do you think we should do?" Tammy rubbed Trapper's dark skin with soap. He kicked his feet, splashing water everywhere.

"We could take a ride around and just look at the sights. Maybe we can drop by and visit with Pete Catches."

"That sounds good," she answered, wiping water from her cheek. "Do you remember the directions to his house?"

"I think so."

As Tammy dressed Trapper, Jeremiah and I secured the camp. The only items going with us today were the ice chest and the pipe bag. Soon we were on our way. The road to Oglala was becoming familiar to me now. We first traversed Pine Ridge, which seemed much busier than the night before. The major stores' parking lots were quite full. Making the bend in town, we saw the hospital on the left. I thought that even though the population's medical needs might not be completely filled here, it was a lot better than when prairie doctors such as Dr. Alexander Brown, the first keeper of the pipe bag, were the only source of medical care. We passed the Red Cloud School. The roads were bordered by sage, and we agreed to gather some prior to leaving.

The first thing we noticed when making the turn into Pete Catches' place was the rather new building housing the local Latter Day Saints group. It dominated the landscape like a peacock with its feathers fanned out in an attempt to attract a mate. It seemed ironic, in a way, that we were here to visit one of the few true medicine men of our times, yet his small old trailer home lay practically in the shadow of the beautiful, neighboring Mormon church. The trailer's precarious position seemed almost a spiritual test.

The next thing we noticed was the terrible condition of the dirt road leading to Pete Catches' trailer. As we approached, I could see that no vehicles were around. To our left stood a lean-to covered with tree limbs and brush for shade. A couple of chairs and some large stumps sat empty beneath it. The trailer was in very poor condition with windows missing. The door had been repaired with a chain and locked with a large padlock. I noticed a sweatlodge up the hill.

I knocked on the door with no luck, after which I left a note:

Pete Catches,
My name is Little Eagle. I came to visit,
but missed you. I will try again later.
Thank you.

Jeremiah said, as we were leaving, "It's too bad we missed him."

I replied, "It's not bad. It's just not the right time."

Something inside me was talking to me about this place and this man. I could feel his presence the entire time we were at his home. His power prevailed, even in his absence. I had been told to prepare myself for visiting this elder, that he would be very skeptical about the pipe bag and my cause. I should keep in mind not to cross him or upset him for his powers were many, and he had the ability to summon nature's fury. As we drove away, I felt some relief, as though I had dodged a bullet. I thought to myself that at least I had tried, and now I could go on with other things. But I knew that trying once was not good enough, and that I would meet this man before I left. I now understood the sensations in my stomach. This elder, Pete Catches, was to be the balancing factor of our journey.

I noticed a medium-sized black raven sitting very quietly and still on top of the elder's trailer. It continued to keep vigil like a watchdog as I started up my car.

As I made the turn back onto the road to Pine Ridge, I noticed in the distance a small cemetery with about three markers. This was not strange, as grave sites dotted the landscape throughout the reservation. But something seemed unique about this particular resting place. As I focused on the road, the feeling left me.

We decided to stop in Pine Ridge to replenish our ice chest and food supplies. As we had seen before, the town of Pine Ridge was a bustling community. The General Store was very large, and you could buy almost anything you wanted. There were people everywhere. Four cashiers were hard at work. After we had made our purchases, we got back on the road again. We arrived at Marie Not-Help-Him's just after noon. She was waiting.

45. KEEPERS OF THE FLAME
Dance Back the Fire

"How did you sleep last night?" she asked.

"Real good until it got too hot."

"Yes, it will get warm around these parts," she said with a smile.

As I was unloading the car, I said, "We tried to visit Pete Catches." Marie seemed surprised. I continued, "He wasn't home, though."

That seemed to relieve her, and she said, "Maybe later, before you leave, you can try again."

"Yes. We have agreed to do that." After I had finished unloading the car I went on to ask, "Marie, do you have any thoughts or recommendations as to what we should be doing next?"

She thought quietly for a moment and then answered.

"Yes," she answered, smiling. "I had hoped that we could go up to Eagle Nest Butte and visit with the Chips family."

"I have heard of the Chips."

"They are one of our most important families. Traditionally speaking, they are the keepers of the flame."

"When you say, 'keepers of the flame' what is it you mean," I asked.

"They're a family who live in the traditional way. Their medicine man is very powerful and has been so for many years. The original Chip, also known as Horn Chips, was one of the greatest holy men in our history. He was a teacher of Crazy Horse. When the holy men of years ago were being forced into obscurity, the one known as Horn Chips kept and protected many of the sacred rites and ceremonies. The one he was most proficient with was the Yuwipi ceremony."

"Do the Chips still do the Yuwipi?"

"Oh, yes! Some say they are the only family who do it the old way."

"You keep referring to the 'family.' Is there more than one medicine man?"

"Yes. They are all blessed with the blood of the old man, Horn Chips. Ellis is the elder, and he has three sons: Charles, Phillip, and Godfrey. Godfrey is the center point of the family. It has been recounted by many that he has the power to call up the first Horn Chip and even Crazy Horse!"

I was taken by surprise and asked, "Call up? What does this mean?"

"Exactly what it sounds like. At certain times the holy men of our past will use Godfrey as a way to communicate with our mortal world."

"You mean like a channeller?"

"They don't know that word. It is a blessing, a very powerful blessing."

"Well, I agree it is vital that we visit them. How do we tell them we would like a council?"

Marie Not-Help-Him smiled and answered, "Oh, they know already and are expecting us."

Things like phones, letters, and RSVP's seemed to have no use within the bounds of this place and time. Instead there was spiritual and mystical communication.

"When would you like to head out there?" Marie Not-Help-Him asked.

"Anytime would be fine."

"Good, let's leave in about fifteen minutes."

"Marie Not-Help-Him darted into the house, and we made our preparations for departure. Once our camp was again secured, I looked out at the driveway and saw Marie and, for the first time, Celane Not-Help-Him, standing by Marie's car, an older Chevy. We walked toward them and as we got close, Marie said, "We should take my car. They will recognize it."

As we were loading up, I reflected on Marie Not-Help-Him's words. They reminded me of a time gone by when a stranger, such as myself, might have entered a Lakota encampment without proper guidance. That stranger would not be able to find what he sought, and might even be placing himself in jeopardy. I was the stranger who sought assistance and wisdom. Marie was the guide who would help me find that assistance. The Chip family was the source of that assistance and wisdom.

Our drive was quiet as well as long. From Marie Not-Help-Him's house we drove in an easterly direction. Eagle Nest Butte rose like a monument from the prairie. The closest town was Wambli. As we made our initial turn off the hardtop road onto a dirt one, I noticed another car behind us making the same turn. The driver had eased toward the left side of the road to avoid some of the thick dust which filled the air behind Marie Not-Help-Him's car. I didn't say anything to Marie, but the other car was slowly gaining on us. I was sure she knew. I suddenly heard the roar of the other car as it accelerated. I quickly looked past her head to glance at the driver. Marie Not-Help-Him cautiously kept her eyes focused on the road. The car was a newer model red Cadillac. The driver never looked at us as he passed, long braids laid back across his shoulders, concentrating intensely on the road ahead. He left a thick layer of dust for us to contend with.

The dust dissipated as we continued. We made a couple more big turns and crossed a few cattle guards before we finally arrived at the Chip residence. The setting was typical of a Lakota home. One of the first things I noticed was the large number of vehicles parked in the area. There was even a large RV. I also found the red Cadillac that had left us in the dust. The rocks crackled under the tires as we brought Marie Not-Help-Him's big car to a stop. I noticed an old trailer and five or six people sitting out in front.

She pointed out, "That's the elder, Ellis Chips, with the red cap on."

We all opened the car doors at the same time. Marie Not-Help-Him looked at me over the top of the car. "Please wait here. I'll be right back."

"Sure," I agreed as she entered the circle of people. I continued to look around. I discovered a large barnlike house near the center of the encampment. To the north, four tents and three teepees were set up. A long clothesline was connected between two of the tents and clothes were drying on the line. To the west side of the large house two sweatlodges stood. To the south was a field of sage and other vegetation. I noticed a number of people, young and old, black and white, bustling about. As I returned my attention back to the east and Marie Not-Help-Him, I realized she was waving for us to come over.

"Little Eagle, I'd like to introduce you to Ellis Chips."

I removed my cap. "It's my honor to meet you, sir."

Ellis Chips looked up from his patio chair, transferred a cigarette to his left hand and extended his right. A big, semi-toothless smile beamed from his face. "Nice to meet you, too. But it looks like you're getting a little thin on your topnotch there. You might get some sunburn if you're not careful. So you'd best put your hat back on, son!"

"You're right," I replied with a laugh and replaced my cap.

I then introduced my wife and sons. Ellis Chips smiled and nodded cordially.

"What brings you out our way?" he asked.

Although I knew he was already aware of our quest, I answered respectfully, "We are seeking guidance and counsel in two areas of great importance."

"Uh huh!" he nodded, then took a drag from his cigarette. I thought it strange that the others around Ellis were so quiet. Even Marie Not-Help-Him had struck a pose of silence, head down, hands clasped in front of her.

Ellis Chips' dark eyes seemed to peer deep inside me. "What are these two things you are talking about?"

Again I was touched by the silence. I felt as though I was alone with this elder. "The first regards a Lakota pipe bag that has been placed in my care. Some say that it once belonged to the sacred one, Crazy Horse!"

Ellis Chips' reaction to this bold statement was unwavering, but I felt a certain shuffling interest in the silent group now gathered around us. I continued, "Recently, the pipe bag came my way and with it came instructions for its care. One of the primary instructions was to bring it to this place and seek guidance as to my duties and responsibilities in its care and protection."

"I think we might be able to help you with that," he said. "Now, what is the second thing?"

"My wife!" I answered.

"Oh, yeah? She looks very cute to me," he said with a smile.

"Yes, I agree, but she is in a great battle, an invisible battle called cancer."

"Uh huh !" A more serious demeanor appeared on his face.

"We found out about her cancer in September of last year, and since then we have worked very closely with many doctors. We have endured the powerful treatments they recommended, and in the end she is still sick. We have decided to dedicate our lives to obtaining spiritual wellness, and with that we hope and pray for physical wellness as well."

Ellis Chips was quiet for a moment and then spoke in Lakota to Marie Not-Help-Him. She answered in the same language. After their short conversation Ellis Chips asked to be excused. He slowly got up from his chair and made his way into the trailer. I was not sure what we should do, so we did nothing. It was a short, but nonetheless uncomfortable wait. Ellis eventually reappeared. With him was a younger man. His shoulder-length black hair was thick and loose. He was wearing Jeans. His muscular arms were exposed by his short-sleeved shirt. As they drew closer, I could see an unmistakable sternness in the younger man's face. But once he arrived, the sternness relaxed into a warm smile.

"This is my son, Godfrey. He will help you," Ellis Chips said.

A feeling of relief moved through me. I realized that Godfrey Chips could have said no as well as yes. I was sure he based his decision to help on his father, who seemed at ease with us.

Godfrey Chips spoke clear and precise English. "I have a couple of questions for you." I nodded for him to go ahead. He then asked, "How is it that you have acquired possession of the pipe bag?"

I explained as clearly and briefly as possible. "It was passed on to me from my wife's father, Vinson Brown. He was given the bag by his father more than forty years ago. Vinson's father was a traveling doctor who spent some time here in Pine Ridge in the 1890s. It was during this time that he was given the bag by a Lakota whose son the doctor had saved from dying. That's it in a nutshell. If you like I can be more specific."

"No, that won't be necessary. How is it that you believe the bag once belonged to Crazy Horse?"

"I have no way of proving its authenticity. Frank Fools Crow kept the bag from 1966 to 1967 for the purpose of using it in his ceremonies and finding out more about it. When the previous pipe bag keeper came to watch the sun dance at Pine Ridge in 1967, he found it hanging on the center pole. It was during that ceremony that Fools Crow announced that the pipe bag was wakan and had once belonged to Crazy Horse."

Godfrey Chips smiled. "Well, we'll be able to tell you the truth about the bag, if you want to know."

I quickly answered, "That's why I'm here."

"Good. And as for your wife, we will do what we can there also."

"Thank you," I replied. "What will we have to do and when?"

Ellis looked toward his son who was leaning forward in his chair, elbows resting on his knees. Godfrey answered, "Your first task is prayer. Your last task is prayer."

I nodded my head in agreement. Godfrey Chips continued, "You must also participate in the sweatlodge, both of you. We will then conduct a Yuwipi." There are certain things you will need to do for the ceremony. First you should prepare 405 tobacco ties. Celane Not-Help-Him has been involved with this before, so she will assist you with this and also the other tasks. You will also need to prepare four flags, using chokecherry sticks. It will also be necessary for you to prepare a meal for all the participants."

Godfrey Chips looked in my direction and I gave an understanding nod. "Good," he said. There are other things also and Marie and Celane will assist you with them."

"When should we plan on doing this?" I asked.

"How much time do you have here?" responded Godfrey Chips.

"Unfortunately, we have come close to exhausting our time, and we will need to be leaving soon."

Godfrey Chips answered quickly, "Then let's do it tonight. You should be back here one hour prior to sunset with all the things you have been instructed to bring."

I glanced toward Tammy, then Marie Not-Help-Him. They both were in agreement. Soon thereafter we were back in Marie's car on the road to Pine Ridge.

The drive was a quiet one at first. I was contemplating the instructions and feelings I had received at the Chips' encampment. Things seemed to be happening so fast. I was concerned that I might be missing something, or worse, doing something out of order. After more thought, I realized that all these fast moving events were out of my control and had been placed in Divine control. The order was not for me to worry about.

46. YUWIPI PREPARATIONS

Dance Back the Tobacco Ties

Tammy broke the silence of our drive with a timely question for me. "Do you think we will be able to get things together in time?"

Before I could answer, Celane Not-Help-Him said, "Don't worry. We do have a big task ahead of us, but I will be helping."

"Me, too!" Marie Not-Help-Him added energetically.

"Thank you, because I'm not really sure where we should even start," Tammy added.

Celane Not-Help-Him went on, "Well, our first stop will be in White Clay. They have everything we need in one store."

"And what will that be?" I asked.

Celane Not-Help-Him took a deep breath as though she was preparing to give a long speech. "We need cloth for the flags and tobacco ties: red, yellow, black, and white. And we'll need tobacco." Contemplating momentarily, she continued, "We'll need some fine string for tying the tobacco ties. Kite string will work fine." Celane Not-Help-Him then looked in my direction. "Our big time consumer will be preparing the meal."

Marie Not-Help-Him added, "We'll figure out what we'll need for food when we get to the store."

Soon after we had made our turn south out of Pine Ridge, we entered the state of Nebraska and arrived in the adjacent town of White Clay. I had no idea we were so close to the border.

"We've found that we get better prices and selection here in White Clay," Celane Not-Help-Him explained.

The town of White Clay seemed to be a typical mid-Western town. A main street was lined with various stores, a gas station, and a cafe or two.

When we entered the store, Celane Not-Help-Him was quickly recognized by the clerks. As we shopped around, we were stopped on numerous occasions by her well-wishers. The woman who cut the four colors of material we required noted that we must be preparing for a ceremony. It was obvious that she had been through the same process many times before. Our shopping took the better part of an hour to complete. Along with the cloth for the flags, we also purchased tobacco and a roll of kite string. But the bulk of our purchases was for the meal: ten pounds of beef, corn, peas, potatoes, flour, salt, baking powder, and a can of shortening for making fry bread. We also picked up a can of coffee, sugar, canned milk, and several cans of berries for making wojapi, a type of pudding. It seemed as though we had enough food to feed the entire camp.

The rest of the day was taken up with the actual preparations for the meal and the ceremony. Tammy and Marie Not-Help-Him worked at the food, and Celane Not-Help-Him rhythmically tied the tobacco ties. Jeremiah and I worked on the flags, cutting and painting the four chokecherry sticks. The day quickly moved into evening, and before we knew it we were all packed and on our way.

The turns and rolling hills on our trip back to the Chips' camp were a bit more familiar this time. Evening had descended by the time we arrived, and it appeared that preparations were already in motion for our ceremony. The fires were going strong at the sweatlodges. As we were unloading the car, I saw Phillip Chips approaching from the ceremonial house. He beckoned to me as he got closer.

"Come over here, please!" he exclaimed.

When I reached his location, he spoke softly. "We will be going into the sweat first. There will be a man's sweat and a woman's sweat." Phillip paused and seemed to be looking over my shoulder. He then said, "Our sweats are very powerful. Someone of distrust entering the lodge may find himself in pain."

This shocked me. I was not sure what to say. Phillip continued, "There are those here who are not to be trusted and they will not be allowed to enter the lodge. There are times when the holy one, Crazy Horse, visits the lodge. He requires a pure heart and clear mind."

"I understand," I replied.

Phillip Chips then added, "Godfrey wants you and your wife to sweat this evening."

I nodded and thanked him. I noticed Phillip looking back toward the ceremonial house. A man stood there. He gestured to the man, who in return ran his left hand in a cutting motion across his right forearm. Phillip then turned toward me. "About fifteen minutes and we'll be going."

"Very well," I replied, "I'll be ready."

Phillip looked at me for a long moment and answered, "Good." Then he turned and walked away.

47. CRAZY HORSE SWEAT
Dance Back the Rocks

The fifteen minutes turned into forty-five minutes before the sweat was ready. The participants gathered for the ceremony. I noticed a number of men were discussing the sweat. The preparation at the sweat seemed familiar with only slight variations. The ceremony was, for all purposes, very much like other sweats in which I had participated over the years. The sweatlodge was one of the larger I had seen. It had a very big fire pit and large rocks lay nearby. A three tier step lead into the firepit. The fire itself had burnt down and the glowing embers lay like a blanket over rocks already placed in the pit, making them nearly invisible. The sweatlodge was close to five feet high at its apex and probably eight feet in diameter, covered with old blankets and sleeping bags. Halfway between the fire pit and the sweatlodge entrance was the ever-present altar. There were a number of items laid upon it. I noticed tobacco ties, necklaces, numerous types of feathers, a couple of rings and watches. It was crowned with an extremely large buffalo skull painted in the traditional way.

We talked as we prepared ourselves. I noticed that all who were present were Indian. No whites were present. I felt this was connected to Phillip Chips' earlier statement regarding a "clear and pure heart" and the possible visitation of Crazy Horse. A rush of adrenaline moved through my entire body. It was not that I was afraid, but rather that I was amazed at the prospect of an actual encounter with the sacred one! Evening had set in by this time and a mysterious quiet had settled over the participants. The faces of these unknown brothers were bathed in the gentle light from the embers of the fire.

The rock man was continuously working with the fire. A shovel was wedged into the ground and a long-handled pitchfork was in his hands. It was as though he awakened us when he exclaimed, "The spuds are ready!"

Now it was time to make our final personal preparation. Some of the nine participants were already set and lined up at the entrance to the sweatlodge. The rest of us put on our shorts or a towel and joined the others.

Among our group were two elders and one young man in his teens. It was only then that I finally recognized our sweat leader, Wallace Black Elk, a descendent of the Lakota holy man, Black Elk, and a powerful leader he was. He moved to each man and touched him on the shoulder. Occasionally he would rearrange the order of entry. He left me where I was.

After a final few words to the rock man, Wallace Black Elk entered the lodge. Once inside he spoke prayers and sang a short song, after which he asked for one rock. The rock man hustled to his duties. With his rake he retrieved a glowing red rock. As he passed the rock by the waiting participants, I heard a low gruntlike noise from one of the elders. Another man waved his hand over the rock in a form of respect. After the rock was placed, I could hear more prayer. Eventually, Wallace ordered the rest of us in. After we had finally settled into position, I noticed that I had acquired the seat opposite the door, commonly known as the hot seat! I realized that the ceremony would be in Lakota and I would have to pay close attention. As I suspected, Wallace did give the order for more rocks in his native tongue. I could see the altar and fire pit from my position. The rock man moved quickly. Rock after rock was brought into the lodge. I tried to keep track of the number of rocks, but soon lost count. The rocks were glowing red, and now rose above the rim of the rockpit. I drew my legs up close to protect them from the heat. And still more rocks were brought. Wallace Black Elk finally instructed the rock man to stop bringing rocks. He quickly followed those instructions with an order to close the door of the lodge.

Total darkness engulfed us, and then the familiar sounds of the sweat filled the lodge. First the water was poured onto the rocks, which emitted a hissing, bubbling sound. My next sense to be tested was that of touch. The heat seemed to rise, roll over my shoulders, and down my back. The other participants spoke softly in recognition of the heat, "Hau!"

"Uh huh!" I heard Wallace Black Elk's voice penetrate the darkness in prayer. Then I heard a new voice begin singing a song, eventually to be joined by other voices. As the intensity of heat, prayer, and song began to increase, I suddenly realized there was a strong, thumping movement under me. I could hear the hissing and bubbling of the rocks as they spoke to us in their ancient voice. The physical heat was beginning to take its toll. I could hear the others singing, chanting, and even shouting. And still the sweat leader poured water onto the rocks! I found myself hunkering down close to the earth, trying to avoid the intense heat which was hottest about head level. The sweat rolled off me and into my eyes. As thoughts of escape crossed my mind, I saw light ahead of me. The door had been ordered open by Wallace Black Elk. A wall of steam obscured a clear picture of the outside. But as I struggled to see cool, clear air, I instead saw the glowing of another rock entering the lodge on the pitchfork of the hard-working rock man; then another and another. A total of four more rocks were added to the still hot rocks already in the pit. Another command from Wallace Black Elk and the door was closed again. The four new rocks glowed red as they sat precariously atop the others. Water was poured again, and for a moment I transcended the discomfort created by the heat, but as the rocks sang their song, I was quickly back to my poor, pitiful, hunkered self.

Another prayer or chant, another song filled the sweat lodge. The thumping returned, this time stronger, louder, and in beat with the singing. The thumping continued, louder and louder, until I felt my body surging uncontrollably up and down from its energy. It was as if someone was physically pushing me, but I knew no one was doing so. As I rolled about, I finally gave up. I heard my voice exclaim, "Yi! Hau! Hyeeee!" And with those words, the sounds that previously filled the lodge were gone. A strange silence came screaming into the lodge as I hung my head low. I realized I was becoming a witness to power. A heavy thump pushed against my chest, as if to wake me. Then a second one came, as if to shake me. A moment later the third strike was laid upon me. I was not sure if my eyes were open or closed. Finally the fourth and last thump struck my deepest being. I was not sure what was happening, but a great force was present. As I looked ahead, I saw a low, glowing orange light appear among the rocks. It seemed to intensify. Eventually it presented a soft but distinct picture on the sides of the lodge. The shadows caused by the wrinkles in the covering and willow framework seemed to come alive. Maps and designs came and went, changing as I moved my head. Things began to happen in slow motion. I finally realized that I was alone within this picture. The walls of the lodge became vast and distant in front of me. The shadowy orange glow began to move again, this time with the waves of steam that were present. I felt at ease and unafraid. The orange steam began to roll steadily into a form. I concentrated intensely on the form. As I did, I saw a face and then a body emanating from the orange steam. It developed further. The steam moved across the face like a stream passing over hidden rocks. The stream of steam gradually ceased and the smoky figure of a man presented himself to me. His face was stern but peaceful. His long hair rested on his chest. His legs and arms were covered with white spots, which seemed to move about while I watched. In his hair I discovered a small clump of reddish feathers. It was at this moment I realized what was happening to me. The holy one, Crazy Horse, had come! I put out my hand to him, fingers extended and nodded, saying, "Greetings!" He remained still for a moment and then nodded his head. This caused the steam to change direction, but it returned. I am not sure how much time passed. The holy one spoke to me within my mind and my heart. "Your answers are in your hands." Then again I heard his voice, which was in Lakota, but I understood clearly, "Your wellness is in your hands."

I contemplated as I sat watching and listening to this most sacred one. Once again he leaned forward in my direction. He moved his hands over the glowing rocks, first clockwise, then counterclockwise, then in opposite directions. Suddenly he stopped, reached into the rocks and picked up two of them, turning his palms upward with the glowing rocks resting in them.

"Take them. They will bring you wellness!"

I was startled at first, but quickly realized that I must do what was required of me. If there had been any fear or skepticism, it was long gone. I extended my hands, palms up, toward his. Once I was within reach, he began singing a chant, so beautiful, so powerful! I soon found myself overcome with a peace, a joy that seemed to ignite my very soul. Tears of love rolled down my face as he placed the sizzling rocks into my hands. They glowed red, but I knew that no harm would come to me. As I held them, he spoke again. "First, believe in yourself; then believe in your people; and then, help your people. Then you will be helped."

His words filled my mind. I could feel the weight of the rocks in my hands, but not the heat! When the work was done, I returned the rocks to the pit, laying them very gently into place. As I raised my head back in the direction of the holy one, I discovered he was gone. I understood that his message to me was, for now, complete. I stared at the place where he had been, and, as I did so, I began to realize that the heat was returning to the sweatlodge. The quiet was changing into the sound of hissing rocks, songs, loud voices, and grunts. I recognized Wallace's voice as he directed the door to be opened. "Mitakuye Oyasin! Open the door!"

The entrance flap was flung open, and the steam rushed outside. I did not dare to move, but sat quietly. I wondered to myself about the events that had just occurred. Had I been dreaming or been a victim to my own illusions, or had that sacred one actually visited the lodge?

The steamy appearance of the sweatlodge and the participants within began to clear. I had a strange feeling of shyness, almost embarrassment. What if I had really passed out and brought shame to the sweatlodge? I slowly raised my head to take a look at my fellow sweatlodge participants. Everything seemed quite normal. They were talking softly to each other. Occasionally, one or two would flash a glance toward me. As I looked about, I was suddenly startled. Across from me at the door sat a man in the exact position in which I had seen the holy one. I strained to see his face and then realized who sat there. It was Godfrey Chips. He was not one of the men who had come into the lodge at the start, yet there he was, sitting, straight-backed with the sweat rolling down his face and body. I looked into his face and found him looking back at me. The slightest of smiles appeared on his face and then was gone. The mystery had happened, and whether or not I wanted to believe it, I was a part of it.

As I sat in wonderment, I watched Godfrey Chips crawl back out of the lodge. He was followed by another and yet another. My turn came and I also left. I was not sure what round of the sweatlodge it was, but whatever it was, it was over. "Mitakuye Oyasin!" I proclaimed as I departed.

I quickly found a seat outside and began to relax and enjoy the coolness of the dark, star-filled night. The other participants did different things. Some were getting dressed quickly. Others walked off into the distance, hands raised, saying their own prayers. Others had joined me on the ground. Wallace Black Elk was in conference with the rock man. I heard a laugh from them and saw Wallace Black Elk extend his hand and shake the rock man's hand. I looked for Godfrey Chips, but he was gone. I thought he must have been one of those who rushed off.

Wallace Black Elk began to dry himself. I got back on my feet and made my way toward him. He was looking up toward the sky as I interrupted him.

"Wallace."

He looked in my direction.

"I want to thank you for your work with the sweatlodge. It was a very powerful one that will not soon leave my memory, if ever."

He smiled and nodded. "You're welcome. I thought it was a little long, but one tends to lose track of time." He hesitated a moment and then asked, "The pipe bag. Do you have it?"

"Yes," I replied.

"Good. The Yuwipi ceremony for your wife and the pipe bag will begin as soon as the women finish their sweat."

I finally figured out what the rest of the evening was about. I asked, "Where will the Yuwipi take place?"

Wallace Black Elk pointed over my shoulder. "There, at the ceremony house."

"Uh huh" I replied. "I will see you there."

I turned to walk away and heard his voice once again. "Wait!" I quickly turned around, and he continued. "Your hands! Let me see your hands!"

At first I was confused, then I realized why he wanted to see my hands. I held my palms up to him. He reached out and held them, his broad thumbs moving gently in my palms. I watched our hands for a moment and then turned my head up toward him. He continued looking into my hands, rubbing them with his thumbs. Eventually he, too, raised his head and looked deep into my eyes. He then proclaimed, "Crazy Horse visited us tonight. You saw him?"

"Yes," I answered, trying to get my breath.

"Do you remember?"

"Yes," I nodded.

"It has been a blessing for you and your family!"

He let go of my hands and turned and walked away. I, too, began to walk away. As I did I brought my hands up to see them. They were quite normal looking. My heart was beating very fast. The mystery of that sweatlodge was no illusion or dream, for the elder, Wallace Black Elk, had seen it too.

Once I returned to our car, I met Tammy.

"How was it?" she innocently asked.

I smiled and put my arms around her. "It was very good."

It was now Tammy's turn to make her way to the sweatlodge. The all women's sweat was lead by one known as "Grandma." Along to support Tammy were Celane and Marie Not-Help-Him. Jeremiah would later participate in a young man's sweat that evening.

48. YUWIPI TIME
Dance Back the Dancing Lights

The sun had long been gone when we were approached and told to prepare ourselves for the

Yuwipi ceremony and pipe bag showing at the ceremony house. I became a bit apprehensive. I really was not sure how this ceremony would go, but I knew the answers I sought would reveal themselves. Like it or not, the truth was about to be seen. The surging emotions of feelings were based upon the enormous power that was present at the Chips' encampment. There was a spiritual electricity on this Eagle Nest Butte that surrounded everyone and everything, like the stars that grace the silent night sky.

Once given the signal, Jeremiah with his clump of sage, and I with the pipe bag, made our way to the ceremony house. My youngest son had long since fallen asleep on the back seat of the car and Tammy remained with him. It also gave her the opportunity to avoid an unfamiliar crowd, which she was always glad to do. While proceeding along the outside of the house, I noticed the windows had been boarded up. The place seemed almost deserted. At the door, a young man stood waiting for us. He nodded to us and then, with four distinct slow knocks, announced our arrival.

Entering, I quickly recognized a number of people whom I had met previously. The amazing thing, however, was the number of people whom I had not met before. A note of caution crept into my consciousness, but quickly left with the realization that no one would be here who was not trusted. The room had been emptied of furniture. The entire perimeter was lined with people, people of the four directions: black, white, yellow, and red. On the east wall sat the Chips family along with Wallace Black Elk and others. On the floor at the center point of the east wall were the four flags which I had earlier provided for the ceremony. Also, in the same area, was a small pile of earth and atop that pile was an abalone shell filled with burning sage. Other items were laid out in a specific fashion around the room.

Whatever conversations had been going on ceased once we entered the room. Jeremiah laid the bed of sage at the center of the room, and I laid the case containing the pipe bag beside it. I looked up to Godfrey Chips, who was sitting at the center position against the east wall, and waited for his go-ahead.

He quickly nodded his head in approval. I took a small portion of sage and lit it with a match. With this I smudged, first myself, then the case containing the pipe bag. I placed the remaining sage in an abalone shell. Praying, I then completely opened the case, lifted the pipe bag ever-so-gently, and laid it upon the bed of sage. Jeremiah had taken a seat on the perimeter with the other onlookers. I took a seat directly west of the bag. Once I had settled down and was comfortable with the position and the arrangement, I looked up toward Godfrey Chips and signaled him.

Godfrey Chips raised his arm in the direction of a hand drummer who sat at the southeast corner of the room, they immediately began to play and sing. Phillip Chips came to the center with a pipe in his hand. He took up a sitting position between the pipe bag and his brother, Godfrey Chips, and began to prepare the Chips' family pipe for smoking. The energy within the room was building with each drum beat and with each pinch of tobacco that Phillip Chips placed into the pipe. An unseen, but felt movement was developing around me. I could see that everyone else was also feeling the energy. As soon as Phillip Chips had completed his work, he laid the pipe down on its rack. Suddenly the drumming stopped. But I could still feel and hear the drumbeat in my head and chest.

In a loud and booming voice, Godfrey Chips began to chant and pray in Lakota. After a few minutes the two kerosene lamps were extinguished and the drumming began again. It started as it had before from the southeast corner of the room, but as the song continued, the beat moved from southeast to southwest in a floating fashion. Then it moved to the northwest corner, eventually arriving in the northeast corner. As I became more and more enchanted with the drumbeat, I realized there was more than one drum. The drums were in every corner, sometimes playing at different times, then playing together. My eyes were finally becoming adjusted to the darkness, but I was still unable to see any forms other than the braids of burning sage. I now detected a pounding underneath me, not like the one I had felt earlier in the sweatlodge. This was produced by many people pounding their feet on the old wooden floor.

At certain times the room would come alive with lights, floating and dancing like fireflies. They were high, low, near, and far. Then they faded away. Growing out of the intensity of this ceremony, I once again heard Godfrey's voice. Even though I could not understand him, the words were powerful. His beautiful Lakota voice was enchanting me. As I listened carefully, I could detect differences in the pitch and rhythm of his voice, lower then higher, slower then faster.

As I became more at ease, I found myself becoming strangely numb. I thought my legs might be falling asleep, but it was different, as though my whole body was falling asleep, except for my thoughts. I began to feel the extraordinary electricity again. I also began to see the dancing lights once again, flickering lights, white like stars, they were changing into what appeared to be rainbow colors. They were at eye level, then at ceiling level, then at all levels.

Even though I felt I could not move my limbs, I willed my hands to reach out and touch the pipe bag. My sense of touch found the bag, but, to my shock, not on the bed of sage. Instead it seemed to be floating about two feet in the air in front of me! For some reason this did not surprise me. It seemed to be in the order of everything else going on about me. I relaxed with soft prayers.

In the midst of these peaceful surroundings, I heard the soft, then loud voice of the spirit bird: the eagle. I thought it might be an eagle-bone whistle, but quickly realized it was more than that. It was an eagle. His voice continued to call from all over the room. At one point, he was just above my head. I felt my hair move from a breeze, not just a draft, but from the flapping of the spirit bird's wings. "Hau!" I called in recognition and honor to the powerful spirit. The flickering lights had lessened in intensity and I could hear others in the room yipping and yelling in excitement. The powerful spirit bird continued to flap his wings. The breeze caused by this action was quite strong, blowing against my face and chest. From within the sounds I again heard the soft, consistent sounds of the drum. I focused my attention on that sound and the other activity seemed to slowly fall away. In due time a peaceful quiet reentered the room. The drumbeat became softer and softer until, with one strong beat, it also ceased.

The silence seemed to scream through my head. After a moment or two I heard Godfrey Chips' familiar voice. I felt as though he was speaking to me, but I wasn't sure. I sat without movement. From the darkness to my left I heard Marie Not-Help-Him's voice, "Little Eagle, it is your turn to talk. Tell them what you are here for."

I really was not sure what to say, but I knew this was the right time and right place to do it. "Hau!" I announced. "My name is Kitpoviosees, better known as Little Eagle, and I thank you for this opportunity to speak. My purpose for being here is twofold.

I have come to this sacred place to ask for your help and counsel. I realize you have no obligations to offer up that which I seek, but I must follow the guidance and instructions I have been given.

"I bring to you this pipe bag. It has been in our family almost one hundred years. There have been other keepers. I am now the one who has that responsibility for its protection. As the previous keepers have done, I am doing now. That is, seeking additional instruction and direction as to my duties."

"What I can tell you about the bag is truth and legend, seen and unseen, alive and dead! The story that stands above all others is that it once belonged to the sacred one, Crazy Horse."

I sat for a moment, but heard nothing from anyone, so I continued. "This place is alive with his spirit and I know that he has visited you in the past, for he has visited me this very night!"

"Hau!" "Uh huh!" I heard exclaimed from a couple of directions.

"I request your interpretation as to the truth. Did this bag at one time belong to Crazy Horse?" I hesitated for only a second because I knew there would be no answer to that question at this time.

"The pipe bag has been held in an honorable and humble way by myself and the previous keepers. I have been told that it would be given back to the Lakota people some day soon. I am here this evening to find out from you, the children of Horn Chips and Crazy Horse, if that time is now.

I once again sat quietly for a moment, then continued, "The bag has been associated with healing in the past, and that is the second purpose for my visit. I am in need of a healing! My beloved wife is ill with a disease that is very powerful. It is called cancer. We have given ourselves totally to making her clear and well. We have received much advice and help from the white man's medical world and we are grateful for their sincere and dedicated efforts to her. However, we have now exhausted those tools, the tools of this physical world. We have now given ourselves to the more powerful spiritual world! I have never loved so strongly nor cared so much for anyone in my life." I felt a lump in my throat and a flush in my face as I thought of my wife. Stumbling with my words, I continued, "I'm sure most everyone who hears my voice understands what I mean when I say, a deep and full love. That is what I have for my wife, Tammy. She has changed me and my life completely. She has entered my life like warm sunshine at daybreak. I could live a million years and never be capable of thanking her and thanking Wakan Tanka for bringing her into my life."

"We are beyond the medical means of curing her and I now humbly come to you, my friends, for counsel and guidance."

Again I stopped, halfway expecting some sort of comment, but realized this would not come. "I thank you again for this opportunity to visit with you and speak to you from my heart. "Hau! Mitakuye Oyasin!"

I had finished and now sat in silence. I finally heard light muttering from in front of me, then the louder voice of Godfrey Chips. The drum started playing again. The songs were being sung again. Soon thereafter the lamps were relit and the room was brought to its original condition.

I glanced down at the pipe bag and saw that it was now lying in a different direction. The bag itself had been turned over. The powerful woman's side was facing up. As I gazed at its beauty, a spark of green caught my eye, then another. I recalled my surroundings and raised my head to face Godfrey Chips. His dark face was filled with peace. As I continued to look in his direction I suddenly saw the same sparks of green in his eyes. I must have shown surprise, because an ever-so-slight smile appeared on his lips.

"Pilamiyah, thank you," he said softly, then redirected his attention to his brother, Phillip Chips, who quickly got to his feet and made his way to the pipe that he had prepared earlier. In due and ancient form he lit the pipe, after which he delivered it to Godfrey Chips. In accepting the pipe, Godfrey Chips spoke soft prayers, looking skyward from his sitting position. The pipe was then passed along to the person to his left and on around the room. Eventually, Phillip Chips reacquired the pipe and brought the sacred instrument to me. I humbly took and smoked it. Then I gave it back to Phillip Chips who sent it on its sunrise pathway around the room. Once the pipe had made a complete journey around the room, the ceremony was completed.

Jeremiah rejoined me and we properly secured the pipe bag. I then returned it to the car where Tammy and Trapper rested quietly. I left the pipe bag with her and returned with Jeremiah to the ceremony house, where the food had been brought out. It was time for socializing and friendly conversation. I spoke with a couple of people, but no one spoke of the pipe bag or the ceremony. A unique event had taken place and filled our memories forever.

It was nearly 4:00 AM by the time we decided to pack up and go our separate ways. My family had long since filled our car. Everyone was sound asleep and I sat quietly preparing to start up the car when I saw Godfrey and Phillip Chips approaching from the direction of the ceremony house. I got back out of the car and waited for them to arrive.

"Hello," Phillip Chips greeted me as he came closer.

"Hello," I replied. "I was about to leave. I'm glad I saw you."

Phillip Chips said, "We have been in council for quite a while and we have come to some conclusions in regard to your two questions."

Excitement entered my body, and a shot of adrenaline shook the sleepy cobwebs out of my head. I said, "Thank you for acting so quickly on my questions. I wasn't sure if it would be now or later, but I thank you anyway."

Godfrey Chips, who seemed to be the leader of the Chips clan, stood quietly as a witness. Phillip Chips continued, "First, the pipe bag. From this day forward you must be very careful about using Crazy Horse's name in association with it. It is no doubt from his time and his camp. That has been told to us. Crazy Horse was an extremely powerful and mystical man. In his life, the bag may have been a gift that merely passed through his hands. Crazy Horse kept nothing! All his possessions were very simple. He owned nothing extravagant or valuable in a physical way. He would always think first of his people. So he may have given the bag to someone else to use."

"We are very impressed with the obvious care the bag has received. Its condition is excellent and you and your family should be thanked. The cherrywood of which the case is made is sacred to our people. Because of your effort to protect the bag, you will be rewarded."

Without hesitation Phillip Chips moved on to the next point, "Concerning your wife: She can be healed. It will take a true, dedicated effort on her and your part to receive that healing. The pipe bag can be used to help bring the healing. What you do and how you present the bag is proper, and with that you will be able to draw a healing power from it. There are other things you both will have to do. Four days and nights of ceremony are required. Each day she will have to participate in the sweatlodge. You will need to make 405 tobacco ties for these ceremonies. You will also need to furnish the food for the participants. In time, after she has been in the sweatlodge ceremony, it will be time to seek guidance, answers, and a vision. In that vision, the final part of her journey will be revealed. Do you follow me so far?"

I was surprised by his rare question. I answered, "Yes. However, will we be starting right away with this next step?"

"That is up to you. When the time is right, you will know. If it is time to start today, we will. However, if it is next year, then that will be the right time. It must be a complete decision on the part of you and your wife."

I asked, "Will it be necessary to do the ceremonies here?"

"No. They can be done whenever and wherever you and your wife feel is right. You are welcome to do them here now or whenever you return."

"I thank you from the bottom of my heart for that offer. We will discuss it and figure out what we want to do."

Phillip Chips glanced back to his brother and said, "As for the pipe bag, you are welcome to leave it here if you so decide. However, whatever healing powers exist within it should be utilized by you and your wife. So we would suggest that you keep it until a later time."

I took Tammy's hand, "We will do that."

Godfrey and Phillip Chips both seemed pleased. They smiled and I shook their hands. Godfrey Chips hand shake was gentle and peaceful. He stared into my eyes and said, "It is good!" I thanked him and they both headed back to the ceremony house.

As we drove back along the dust filled roads that brought us here, I realized that even though we had been up for nearly 24 hours, I felt fresh and peaceful.

49. YOUNG BEAR

Dance Back the Powwows

We were able to get a couple of hours of sleep before we took up the rest of the next day. Marie Not-Help-Him felt there was one remaining segment to our trip. I felt there were actually two. The first, as agreed upon by both of us, was a visit with Severt Young Bear, a medicine man highly respected among the traditional Lakota. The second was my choice, Pete Catches, a renowned and powerful medicine man and sun dance leader. Marie Not-Help-Him felt that he might be too negative or skeptical for our purpose. She expressed concern regarding his undeniable power and his ability to affect things and people in a supernatural way. I thanked her for her concern but felt that I had received so much positive energy that if a negative energy was to be revealed, it was necessary for the overall balance of the journey.

After a short ride we found Severt Young Bear. The day had again heated up as we came to a stop at a makeshift parking area. He was working on his powwow arbor just outside of Porcupine. It could have been a sun dance arbor, but there was a difference. I saw about ten young men working at different jobs all around the fifty foot diameter grounds. Marie Not-Help-Him identified Young Bear, who was in conversation with a couple of other men at the far eastern corner. She preceded me while I filled my pipe to present to him. She was greeted with a big smile and a hug. They spoke among themselves for a moment, then the other men departed, never looking in our direction. Severt Young Bear, however, did raise his head and took a quick, almost disapproving, look at us, after which Marie Not-Help-Him turned and went back to our car.

"Severt will see you now," she announced as she leaned into my window.

"Thank you, Marie." I climbed out of the car and proceeded in his direction. Young Bear was yelling directions to a young man in the distance. He turned to greet me and I realized that he was, physically, a very large man. My six foot three, 230 pound frame was dwarfed by his huge presence. He wore a red cloth in his long hair, a symbol of his position. I introduced myself and he stuck out his big hand, smiled, and said, "Hello."

With the pipe cradled in my arms, I said, "Severt, it is an honor to meet you. I have come to seek counsel. I present this pipe to you in recognition of my respect for you and my hope that you will be able to assist me."

He was quiet for a moment, then put his big hand on my shoulder and said, "This is good. Follow me, please."

Severt Young Bear escorted me to a rare shady spot just outside the arbor near what would be the speaker stand for the ceremony. He took a sitting position on the dry grass. "Pull up some dust," he instructed with a laugh.

I offered the pipe in a traditional way. After three initial attempts, Severt Young Bear accepted the spiritual implement on the fourth try. We smoked.

After we had completed our ceremony and the pipe had been cleaned and put away, I said, "Severt, I thank you for taking the time from your busy day to talk with me."

"No problem!" he said. "I needed a break anyway."

I continued, "I have been here at Pine Ridge for a few days and I was at Greengrass before that. I am on a quest for guidance. I'm not sure if you are aware of what guidance I'm seeking."

He smiled. "I have listened to the radio and to Marie."

I followed his smile with my own. "So, you probably have some idea..."

"Yes, the pipe bag," he interjected.

I nodded in agreement. "What I am trying to determine are my duties and responsibilities in regard to it."

"Haven't you already been given instruction?" he questioned.

"Yes, I have received instruction as to its care and to whom and when I should show it. Another instruction from the previous keeper was to bring it to this place and seek additional guidance."

I paused for a moment. "Can you help me?"

Severt Young Bear's voice was gentle and understanding. "I'm not sure. I can only tell you what comes to me right now. I do not know when, but someday you must return the bag to the Lakota. Take it to Greengrass. That's where the Wakan

Chanunpa, the holy pipe is resting. By bringing the two together you could be given an answer."

I nodded. "We have been to Greengrass and Arval Looking Horse has suggested the same."

"Uh huh!" he said with his easy smile. "Arval Looking Horse is a good man. It is his responsibility to set a good and proper example. He has been giving people help his whole life. He was born to keep the pipe."

I added, "He suggested that we bring the pipe bag back next year for the sun dance."

"Uh huh! That sounds good," Severt replied.

He paused momentarily. "I see another step in your journey. I have heard the stories of the Crazy Horse connection with the pipe bag. I am sure you have spoken with a number of people on this subject."

"Yes," I agreed, "specifically with the Chips family on Eagle Nest Butte."

"Good. They have a very special connection with Crazy Horse. But with all the information that you have received, I will add one more thing."

I listened intently, with an inner excitement, as Severt Young Bear continued. "I would tell you to take the bag to the most sacred place in Crazy Horse's life, the place where he was given his ultimate vision, the place where his blood spilled into the ground when he was assassinated. To the Lakota that is a sacred place, and there you might find more answers."

"You mean Fort Robinson?" I asked.

"Exactly! We believe that a person's spirit is most accessible at the place where he left these earthly bonds. So it only makes sense that you will find an answer about the pipe bag at that place."

"Yes," I said. "That makes sense to me. But is it still there and could I get to it?"

"Oh yes. It is a national monument and the exact place where Crazy Horse was killed is marked and preserved."

One of the young men yelled at Severt Young Bear and he got to his feet. I followed suit. Looking in the direction of the young man, he continued, "You would need to contact the National Parks people. I believe they would allow you to visit at a private time, especially if you tell them why."

Another man called to Severt Young Bear. He waved and yelled back at him to hold on for a moment. I could see that he was busy and his presence was needed with the work on the arbor. I then pointed out the obvious. "Well, it looks as though you've got a lot of work ahead of you, so I won't take up any more of your time. I am very grateful for your time and counsel regarding the pipe bag. I will not soon forget it."

"It's been my pleasure," he replied with a broad smile. "I hope I have been of some assistance."

Severt Young Bear once again extended his big hand and I took it proudly. "I hope to see you again when we come back here next year."

"Oh," answered Severt Young Bear. "I'm sure we'll cross paths again somewhere. Take care!" He turned and walked away, but only in a physical sense. His words rang in my ears. His counsel rang in my heart.

On our way back to Marie Not-Help-Him's house she noted, "He's a very good person!"

"Yes," I agreed. "We had a good talk."

She continued, "Severt was one of our most powerful politicians on the reservation. He drove a real fancy car, lived in a real fancy home. He was in that circle of people who work very hard for material things. A few years back he received a vision which put him on the medicine path. He gave up everything and took up the work of being a medicine man. He is materially poor now, but he is happier and loved more than he had ever been. He's one of our medicine men."

It was just past noon when we settled in at Marie Not-Help-Him's for lunch. She prepared some sandwiches and chips. We shared some conversation. Then I said, "I think I'm going to try once again to see Pete Catches."

She had given up trying to change my mind. "He'll probably be home now."

"Yes," I replied. "I have that same feeling."

After straightening up a bit we were on our way. Marie Not-Help-Him had decided to stay. I still detected uneasiness about our visit with Catches. I, too, harbored a feeling of strangeness, but I knew it was time to become acquainted with the man. To refuse his input would be counterproductive as well as unbalancing.

50. PETE CATCHES' MEDICINE

Dance Back the Raven

As we approached the long dirt driveway that led to Pete Catches's trailer, I spotted a person standing in the field where I had previously seen a small cemetery plot. Once again I felt a pulling to that place and said aloud, "We need to visit out there before we leave."

Tammy didn't say anything, but I was sure she felt the urgency that welled up inside me. My focus returned to the dirt road we were traveling and the man at the end of it. Once the trailer had come into sight, I noticed that it appeared to be empty again. As I surveyed the surroundings, however, I noticed an elderly man sitting under the makeshift shade arbor. He was very still, like a fox that had just been spotted. I brought the car to a stop and climbed out.

I had previously filled my pipe for the purpose of honor and respect to this man. I placed the pipe in my arms and strolled purposefully to where he was sitting. As I got closer, I became aware of his stern and penetrating eyes. He still had not moved. As I reached the perimeter of his shade, about ten feet away from him, he held up his left hand in a stop fashion. I immediately obeyed.

"I do not want to smoke the pipe!" His old but powerful voice filled my ears. This was followed by a noise like a clap of thunder. However, the skies were clear and rain seemed unlikely in this place. I realized that my attention was still on him, and it was apparent that the supernatural noise I had heard had been generated by him. I was now feeling an unseen force, like a pushing sensation against my chest. Pete Catches's left hand was still extended in my direction as if it were producing that unseen force. As I focused on his face and then his intense eyes, a fear grabbed at me and I knew that if I did not act quickly and effectively, this opportunity would be lost, or worse, turned against me. A roar began to fill my head. I said, almost shouting, "O Wakan Tanka, Niskaminu, Oshimalayi-Oyate Wanee wa'chi cha," then in English, "O God and all good spirits. Have mercy on me so that my people may live!"

The roar quickly dropped off and I answered, "Pete Catches, I respect and understand your desire not to smoke. I will withdraw the pipe in an honorable way. I have come not to cause shame or harm to you. I come as a lost person who is seeking guidance and help from one who is known to be caring."

Even though the roaring had ceased, I could still feel a pressure at my chest. I offered, "If you must strike me down, then go ahead. I am not here for myself alone, but for many, especially for that one I love above all, my wife!" I felt tears begin to roll down my face. I felt like it was over and I had unintentionally crossed a line that would kill me.

"Help me, God! I cannot help myself," I said.

With that Pete Catches lowered his hand and the pressure left my chest. My legs felt limp and unsteady. The roaring in my ears and head was completely gone. He got up slowly as I cleared my head and thoughts. A large stump seat was beside him. He lifted the four-foot diameter stump by grabbing it with a bear hug from the ground and placed it at my feet.

"Sit!" he commanded.

I stood in disbelief for a moment, but quickly obeyed. Pete Catches sat, arms folded across his chest. His shoulder length hair was thin and gray. He wore an oversized pair of jeans with the belt cinched tight to keep the jeans up on his frail 110 pound body. He also wore a typical long sleeve, blue shirt and a pair of old tennis shoes. He looked around and by me a couple of times and then opened the conversation.

"Most people would run or at least go away when faced with what you have experienced. Why is it that you've stayed?"

The answer popped into my head without thought, "Because I must stay. If it were just for me, I would have run. I would not even have come. But I am here for others as well."

"I see," he replied, looking over my shoulder toward the car and my family. "Now why are you here?" I could still sense a bit of irritation in his voice.

"I come to seek guidance and direction in two matters. The first is the pipe bag with which I have been entrusted."

Pete Catches interrupted, "I have already heard of this pipe bag and I understand your need for guidance. Sounds like a bunch of bullshit to me! But let me tell you something first. About ten years ago, some anthropologists came out to see me. They had come all the way from the Smithsonian Institute in Washington, DC. They, too, came for guidance. With them they brought a drum. They told me that this drum was once the property of Sitting Bull." He paused for a moment.

"They wanted me to go with them to Washington, DC to do a ceremony for this so-called drum of Sitting Bull. Once the ceremony was completed, the drum would be placed in a special place for viewing by the visitors to the museum."

Pete Catches's wrinkled face tensed up, and an obvious anger swelled up in him as he continued. "They brought the drum to me. I looked at it, then I looked at them, and said that this was not Sitting Bull's drum. One of them suits jumped up and said that it was his drum and that it had already been verified. I told him that he was a damn liar!"

Pete Catches's cold and powerful eyes pierced me. I did all I could to avoid them. He continued, "Just as Sitting Bull was cut open by the army's bayonets, so was his drum. All his personal belongings were destroyed. They feared his power so much that they wanted to be completely free of all physical connection to him. So it is with all sacred things. They represented an unseen, unconquerable part of the Sitting Bull's life. The drums, the pipes, the pipe bags were piled high and torched! Even the teepees were set fire, leaving our people either dead or stranded without shelter."

A deep sadness appeared on his face as he seemed to relive those horrible times. "So you see, it is very hard to believe that a thing such as Crazy Horse's pipe bag still exists. If it does, how is it that it has found its way to you?" Pointing his bony finger in my direction, he added, "Who the hell are you anyway?"

I opened my mouth to answer his question, but he immediately interrupted, "Crazy Horse's family and certain medicine men are the only ones who know of Crazy Horse. He was also killed because of his power. When the soldiers turned over his body to his family, they took it into the Badlands where it was secretly put to rest. With it they took all his belongings, which were very few; that is, what the soldier's fires had not already found."

He paused for a moment. "I am one of the last ones who actually knows the place where Crazy Horse rests, and when I die I will take that with me!"

I finally spoke. "I am very honored that you have shared these thoughts with me. I must say that I come here, not to show you a pipe bag that once belonged to Crazy Horse, for Crazy Horse is the only one who can truly say whether this bag is his or not. I come to ask your advice as to what I should do with the bag. I will not just give it to anyone or sell it to a collector or museum. I do not have the right to do that. I do not own this pipe bag. I am merely the keeper of it." I paused for his reaction, but there was none. I continued, "You asked who I am. I am Lionel Little Eagle; my people are the Micmac from eastern Canada. I did not find the pipe bag; it found me!"

Pete Catches sat silently. I then added, "The other reason I have come here is much more important to me in a very personal way!"

"Your wife!" Pete Catches's voice interrupted. I was stunned for a moment, but then realized that I was sitting before an uncommon man.

"Yes, my wife. If it would deliver her away from her illness, I would take this pipe bag into the Badlands and secretly release it to nature. I would lay down here at your feet! The bag has an importance, but the wellness of my beloved wife has even more. I have asked God to help and I am still waiting, and because of her I am still believing. So, Pete Catches, I am not here to trick you or cheat you. First, you would not let me, and second, I have no reason."

Once again I stopped in hopes of some sort of acknowledgment from him, but he still sat in silence. After a bit, he finally spoke. His voice seemed more at ease now. "You know, I've been busting my ass all day. I've been working on our sun dance arbor, that is, working along with my helpers. To us Oglala, the sun dance is the most important and sacred thing we have. Through it we are able to find answers to the unknown. Every day for the last couple of weeks I have been at the arbor. Today I left early because a raven told me that you were coming. I wanted to see you, to see what kind of a man you are. But when I tested you, you stayed." He paused, slowing his speech. "And now I understand why."

A recognizable gentleness had drifted over him, like the cloud that was presently blocking the sun. "Your work with the pipe bag," he continued, "is just beginning and just ending. You will know what to do with it when the time is right. The bag will do the guiding. All you have to do is hold onto it. If this bag does contain the mystery force, then it will not matter what I say to you or anyone says to you. Things will happen in a proper order. Don't rush it."

"As for your wife..." He paused once again. "The sun dance has helped many Oglala with directions and answers. It has been known to actually cure the worst illnesses. You must be careful of who puts on the sun dance now. I am the only one who is doing it the old way. Others give too many breaks, and even water to the dancers. They also give the dancers shade. This is not the old way! But because of the effort and strength needed for my sun dance, I do not recommend it to everyone!"

I jumped in, "Do you mean that I need to participate in the sun dance in order to make my wife well?"

"No. Are you not listening?!" he quickly responded. "I said that the Oglala use this ceremony for such help. It may or may not be right for your life. It is a decision that is with you and your wife. I can't tell you that you should dance, nor can anyone else. I can suggest it, but it's completely up to you."

As I sat contemplating his words, he went on. "Another possibility that you should keep in mind is a vision quest. "Many people find answers that way, too."

I said, "We have been considering both those options, but have made no decisions or commitments yet. Thank you for your suggestions. They mean so much to our efforts."

Pete Catches climbed to his feet and looked back over his shoulder. "Well, I've rested enough now. It's time for me to get back to the arbor and it's time for you to go!"

I understood and was not about to remain sitting for any more challenges. I felt very fortunate to have even met him. "Thank you for your time, Pete Catches. I will take your words and counsel with me."

His gaze still roamed over the plains. He raised his head, and with a half smile, bid me farewell. That was good enough for me. I turned and started back toward the car. After only a couple of steps, I heard his rough voice call loudly from behind me. "Next time you come, we will smoke the pipe!"

I stopped and smiled. "I would be honored!"

I finally arrived at the car, where Tammy and the boys sat patiently in the hot sun. "How was it?" Tammy asked.

I raised my head in Pete Catches's direction. He was nowhere in sight; it was as though he was never there. On his silver trailer sat a black raven. I nodded in its direction and answered her question. "Fine. Just fine!"

She understood my answer.

On our drive back to Marie Not-Help-Him's, I contemplated my visit with Pete Catches and the medicine power that was evident there. Something down deep inside told me that it was time to move on. It was time to wrap up our extraordinary visit. We had been given our answers. I had found the guidance I had sought, or should I say, it had found me.

Marie Not-Help-Him and her wonderful mother, Celane, were waiting for us when we arrived. I could detect concern in their eyes. "How was your visit?" Marie Not-Help-Him asked right away.

"It was like you said. At first I had a very hard time and came close to running out of there. But I was able to muster up a little courage, and, once Pete saw that I wasn't going to turn and run, he loosened up his powerful grip on the air, and on me, too."

I heard Marie Not-Help-Him release the pressure caused by her true friendship and concern for us. Celane Not-Help-Him simply turned and went back into the house. I knew that she, too, was concerned about us. She also possessed a special medicine power.

51. CELANE'S MESSAGE
Dance Back the Eyes

Evening began to set in after our very long day. We had covered the ground that we wanted to cover. All of us sat around our campsite outside Marie Not-Help-Him's house. We laughed and talked. Celane Not-Help-Him was such an easy person to like and listen to. I could see why Marie was so proud of her and loved her.

"I believe we'll be leaving in the morning," I said, sort of out of the blue. There was no other way to say it.

"Ah!" Celane Not-Help-Him moaned. "But you just got here!"

"Yes, it does seem like that. But we have accomplished most everything we wanted. We have visited with a lot of people, and with those visits we have received a lot of very important information and guidance."

I hesitated for a moment, then said, "You know, without your help it would not have been possible. Both of you have made this visit complete. There are no words to express my thanks and gratitude for taking us into your lives."

Celane Not-Help-Him, who was listening quietly, smiled and added, "You know that if we didn't believe in you, we would not have helped you. You are a good young man and what you are doing with the pipe bag and with your wife is good. The Great Spirit looks down upon you with pleasure and pride."

"Thank you, Celane. Coming from you, that means a lot to us.

Marie Not-Help-Him interrupted, "I can't believe you have to go already. It seems like you just got here."

Celane Not-Help-Him added, "Well, maybe you can leave Mato Cikala, your Little Bear. I'm sure I can teach him to stay on his feet!"

We all got a good laugh out of her joke.

"Will you be coming back soon?" Marie asked.

"Yes, we plan on coming back again next year, and we'll be sure to look you up!"

"Good!" Celane Not-Help-Him smiled.

"Maybe you two can get out to our neck of the woods in Washington State," I offered.

"That sounds nice," Celane Not-Help-Him answered. "What's it like there? Would I like it?"

"I'm sure you would. We live in the town of Suquamish on the Port Madison Reservation. It's a small but proud community snuggled under the loving arms of the beautiful Olympic Mountains."

I sat back and thought about home. "The trees are taller than any of the buildings here, and if you love fishing, you'll fall in love with our waters."

"I love fish!" Celane Not-Help-Him replied, eyes twinkling.

I went on, "People are nice there. They seem very content and happy with the life and environment. I'm sure you'd like it and you will always have a home there."

They smiled. Marie Not-Help-Him answered, "Thanks! Well don't be surprised to see us out there!"

Celane Not-Help-Him said, "They have invited me to a place in Oregon called Mt. Hood for a sun dance a couple of times. A relative named Martin Highbear runs it. I just haven't had the chance or the time to get there yet."

"Well, when you do, come visit us, too," I said.

"Yes," Celane Not-Help-Him replied. "I feel like we are family with you now."

52. GOING HOME AGAIN
Dance Back Anna Mae

We quickly fell asleep that evening, and before we knew it, it was morning and time to make our departure. Even though it had been a number of days since the last time we had broken up camp, the process of taking down and packing up came back quickly. Upon its completion, we stood by the car. Tammy had made a beautiful, log-cabin style quilt, which she had finished just prior to our departure almost a month ago. Her quilt making brought peace and joy to her life. It simply made her happy. To her, it was a way of wrapping her love around those whom she cared so much for. She knew that the right person would eventually come along to receive this special offer. We had no idea who that person would be, that was, until this moment. She handed it over to Marie Not-Help-Him.

"I want you to have this gift from our family to you." Tammy spoke softly. "Without your help, our time here would not have meant as much. Thank you."

I detected a trace of a tear on Marie Not-Help-Him's cheek. She pushed her glasses back on her nose and wiped it away. Tammy continued, "You gave us access to your home, and even more importantly, to your people, especially your wonderful mother. You have been a true friend and we thank you from our hearts."

Our good-byes were completed and we found ourselves back on the road. We drove down the now-familiar main street of Pine Ridge and by the Red Cloud School. As we approached the Oglala area, I spotted the small cemetery plot to the right of the road, the one I had felt drawn to before. I pulled over to the shoulder of the road. I knew I would have to go and pay my respects. The cemetery was about 100 yards off the road, and Jeremiah accompanied me. There were four plots altogether. Each had certain spiritual articles laying on them: abalone shells, sage, sweet grass, tobacco ties, a few beads, and leather pouches. It looked as though it was a memorial, and it was! Within these earthly bounds lay the remains of a blood relative, a Micmac sister, Anna Mae Aquash!

Anna had made such an impact on this community that she was allowed burial on their reservation. Her people, and mine, were from the New Brunswick and Nova Scotia regions of Canada. She had fought and died for her belief that the Indian peoples of this continent should not be forced to give up their traditional way of life. For this she was murdered! I felt as though she was here, not in this small, unmarked cemetery, but here on this reservation. She maintained her power, even from the spirit world!

I left a small crystal offering and some tobacco ties, then returned to the car. We were soon back on the road. I daydreamed as I drove on. All of a sudden, I heard Tammy's voice, "That looks like rain!"

I could not believe it but it was true. Directly ahead a large sheet of rain was approaching us. "Yes," I replied.

"That's great!" Jeremiah exclaimed. "Here we sweat and burn up for five days and now that we are leaving, it begins to rain. What rotten luck!"

"Not really, Son," I assured him. "We are going to be blessed by this rain. It has nothing to do with bad luck; it has everything to do with good fortune. It hasn't rained in these parts for four months and now here it is."

I reached across and held Tammy's hand. "We are truly fortunate and blessed that this is happening to us!"

Tammy squeezed my hand and I could feel her smile without seeing it. We came seeking answers and directions. As the heavy raindrops began to plop against our windshield, I was grateful that our answers and directions had been given.

BOOK III

RELEASING THE DANCE

"For the dead are not powerless.
Dead did I say?
There is no death, only a change of worlds."
Chief Seattle (b. 1786, d. June 7, 1866)

"Honey, I'm not dying;
only changing worlds."
Tamara Lynn (b. 1952, d. June 7, 1990)

CAN-WAKAN, THE MYSTERY TREE

53. TRUTH
Dance Back the Pain

In May 1990, I again found myself on familiar roads, but these were not the roads of South Dakota, but of my home, Washington state, specifically Highway 16 north, which runs from Tacoma to Bremerton through the Olympic Peninsula. This route has become all too familiar to me now. It connects our home with the hospital were Tammy receives her treatments and advice. It's beautifully lined with evergreens. The majestic Olympic mountain range occasionally peeks through the tall trees. This was a typical Northwestern day, overcast, with showers here and there. The temperature was mild. With me was Tammy, my wife and dearest friend.

In all my life, I had never experienced a moment such as this one. We were silent, our faces wet with moisture from the miles of tears. I was having trouble breathing. I could hardly concentrate on driving. My heart was breaking; I was dying on Highway 16 somewhere between Tacoma and Bremerton.

Tammy broke the long silence. "Lionel, I love you."

"I love you too, Honey," I choked out my response.

"We knew this was a possibility," Tammy stated.

I was silent again. My face felt flushed but I couldn't think of anything to say. She went on. "We'll need to make some preparations." She paused for a second and then said, "I want my sons here; I want them to be with me."

I was sobbing, nearly out of control. The tears and snot mingled together. I did not have anything to blow my nose with so Tammy opened her purse and handed me a dainty purple and white lace hanky. I blew it to smithereens.

"Honey," I said, "I don't think I'm going to handle this very well. I'm a terribly weak man." By this time, what little bit of control I had was completely gone. I cried, looking for sympathy and understanding from the one who deserved it more than me.

It was so hard to believe that this was happening. Tammy sat quietly with her hands in her lap. Her golden brown hair, streaked with occasional silver-gray, rested on her shoulders. Her heart-melting, sky blue eyes sparkled with beauty and life. But her life was the question. The doctor we had just left told us that we had two, maybe three, weeks left before the cancer, which was invisibly ravishing her gentle 120-pound body, would win the battle and the war. Two or three weeks seems so long unless you are talking about dying; then it's ridiculously short.

The vicious cancer had made its way to her spine, liver, and lungs and was causing an unrelenting pain throughout her fragile body.

"It worries me, Lionel, that it's in my lungs. I'm scared of choking or suffocating. If only it would have stayed away from my lungs, I would have been better able to handle it."

"I know Honey, but it's there and we are going to have to deal with it," I managed somehow to reply.

Our drive became a silent one, both of us in our own thoughts. My thoughts roared through me like an out-of-control locomotive. We were so wonderfully in love; our plans were well thought-out; our children were still young. I didn't want this to end. I wanted to be with her for a long time, to love her, laugh with her, cry with her. God, turn this night into day, I prayed. My mind was racing, my heart was pounding so hard and loud I could actually feel it. Tammy broke the silence once again. "Lionel, you're going to have to go to Greengrass for both of us."

What little bit of control I thought I had regained was completely shattered. She was saying, in her knowing way, that she would not be going with me! I wanted to die right there. It's a feeling that you can't touch or see or hit or kick or bite or anything. You are completely and utterly annihilated by it: the recognition of imminent death. Things took on a different meaning. What was once important was not important anymore. What was once taken for granted became incredibly important, like a kiss or a smile. Greengrass seemed to be the least important thing to me. The circling raven, high above us in the distance, carried the greatest importance.

"Is that a raven?" Tammy asked as if reading my mind.

I squinted to see. "Yes, I think so." She watched it with great interest. I changed the subject. "Honey, what good would Greengrass do now? We gave of ourselves; we met with the medicine men; we participated in their ceremonies. But it gave us nothing back! I don't see a purpose in returning. I don't even want to see the place."

It was then that I noticed that the peaceful and almost holy aura, which had always existed around her, was now becoming even more vibrant and radiant as she spoke. "That is why you must go back. There is something there for you and for me. You have to go back for both of us."

54. TIME FLIES WHEN YOU'RE DYING
Dance Back the Prayers

Over the next few, very short weeks we all dissolved into an almost blissful state of existence. Time, which had become so dear and important to us, was now merely a formality, much like sleep, which we got little of. Our families were gathered by the circumstances, and our hearts were opened. We recited prayers and shared love.

On June 6th, 1990, at our home in Suquamish, Washington, Tammy called us together around her bed. To each of us she gave a promise of prayer from the other side. After we all had our private visit, she said to us together, "Pray for me, help me. I want to go now! Please pray for me!" Her desperate plea was heeded and we began a vigil of prayer. I prayed as hard and sincerely as I could. So did the rest of the family who made the hoop around her bed.

"Please God!" I prayed. "She has suffered enough within this world. I pray you release her from her tired and sad body. I pray you receive her spirit into the bosom of your joyous and everlasting glory. Wakan Tanka, Niskaminu, Tunkasila, Spirit Family of the other side, come now and assist your humble and beautiful child. She is ready to do that work you have for her and you will, indeed, be pleased with what she will produce. Hurry God! Hau!"

Time marched on in a void. Nothing seemed to be important, nothing but my beautiful darling wife, my Tammy. After nearly six hours of continuous prayer by the family, Tammy went into a deep sleep, her last sleep. She breathed irregularly. I watched for a while longer and then the image of my father appeared in my mind, a father who so dearly loved his daughter-in-law. He was 2,000 miles away, but I knew his presence was necessary, if not in a physical way, then in a prayerful way. It was around 9:45

PM when he answered the phone and I heard his familiar voice on the other end of the line.

"Dad...," I said.

"Yes, Son, how is she doing?" he asked.

"Very, very bad, Dad. She is ready to go, but she is having a very hard time letting go."

"Oh God!" I heard him moan, "Oh God! Why Lord is this happening!"

He was quiet for a moment and I could hear the rare sounds of my father sniffling back tears and clearing his throat as he prepared to say something to me. I interrupted his awkward search for words. "Dad, I need your help. Tammy needs your help. Please use your rosary, your medicine to help her let go. She is ready. She is suffering and wants to go on."

His soft sobbing was now much louder. "Oh, Son, I am so sorry, so sad that this has not turned out the way we wanted." He was again silent for a moment and then added, "I will do that for her and for you too, Son."

"Thank you, Dad," I replied. He didn't acknowledge my reply. He simply, sadly hung up the phone.

Hours, minutes, seconds and the tears of a loving family rolled by. Our prayers continued to fill Tammy's sensitive and gentle ears. At some point, I observed the saddest tear drop I'd ever seen before form at her right eye and then slip, ever so gently down her soft cheek. Like a cat, I leaped to that sweet tear drop, scooping it up with my right forefinger and then shoving it quickly into my mouth, savoring and cherishing my beloved wife's last precious gift to me on this good earth.

At twelve minutes after midnight on June 7, 1990, as I held her hand, she took her last mortal breath in, and then released it. A mixture of sadness and joy immediately filled my heart and then the room. As I had promised her, I raised my eyes upward to the plain white ceiling in our living room. I did this to see her make her glorious exit from this good earth. At first there was nothing but that white insensitive ceiling. Then, like the moon appearing from behind the clouds, her peaceful face appeared smiling, her mom's smile, a smile of freedom and love. Around her were translucent-like spirit beings, gently touching and caressing her.

She was gone in a physical way but powerfully present in a spiritual way. I smiled through my tears. Life was now and forever changed.

Less than a half hour later the phone rang. I happened to be standing beside it at the time. It was my dad. "Lionel," he said, and then before I could say anything, he continued, "It's over now, Son. She's gone. Her pain is over."

I was still in shock from the events of the past half hour, and now my father was telling me something that he could not have known, but did anyway. "Yes, Dad, she just left." We were both quiet for a moment and then I asked the obvious question. "How did you know, Dad?"

"Because she just came by here on her way to heaven, Son!"

The power of the moment and that statement was unbelievable! It was something I'm sure I'll never experience again. I thanked him for his prayers. He, once again, simply hung up the phone.

55. MOON OF THE GREENGRASS SUN DANCE

Dance Back the Grasshoppers

Two months later, in mid August of 1990, I once again found myself zipping along the hot roads of South Dakota. Being there seemed almost unreal. She'd told me I would be going to Greengrass, but I had no idea it would be so soon. But here I was and I wasn't alone. With me were my sons Jeremiah and Trapper. Also with us was a family friend, James Old Coyote. The past two moons had been very difficult, more so than I had previously imagined. I had fallen into a hole of grief, a bottomless pit of sadness. So strong were these feelings that they were literally controlling and disrupting my everyday life and the lives of those around me. Greengrass was screaming out my name.

A unique dream became my guide. In it I found myself standing on a butte, somewhere in the South Dakota landscape. I was alone. It was nighttime, the sky was clear but no stars and no moon shown above. I felt a sadness and longing for those sacred images of light, yet no matter what direction I looked, I was unable to find any sort of light. As I pondered my sad situation, I suddenly saw what appeared to be a campfire on a distant butte, and, in time, a voice from the darkness filled my ears and heart with mysterious words: "I will dance your sadness away, my Love." Then I'd awake with no answers to the questions raised by my dream.

Now I had followed my heart to Greengrass to look deep into myself. Two men and two young boys waited for us at the main entrance into the sun dance grounds. "Security!" one of the young boys announced with distinctive pride in his voice. "You have to turn in all cameras, recording devices, drugs, and alcohol."

James Old Coyote, who was sitting in the front seat, reached through the window and handed his walkman to the youngster. The two older men stood off from the car. The second teenager moved around to the opposite side of the car and pointed out, "You're going to have to open your trunk!"

"Okay, no problem," I replied. Once I had opened the trunk, the boys quickly realized that it was filled to capacity and instructed us to close it up. Finally, one of the older men eased up to the rear of the car, leaned against the trunk, cigarette in hand, and without looking directly at me, asked, "You folks been here before?"

"A couple of times," I replied.

"You know the rules of the camp then, right?"

"Yep," I answered, and then thought to myself, I hope I do.

One of the teens tied a small piece of red cloth around our antenna to serve as a quick look reference for security. The man looked into the car. "I see you got a couple of young men with you." He then added, "We'll be needing some help with security."

"Sure," I answered. "I'm sure the boys and myself will be able to help out wherever we can."

"Okay, great. We'll be in contact." He then looked over at one of the boys, who had stationed himself near the rope gate that was across the road. He nodded, and the boy dropped the rope on the dusty road. "Go ahead!" he instructed as he waved us on.

I climbed back into the car and thanked him; then we drove on. The road dipped, curved around to the right, then to the left. As we climbed out of the small valley, I noticed that the areas around the road seemed dryer than I had seen before, but I had been here later in the year, too. The familiar odor of sage filled the air and the plants spread abundantly as far as we could see. Eventually, the site of the sun dance grounds and cabins, including the pipe house, came into view.

The first thing I became aware of was the absence of the arbor. It was gone! Only a couple of tents were set up and my first thought was that the sun dance grounds had been moved. I brought the car to a stop beside a couple of young Indian men parked in a pickup.

"Excuse me, can you tell me where the sun dance grounds are?"

"Sure," the driver answered. "Just drive that way," he pointed, "until you hit the river, then take a left and follow it until you find a spot where you can cross. From there follow the road that looks like it's been used the most. It will take you to the camp and arbor." Pretty simple directions I thought to myself, except maybe the part about crossing the river.

The wheels of the car sank deep into the dry sand as we bumped, humped, and jumped along the dusty road. We finally came to the river, and I noticed many others had also made their way along the same route. Water still flowed in the river, but at that time of the year it had dwindled to a small trickle about fifteen feet across and only a few inches deep. About a quarter of a mile up the river, I found the crossing point. The river was mostly thick mud at this area. I dropped the car into low gear and chugged on across with no problem. Upon exiting the river, I was immediately back in the thick and treacherous dust. I gunned the car up the bank and found the main road. It was not very far until I spotted the arbor. It was new, only the second year of its use. Beyond the arbor, I could see the camp.

I counted about twenty campers scattered over a half mile of prairie. Tents and lodges were mingled together as were the people. Red flags marked the boundary or limits within which we could not set up our campsite. This was done to give the sun dancers plenty of room with the least number of distractions. No activity was visible in or around the arbor.

We nuzzled into the northern side of the camp area and began to set up. But before we could drive in the first tent peg, a young man approached us and announced, "We're digging on the firepit for the campers, would you like to help?"

"Sure," Jeremiah and James answered in unison, and off they went. Trapper took off to explore the area and I finished setting up our camp. We were in a good location, close to the river and within a reasonable distance from the sun dance arbor. A couple of other campsites were in close proximity to ours. No one was home at either site.

Once done with the setup, I took a quick look toward the firepit where the boys were hard at work. Spades and shovels banged and clanged away. Grayish dust rose around them, itself like a fire. I found Trapper and we both took a walk down to the river bank. The sage was knee-high to me and chest-high to him. He bounded through it like a young deer. The grasshoppers were everywhere and the youngster quickly realized that they were a lot of fun to catch.

The Moreau River seemed higher and more like a river at this location. There were kids and adults in it trying to cool off from the ninety-degree-plus temperatures blanketing the plains at the noon hour. I sat quietly as Trapper chased his newfound friends, the grasshoppers. I began to reflect on my last visit to these special grounds. Tammy, sweet Tammy, I thought to myself. The tears that flowed so easily were once again flowing. I felt a tug on my arm. It was Trapper. "What, Son?"

"More, Mommie!" he answered.

"What?" I asked in surprise. "What are you talking about, Trapper?"

"Mom, Mom," he said matter-of-factly. "Momma there!" He pointed toward the puffy white clouds overhead. A large one caught my eye. It appeared like hair blowing in the wind. "You see your Mom in the clouds?" I asked. He nodded yes and then took off for his grasshoppers. "Hoppers, Dad. Catch 'em!"

I watched him run off and then returned to the clouds. "Mom," I said softly to myself. "Tammy," I said, closing my eyes.

On our way back to the camp, I decided to stroll by the area of the arbor. I met people along the way. We waved or said hello but not much more than that. Certain men had a certain way about them that identified them as sun dancers. I found the kitchen area. A couple of women were hard at work. I looked around but didn't see the familiar face of Shirley Calfrobe, the kitchen boss we had gotten to know in previous visits. Two young men were busy splitting wood. The arbor showed activity now. Two pickups were parked along side it with six men hard at work unloading cottonwood branches to be used to shade the observation area around the perimeter of the arbor. The wind had picked up a bit, making the process of throwing the branches on top of the arbor frame more difficult. As I walked toward the arbor, I could see its layout better. To the west of it was the dancers' resting place, where a large preparation teepee had been erected. Four sweatlodges had also been built in that special compound. One very large firepit was set up at the center of the sweatlodges. A few men were working on the woodpile and other preparations. By the time I arrived at the arbor, the trucks had taken off to collect more shade. I introduced myself and Trapper to the group of men. Three were from South Dakota and one was from Massachusetts. We shared some small talk until the trucks returned with the next load, and we set to work.

The area we were covering was the outer eight feet of the arbor's perimeter. The dancers would not feel the shade during the ceremony. The shade was for the sole use of the observers. The process of throwing the branches up on top of the arbor frame was becoming more and more difficult as the wind blew harder across the dry, treeless prairie. However, we did finish the job in about two hours. It was good work.

Trapper had done very well. It helped that he found a little girl to share his grasshopper hunting adventures. Upon returning to the campsite, we had some cold water and relaxed. The wind was still blowing hard. "I'm hungry, Dad," announced Trapper.

"Oh, yes!" I replied. As I went to work preparing our evening meal, a familiar thought re-entered my mind: I'm a single parent; I've got to remember things like feeding my son and washing him. I did not dread it. In fact, it was very satisfying and I could hardly call it work. Caring for my son was more like worship. I thought of something that Tammy had once told me: I should never re-marry, she had said, for the purpose of giving Trapper a mother, as I was capable of doing that work. Even though I knew I could never replace his mother, her statement was the most important recognition I had received in my life. I will forever cherish and hold her words close to my heart.

Later that evening, Trapper and I joined a group who had gathered near the arbor. A middle aged man with an abundant body was speaking. "My name is Harry Charger. I am the chief of security for this sun dance. My job involves keeping an eye open for anyone who may be unfamiliar with the ways of our ceremony. I also watch for the ones who think they already know everything!" He smiled and added, "Sometimes these ones can be more trouble than the new ones!"

Charger carried himself with a great deal of confidence, complemented with a robust laugh and strong Lakota pride. On his rather large head he wore an old, ragged Cincinnati Reds ball cap. He often boasted of how his team was going to win the World Series this year.

"It's very simple," he continued. "If you are not sure about something, ask me. Or, just don't do it. You are all part of this sacred ceremony." Pointing to the sky, he added, "The Creator has brought us all here for his purpose. Don't try too hard to figure it out. Just let it figure itself out. Some of us do have a specific purpose: the dancers, the drummers and singers, the intercessor, and the medicine men. It is primarily for them that we are here. It is their personal vows that have brought them here."

A larger group had gathered and Harry Charger gazed over them. He removed his ball cap, and then took a red bandanna from the back pocket of his well-worn Levi jeans. Wiping the sweat from his brow, he went on, "We will need a lot of help. Help with the fires for the sweats, splitting wood; and once we start the dancers' fire, it must stay lit for the whole four days! That fire must not go out!" Shoving his bandanna back in his pocket, he then carefully replaced his cap. "We will need help in the kitchen area also. With the fire, and cutting up the meat."

He stopped and directed a question to someone in the crowd. "How many animals do we have?" A man from the crowd replied, "Two cows and a buffalo."

"Uh huh," Harry Charger noted. "We will be very busy with that work. The more people helping, the easier it will be."

About fifteen people were gathered near the arbor by this time. Harry Charger tapped a cigarette from its pack and lit it. "Cameras and recording devices are not allowed at any time, anywhere, for any reason. If you should forget and bring one here..." He paused to get his point across, "you will be asked to leave!"

"There are certain people designated as security. You will be able to identify them by their red arm bands. However, security is the responsibility of everyone." He stopped and peered through the crowd. "You are the security! If you see something that doesn't look right, let one of us know. A few can't do it alone. All must help!" He directed another question in Lakota to the man he'd spoken to earlier. The man pointed back over his shoulder and replied back in Lakota.

"Oh yes," Charger went on, "the buttes around here are off limits. We have at least seven men and women on Hanbleceya, vision quest. They must not be disturbed, so keep off the buttes."

Again he asked something of the other man, who simply shrugged and gave no reply. Charger thought for a moment. "The sweats for the observers will soon be ready. They are not just for looks. They have a very important purpose, the purpose of purification. Everyone who plans on attending the sun dance ceremony should cleanse themselves. If you do not, you could affect the dancers! Each day before you come down to the arbor, steam yourself off. Steam off the little ones too. It doesn't have to be a long one for the little ones, but steam them anyway."

He then pointed to the opposite side of the river where some cars and tents were set up. "Over there is the Moon Lodge. It is for the women who are in their time. We will have a sweatlodge built for them over there. That is where the women must be who are in their moon. Please, do not try to deceive this ceremony. It is a very sacred and powerful time for our women. If you do not treat this matter in a proper way, it could cause harm to the dancers, so don't take the chance. Women are there now. It is sacred."

Harry Charger broke apart his half-smoked cigarette as he continued his remarks to us. "When you see a gathering such as this one, go find out what's going on. When you do receive information, pass it along. Help your neighbor get to know the ones who are around you. We are brought here for a common purpose. We are family here. Keep that in mind." After these words, the crowd dissipated and we made our way back to our campsite.

56. "CHANUNPAMONY"

Dance Back Mom

As evening settled in, I gathered up my pipe bundle and decided to take a walk into the quiet prairie, Trapper in tow. We waded through a lake of prairie grass and grasshoppers. Trapper chased and jumped and laughed along the way. Eventually, we found ourselves far from the camp area on top of a small hill. The evening sky was beautiful, the stars were just beginning to come into view. A couple of large puffy clouds roamed the vast South Dakota skies.

"This looks like a good place," I said to Trapper. "Let's sit here for a while. We will do our Chanunpa ceremony now."

"Oh boy!" Trapper said excited, "I like the Canupamony!"

I smiled to myself. Close enough for a three-and-a-half year old.

The winds were still blowing but with less intensity as I prepared for this private ceremony. A good thought entered me. I recalled the elder Tom Calfrobe from our last visit and his most special talks of the clouds. I wondered how he was and if I would be able to meet him this trip. I hoped so.

I watched the many forms and figures made by the drifting clouds floating through the sky. "Hmmm, I wonder what Calfrobe would say of these?"

"Dad, Dad!" Trapper's panicked voice grabbed my attention.

"What is it, Son?" I asked.

He pointed at my cap. "A grasshopper, Dad, it's on your hat!"

"Oh that's nice!" I said with a smile.

"No Dad!" he protested. "Get it off!"

"Oh I think I'll just let him stay there. He'll leave when he's supposed to." That seemed to ease his concern a little, but he still kept a watchful eye on it until it did leave.

It was here that I unpacked my pipe bundle and began my preparation. As always, I described what I was doing for Trapper. I held the bowl of my pipe in one hand and the stem in the other.

"Trapper, this is a very important thing for our people. It is a special gift from the Creator. It should be done very carefully and handled with great respect and honor." I then eased the bowl onto the stem. "Now this pipe has even more power and importance." Trapper listened carefully. "Now it represents our ancestors; it stands for our family on the other side, with God."

"Like Mom?" he quickly asked.

"Yes, like Mom," I replied. I then held it vertically with the bowl at the top. "It is like a man. You see the bowl, here, is like a man's head. He thinks here, he learns here, and in time, he becomes wise here. The stem is like the body of a man, his backbone. With it, we have strength and courage. The color of the bowl is red. This represents the blood of our family and the families of all Indian peoples."

"Blood?" he asked with some concern.

I smiled and rubbed his back. "You'll understand better later on. Just remember that it is very important to me and you."

"Okay. Does Mom have a pipe too?" he asked.

His question caught me a bit off guard. It was becoming routine to hear eighteen-year-old questions coming from his little three-and-a-half year old mouth.

"We use the pipe in our prayers to God." I paused for a moment, searching for the right words. "It is like a telephone to God. When we smoke it, we can be assured that the Creator is listening. Mom, doesn't need the pipe now because she is with God and can talk directly to him if she wants."

His little brown eyes appeared to understand. "Oh, I see, Dad."

I pulled some sage from my bundle and placed it into a small abalone shell; then I lit it. The fragrant grayish smoke gently moved upward. Opening my tobacco pouch, I drew a pinch from its contents. "Now we will load the pipe for smoking." I swirled the pinch of tobacco through the blessing smoke and then held it to the east and prayed aloud, "Wakan Tanka, Niskaminu, Tunkasila, O God, Creator of all things, I send my first tobacco offering to the east in remembrance of the new dawn and in honor and recognition to the red race of man who lives on this good earth. I pray this ceremony will be done in a proper and respectful manner, pleasing to you." I then placed that pinch of tobacco into the bowl, drew another one from my pouch, and passed it through the smoke. "Niskaminu, Tunkasila, I offer this second tobacco to the south in remembrance of all things that grow and for the continued growth of spirituality among all people on this earth. I hold honor and respect for my yellow brothers and sisters." After placing this pinch into the pipe, I gathered my third offering, ran it over the sage smoke, and prayed. "Wakan Tanka, Niskaminu, I pray to the west, the dreamworld place, the direction representing your eternal promise of a new day. I recognize and honor the brothers and sisters of the black race." With the third pinch placed into the pipe, I obtained a fourth portion and passed it through the smoke. "Wakan Tanka, Tunkasila, Creator of all things, healer of misery, life-giving and life-taking force. I pray in the direction of the north, from which the purifying winds blow, in honor of the white families who share this sacred Mother Earth with us." I carefully gathered a fifth pinch of tobacco and, holding it against the earth, prayed, "O Sacred Mother Earth, I hear your suffering and pray for your healing, your peace. I pray that the people who walk on your holy being will do so in a humble and loving way. In honor of the four-leggeds and swimmers I send my prayers."

I pulled the sixth and final tobacco offering from my pouch. Holding it skyward, I prayed, "O Wakan Tanka, sacred and all powerful God, I love you dearly and pray that you will love me and my son in return. You are the most powerful, most generous, most merciful, and most loving. To the ancestors who call your shelter their home and to the winged ones who share the vast sky, I send my prayers. Hau!"

With this the pipe was loaded in due and ancient form. I then lit the sacred tool and prayed again in a silent way. In all six directions, I blew the smoke. Trapper sat attentively and patiently as I conducted the pipe ceremony. I was very proud of him. After a bit I held the pipe, stem first, toward my young son.

"Now, Son, I will touch this pipe to your shoulders, then your heart, then I will rest it on your head. You can say your prayers if you want." He was very cooperative and recited a special prayer.

"O God, Guide me, protect me, illumine the lamp of my heart, make me a brilliant star. Thou art the mighty and the powerful."

"That was a wonderful prayer, Son," I congratulated him.

"Dad, can I hold the pipe?" he asked.

"Sure, Son, but be careful. The bowl is warm," I cautioned him.

I handed him the pipe and he looked at it very seriously for a moment; then surprisingly, he held the stem to his ear and spoke into the bowl. "Hello God, can I talk to my Mom, please?"

I was stunned by his sincere and beautiful request. I did not realize that my earlier reference to the telephone conversation with God had struck him so deeply. I was a bit concerned that he might be set back by the obvious non-response to his request, but decided to just wait for a while.

He listened intently for a few seconds and then announced, "Mom's gone on a walk, Dad. She can't talk now."

"Okay, Son. That's fine." He handed me back the pipe and jumped to his feet yelling something about the grasshoppers. I just sat for a moment in amazement at what had just occurred. I lit the pipe again and finished the special ceremony or, should I say, long distance phone call!

Now I know what a "Canupamony" is.

James and Jeremiah didn't return back to camp until close to midnight. They both had been at the front entrance serving as security. We were all very tired by that time and quickly fell asleep.

57. SWEATLODGE VISIT
Dance Back the Smile

Morning was announced at 6:00 AM by Harry Charger banging on the tent pole. "Rise and shine. Rise and shine. It's mornin' time!" I stuck my head out the front door and saw him a few campsites down, banging on tent poles and singing some sort of morning song.

The next thing I noticed was the popping sound of wood burning near the sweatlodge a couple of hundred feet away. That sounds good to me, I thought to myself. I knew the boys would be sleeping for a few more hours, so I gathered up my shorts, towel, and a handful of sage and off I went. Once I arrived, I could tell that the fire had been going for a while. There were a number of men and women lounging around. I saw a young man I had met earlier at the arbor and walked over to him.

"Good morning!" I announced.

"Morning," he replied. "How'd you sleep?"

"Oh, real good," I answered. I noticed an elder man to his left and I removed my cap and greeted him. He nodded in reply. I looked back to the younger man. "Do you think it would be okay to sweat with you all this morning?"

"Sure, no problem. We'll begin in about half an hour or so."

"Great, thanks!" It made me feel good to be with friends. I was becoming more and more comfortable. The young man introduced himself.

"My name is Max Strongheart." He stuck his hand out to me and I accepted it with honor.

"Uh huh, nice to meet you. My name is Lionel Little Eagle."

"Little Eagle," he said in a curious way. "Any kin to the Little Eagles up toward Mobridge?"

"Maybe. I've got some family from these parts." I then asked, "Are you from around here, Max?"

"Yep, Eagle Butte born and raised," he answered with a pride in his voice.

After more small talk, the elder, whom I'd met earlier, announced that it was time to begin the sweat. Not long after that I found myself cross-legged in the rather large sweatlodge. There were six men and six women sharing this ceremony with me. The elder quickly went to work. He called for seven rocks and as each one entered the lodge he sprinkled them with a cedar-sage mixture causing a plume of grayish smoke to fill the lodge. The sweet aroma penetrated my senses. Once the rocks were in place and blessed, he ordered the door closed. We became surrounded by darkness. Singers to the left of the door struck up a song. The elder prayed softly. I could barely make out his voice through the strong songs of the singers. I released my focus on the songs and prayer and began to concentrate on my own song of prayer. As usual, the first form to appear to me was that of my wife. I knew she was physically gone but in this forum of prayers she was all that I could see. With the sweat rolling off my face and eyes closed, she seemed so real, so beautiful. This sensation seemed stronger than before. I watched her with my inner eye and my inner being. She smiled her familiar smile. A pure and clear light seemed to radiate in and around her. A strange and peaceful stillness settled in. I became engulfed by her very powerful presence. I had witnessed the same image in other sweats, dreams, and ceremonies but never with such realism and clarity. My heart sprang up with amazement as her soft lips parted as if to say something. This was new. I watched intently.

"Hello Love." Her voice was all that I could hear. I felt she had actually communicated with me! I watched and then listened carefully. In a short while her presence began to fade into the radiant image around her. I had been blessed and I thank God for that. The voice of the elder boomed through the lodge as he announced "Mitakuye Oyasin! Open the door!"

The rest of the morning eased along. We had breakfast and a short walk down to the river. Trapper did his best to throw a rock completely over the river, but even in its dry, shallow state his arm wasn't strong enough to reach the opposite bank.

"Someday, Son," I reassured him.

58. Can-Wakan, Mystery Tree
Dance Back the Honor

It was near noon when the word went out that it was time to go for the tree. We were a long way from our campsite and transportation, so I waved down a pickup and asked if Trapper and I could catch a ride with them. The front seat was full with three people plus the driver. I lifted Trapper up and into the back of the truck and climbed in myself. We both sat on some old tarps and blankets. Before we pulled away, a couple more people joined us. Little did I realize as we pulled away that it would be a ride we would never forget. I learned, the hard way, an important lesson while riding in that open-bed pickup on a thickly dusted road filled with bumps, holes, and hills. The dust literally and completely covered us! All I could do was feel for Trapper, who quickly began to cry. I finally realized that the covers and tarps we were sitting on were the only things that would keep us from suffocating in the overbearing dust cloud. I pulled them up and over us both, and sure enough, we were semi-protected. We were soon joined by our co-riders. Although Trapper continued his frightful crying, the heat of the day and discomfort of the covers were far better than the killing dust.

We must have driven about five or six miles before the truck came to a stop. We slowly uncovered and found we were completely covered, head to toe, with South Dakota dust. Even my ears, nose, and mouth were full! Trapper's face was streaked with mud from the tears on his face. We brushed ourselves off as best we could and joined the others in a nearby thicket of cottonwood trees. What I observed at this point was one of the most important parts of the entire sun dance: the taking of the tree to be used as the center pole at the arbor. More than thirty people were present to help with this sacred duty.

The cottonwood tree that had been selected was at least thirty feet high with a distinctive "y" shape at the twenty-foot level. Its leaves sparkled in the sunlight as the wind gently blew them. A yellow ribbon was wrapped around its three-foot trunk with four different bundles of sage tied to the ribbon. A shirtless elder stood proudly beside it. I would later find out that he was a medicine man named Vincent Black Feather and that he would be the one to serve in the honored post of intercessor for the sun dance. In his hand he held his pipe. To his left stood a young boy, the one who had been given the responsibility and great honor of actually selecting the tree.

Everyone drew closer as Black Feather prepared his pipe. I also observed four young girls, ages seven to about ten, standing close to the tree. Each one was holding bundles of sage. Another elder man was busy with a large Folgers coffee can that had been converted into a smudge bucket. He held this in his left hand by a three-foot-long broom handle. In his right hand he carried an eagle-wing fan. With these tools he was working on the tree and all the people directly in the area. Soon he had smudged everyone with the blessing smoke.

Once Black Feather had finished with his pipe, he called the young girls, one at a time, to the tree. He then handed his pipe to them. Each took it in turn and humbly prayed with it, finishing by touching the stem to the tree. Each girl represented one of the four directions. After this portion of the ceremony, Black Feather retrieved his pipe and placed it on his bundle. The next process was the symbolic cutting of the tree by the girls. A small, brand new ax, about four feet long, was brought out tied with colored ribbons. Each girl took her turn with the tool, striking the tree with a gentle blow. Once they had completed their work, Black Feather whispered something to them, hugged them, and directed them away.

It was then time for the big boys to take their turn with a full-sized ax. The first man would take four or five mighty cuts into the tree and then pass the ax onto the next person in line. The line was about twenty people long. The cutters were the sun dancers and it was their honored task to bring the tree down. Soon the tree began to give way to the efforts of the men. A call went out to everyone.

"Don't let the tree touch the ground!"

The thirty-foot-tall tree was full of branches. Not letting it touch the ground was going to take some good coordination and positioning. I rushed to the tree along with everyone else and found myself stationed at the halfway point of its length. It seemed impossible, but somehow the tree was staying up and off the ground. Another instruction was called out.

"Okay! Let's get it to the truck!"

A large 4x4 pickup truck sat ready to receive the tree, so off we went, tugging and lifting, until it lay precariously on the truck, just off the ground at its lower end.

"Load up!" someone announced. I quickly grabbed up Trapper and headed for the pickup truck we had come in. I thought of the discomfort Trapper had endured on the way over. I heard a voice behind me.

"Need a ride?" I turned and discovered a huge mountain of a man, about six foot tall and probably well over 350 pounds, smiling at me.

"Yep! Sure could use one," I happily replied.

We then climbed into the front seat of his pickup. He started it up and then to my surprise rolled up his window! I quickly figured out why when he turned on the truck's cool, refreshing air conditioning. "Big difference from our trip out here," I pointed out to Trapper.

The driver introduced himself to us as Keven Brown Eagle of California. We had a nice, short conversation on the way back to camp, and he invited us over that evening to have coffee. Back at the arbor, the next phase of the operations began rapidly. Blankets, quilts, tarps, and coats were laid out next to the hole which had been dug at the center of the arbor. The hole was about five feet deep and a two feet in diameter.

"We need more coverings!" someone announced from within the bustling crowd.

"The tree cannot touch the ground!" another voice reminded us.

The reason for the blankets and such became evident then. The truck backed up as close as possible without actually entering the arbor. Black Feather studied the path by which the tree would be taken. He then gave the order to move it. Grunts and groans filled the air as the tree was unloaded. The tree was gingerly carried toward the hole, the carriers stopped four times for prayers along the way. Finally, it was carefully placed on the ground coverings with its base next to the hole. The intercessor once again made rounds about the tree, peering into the hole as if he were looking for something. Certain selected elders joined him and made some offerings that were placed into the hole. The crowd had backed off as he continued his diligent inspection. Eventually, he stopped at the tree's base and, in Lakota, summoned a couple of men with buckets of red paint. These men, under his specific instructions, painted a red strip running from above the tree's half-way point to the base. This red strip symbolized the good red road. When the painters were done, he announced the next instruction. Everyone moved in quickly and began to tie offerings on the limbs of the tree. Among them were tobacco ties, sage bundles, and four-colored flags.

I realized what was going on but I was too far from camp to make a dash back for my cloth. I finally remembered my red bandanna in my back pocket and the bag of Top tobacco I always carried. I quickly put together an offering and with Trapper's help, we tied it to the highest point on the tree. As we did that we both said our prayers, my Tammy prayer and Trapper's Mom prayer. Once we had finished, I found the sun dancers also hard at work tying their pledger ropes to the midpoint of the tree, pulling and stretching and testing them to make sure they were securely attached. From top to bottom I saw red, white, black, yellow, blue, and green flags tied to the tree's branches. It was a very inspirational sight. When the tree had been prepared, the intercessor, always speaking in Lakota, ordered the tree to be raised. Like the flag raising at Iwo Jima, the Can-Wakan mystery tree was gallantly and proudly raised. The sun dancers, with pledger ropes in hand, quickly spread out to assist with the balancing of the tree. About six of us gathered at its base. Under the direction of Black Feather, we pulled, pushed, and twisted, then pulled some more until he was finally satisfied with the tree's positioning. The red paint that adorned the tree now adorned my arms and chest. I felt a certain pride and honor in its red color and even though I would not take part in the actual dance, I felt I was more than just an observer. I felt I was a part of this sacred, age-old ceremony!

The hole was quickly filled in. The men dancers then looped their pledger ropes for easier access during the ceremony. It was then that I discovered the beauty of those pledger ropes. Some were decorated elaborately with colors and/or eagle feathers. Some were made of fine leathers and others more simply made from hemp or nylon. But each served the same sacred purpose. I found the man with the smudge bucket again and realized that he would serve as the intercessor's main assistant. He was walking about with his smudge bucket, blessing the tree, the pledger ropes, and all the people who were present. I later discovered his honored title to be buffalo dancer. By this time most of the crowd had broken up into smaller groups carrying on conversations. Others were gathering up their now blessed blankets and other coverings. Somehow the mystery tree had taken on a different, more powerful presence. No one would touch it now or even approach too close. It had been transformed into a sacred being, Can-Wakan!

I watched as the wind picked up again, and the leaves, branches, and flags all seemed to come alive. It was a very exciting and moving moment. As I looked through the tree, I searched for the tobacco offering we had placed on it earlier. The wind blew the leaves so hard it had become invisible to me. By now the crowd had dissipated. I looked harder in an attempt to locate our offering. All of a sudden, a shock leaped through my body as if I had been touched by an electrical current. Atop the tree in the area where our tie had been placed, I saw the image of a woman.

Before I could attempt to understand what was going on, thoughts of Tammy exploded into my mind! "Honey," I said softly to myself. My heart pounded as the image became clearer, gradually becoming the image of my wife. She was sitting peacefully among the branches of the cottonwood tree. As before, in the sweatlodge ceremony, her presence seemed so real, yet I could see an illumination in her being. She was wearing a colorful dress with a single white daisy in her flowing brown-blond hair. Her soft blue eyes and smile beamed into my eyes and soul. In her left hand she held the tobacco tie that Trapper and I had tied to the tree. I watched like a child on Christmas morning as she watched like an angel. Then she looked away from me to where Trapper had gone to play near another, larger cottonwood tree. I turned and found him staring intently in her direction! His eyes focused sternly for a moment and then eased into a more joyful expression. His right arm shot up to wave. I felt my face wet with tears of happiness. I slowly turned back to the tree and she was gone, our tobacco tie hanging in the exact spot where she had been.

I found a restful spot under the arbor where I could see Trapper as well as the tree. I prayed and thanked God for the wonderful visit. After about an hour, Trapper came and sat next to me.

"Dad, I'm thirsty!"

As we strolled our way back to camp, Trapper spoke with excitement about a new friend he'd met at the big tree near the arbor. The little girl's name was Sita.

"She's my sister!" an expression he liked to use for new girl friends.

"That's nice, Son," I said. "Did you watch the people putting up the tree?"

"Yep! I'm thirsty, Dad!"

"Okay, Son. We're almost there."

It was apparent to me that whatever this gentle child of love had on his mind, it was his alone: a private moment in time with his mom. Then again, he may not have seen her. The most important thing to him at this moment was a drink of water on a hot and dusty day.

59. KEVEN BROWN EAGLE
Dance Back the Sun Dancer

The wind picked up again around sunset but then tapered off as night eased over the campsites. We finished our dinner. Jeremiah and James had returned from another long day's shift at the front entrance. Both boys seemed to be dragging and were in their tents early to catch up on some needed sleep. After I had finished with the dishes, Trapper and I decided to find the camp of Keven Brown Eagle.

By now, about twenty-five different campsites dotted our area alone. As we slowly walked, I found cars with tags indicating people who had come from California to Maine. The individual camps were active with kids and music. Laughter filled the evening air. I finally found the Brown Eagle camp and big Keven. He was lying back in a his rather large lounge chair; a tall glass of water rested in his hand.

"Hello!" I announced as I entered from the shadows.

"Why hello there!" he replied. "Come on over."

I saw that his camp was a big one. A kitchen had been set up between a tree and the tailgate of a pickup. At least three more adults and a handful of children were in the area as well.

Brown Eagle said something in Lakota to a young man who sat in a nearby chair. The young fellow jumped up and Keven pointed at the chair and said, "Little Eagle can roost here for a while."

"Thank you." I sat and Trapper quickly snuggled in between my legs, cautiously watching the older kids playing in and out of the camp. Eventually, the young man whom Keven had rustled out of the chair returned with a glass of water. Trapper intercepted it and took the first big drink. He handed me the half full glass over his shoulder.

Brown Eagle noted, "That there water's from town. It's bottled water. The water around here could cause you problems."

I thanked him for the water and the advice.

Brown Eagle asked, "Where you from, Lionel?"

"Oh, we're out of Seattle, Washington area. However, my people are from Nova Scotia, Canada."

"Oh," he responded, "Micmac?"

"Yes," I replied. He told me he had a couple of friends from that area, and that he saw them on the powwow trail here and there.

"Are you dancing?" I asked.

"Yep, how about you?" he followed.

"Well, I have given it some thought, but I'm not prepared for this year."

He nodded his head in agreement. "It does take a good bit of preparation. You have to have a sponsor to assist you. You also need a dance robe, and a pledger rope, and many other items."

I explained, "A lot has gone on in my life lately, and I really haven't had the necessary time to dedicate to the preparations." He nodded again and took a drink of water. I continued, "I have come to help and, hopefully, by giving that help, I'll be helped."

"Uh huh," he said. "It is good. Before someone takes that important step they should help first. They should watch and learn and find out if it's really what they want." After a pause, he added, "You know, it's not for everyone."

"Yes," I agreed.

Brown Eagle then asked, "You mentioned that a lot of things have gone on in your life recently. Do you mind if I ask you what type of things?"

"No, not at all. In June my wife crossed over to the other side."

"Humm," he said with his eyes closed. "I am sorry to hear that. You are a young man and you have a lot of life left ahead of you. You also have that little one. Your wife must have been young, too."

"Yes sir. She was thirty-eight years old," I answered.

"Cancer?" he asked.

"Yes," I replied.

"It is too soon for you to dance, but I will keep her in my prayers during my time at the tree."

I pulled a pack of tobacco from my pocket and gave it to him, shaking his hand. Brown Eagle thanked me, and I him, expressing my gratitude for any prayers he would offer on our behalf. Since I would not be dancing, I felt much better that a dancer would be carrying the name and memory of my wife into the sacred arbor.

One of the women who had been busy cooking at the kitchen showed up beside me with a bowl of boiled meat. I thanked her and glanced around for Trapper. He had also found the meat soup and was sitting near the kitchen with the other children enjoying it very much.

After the good soup and conversation, I gathered up Trapper, who was reluctant to come, and headed back to our camp. Just before we left the campsite, Brown Eagle asked, "What is her name?"

"Tamara, but I called her Tammy."

Brown Eagle smiled. "Tamara, that's a nice name."

The hour was late and the next morning would mark the first of four days for the sun dance ceremony. My little son cuddled in my arms, I thanked the Creator for the ninth time that day for this special day.

60. DREAM BAG
Dance Back the Voices

In my sleep, a dream came. I stood on a beach looking out over the majestic silver and blue waves. The sun had just dropped out of sight. The sky shone with vivid colors. Where the ocean's horizon met the sky, the clouds parted. The two blues blended and before me two wonderfully blue eyes appeared. In these eyes I saw the undeniable beauty of my wife, Tammy. I felt her love and her breath on my face. I heard her words in my heart.

"Listen to the voices." The voices, I thought to myself. "Yes, the voices will guide you." Her voice was familiar and clear, "Remember, I love you with all my spirit."

Once again, I found myself gazing into the distant blue ocean. A rolling wave presented something to me, but I could not make it out. It was flat and about the size of a folded towel. As I watched closer, it seemed to be sparkling. Suddenly, I realized that I was watching the pipe bag of our family. I watched closely as it dipped and peaked on the waves. Eventually it was gone; it seemed to have sunk quietly away. Again her voice came.

"Listen, Love." Then a new voice came, this time more masculine, "Listen, Little Eagle!" Once again, this time with deeper tones, "Listen and see!" I now saw myself turning away from the cool ocean and discovering the dry, rolling hills and buttes of South Dakota. The sounds of the ocean were gone. The smell of the crisp, clear air was gone. I now stared into familiar buttes and in the distance I saw the pipe house, the place where the sacred pipe of the Lakota people was kept. The house glowed with a bluelike color and seemed to vibrate in the hot prairie air. Once again, the strong spirit voice spoke to me, "Listen and see!"

I then found myself wide awake, staring at the top of my tent. Trapper was sound asleep under my arm. The message that had just been given to me seemed obvious: The pipe bag, which had been carried in our family for nearly 100 years, would soon be leaving this family and would find its way to that pipe house. Exactly how and when was not yet clear to me, but I knew that it would be done soon and in a proper way.

61. DAY ONE OF THE GREENGRASS SUN DANCE

Dance Back the Sun

The next morning the familiar tent pole rattling of Harry Charger awakened us. I quickly got dressed and headed for the sweatlodge. Once again, this wondrously refreshing ceremony prepared me both physically and spiritually for the day's work.

The dancers were in their rest area when I arrived. I could tell that they had just completed their morning sweats as well. I eased my way to the arbor and joined close to thirty people there. I could see the intercessor, Vincent Black Feather, visiting with the dancers. The men dancers were dressed in long robes; some were elaborately decorated and others were more simple in design. Around their ankles and wrists were braids of sage. Braided sage halos also adorned their heads. All were barefoot. The intercessor and his assistant, the buffalo dancer, were going back and forth between the preparation area and the arbor, checking on all the details. Eventually, everything was ready. One drum with several singers was set up under the shade area near the south gate.

These men would alternate with others over the next four days, but the music would not stop during the dancing portions of the ceremony. The previously unnoticed silence of the area was shattered when the dancers signaled with their eagle bone whistles that they were ready. The intercessor, who was holding the lead male dancer by his sage bracelet, began slowly to lead the honored group of both men and women to the entrance located on the east side of the arbor. Once they arrived at that point, he then guided the dancers into the Mystery Circle with four distinctive stops along the way. Once inside, he led them clockwise around the sacred tree four times. The east entrance was now closed, and a man guarded that position. He would stay there, sleep there, and eat there for the next four days. Like the fire keeper of the pledgers' sweatlodge, he would have to be dedicated.

The ceremony became very familiar to me over the next four days. The process rarely changed. The sounds of the drummers and eagle bone whistles became second nature. The pace of events ran smoothly and efficiently under the watchful eye of the intercessor and his assistant. During the four-day ceremony the dancers would only be allowed to communicate with the intercessor. If necessary, he would communicate with his primary assistant, the sole buffalo dancer. This post was being filled by a respected elder named Rufus Charger, Harry's big brother. Rufus Charger would be the only person allowed to communicate with the observers, a station of special honor. He would always be hustling, never resting, and continually on the move.

As the sun made its way across the sky, the ceremony continued. The dancers were first led to the eastern gate of the arbor, which was marked by two yellow flags where prayers were offered. After about forty-five minutes, the buffalo dancer led the dancers to the southern gate, following the path of the sun, where prayers were once again offered. This gate was marked with two white flags. At this point he, along with Black Feather, randomly selected four pipes from the altar located on the west side of the arbor. The altar was marked with a buffalo skull. The pipe rack was about four feet long and six inches high off the sage-covered ground. These pipes had been filled and prepared by the dancers that morning. With the pipes cradled in their arms, the intercessor and his assistant proceeded down the line of fifteen male dancers. When a dancer recognized his pipe, he took it from the men and joined them.

The intercessor and the buffalo dancer avoided touching the sun dancers as much as possible. After each pipe had been taken, they led the four dancers by their sage bracelets to a bed of sage located near the buffalo altar. There the dancers would be allowed to sit while the next segment of the ceremony was readied.

This portion of the ceremony required the participation of the observers. The buffalo dancer trotted around the perimeter of the arbor and selected, with the point of his finger, four elders to help. Both men and women were eligible to assist and did so readily. The elders slowly made their way to the south gate, where they lined up and waited. The buffalo dancer then retrieved the four sun dancers who had been selected earlier, and led them clockwise around the sacred tree and to the waiting elders. Under the command of the buffalo dancer, each dancer held his pipe out to an elder, then pulled it back to his chest. This was done three times until on the fourth attempt the pipes were received.

Once the pipes had been received, the dancers were returned to their bed of sage. The elders who had been given the sacred trust of the pipes moved around the arbor until they had each taken a position at a different point. Then they lit and smoked the pipes, eventually passing them on to the people in their immediate areas. The people were helping, and as they drew on the pipes you could see the prayers in their faces. Each person who participated cradled the pipe he or she received in a very sincere and humble fashion.

The elder on our side stepped in front of me, pipe in hand, and in a respectful way I accepted the pipe and smoked it. The aroma filled my senses. I held it to my shoulders and said my prayers. I then returned it to the waiting elder. Once all the pipes had been smoked, the elders met back at the south gate with the pipes. The buffalo dancer then gathered up the four sun dancers once again and led them over to retrieve their chanunpas. In four distinctive motions of offering and withholding, the pipes were returned. The elders, as well as the buffalo dancer, were always careful not to touch any of the dancers. The elder helpers were done and returned to the shade of the arbor. The dancers returned to the buffalo altar, where they placed their pipes on the opposite or east side of the pipe rack, indicating that these pipes had completed their work for that day. Those dancers then gathered at the Mystery Tree, where they were joined by the other sun dancers. After prayers, they all filed out of the Mystery Circle through the west side and went to their preparation area.

Female dancers participated with the male dancers in their own sacred way. Each time the men entered the Mystery Circle, the eight women would join in the procession. They would always take up the same position at the northwest side of the arbor. This was the place for their most sacred and holy work. Each was beautifully dressed in a long colorful dress, especially designed for this particular sun dance. Halos of sage crowned their heads and adorned their wrists and ankles. Just like the men, they wore no shoes. Although the women did not pierce, they would be witnesses to the suffering and sacrifice of this blessed ceremony.

The hot grayish ground, with which the male and female dancers would become intimately familiar over the next four days, was filled with many obstacles, such as little pebbles and slivers of sticks. For the feet of these dancers, it would be a very painful and memorable ceremony.

While the dancers rested in the preparation area, the observers mingled and moved about, some going back to their camps for refreshment. No water was allowed around or near the arbor. The drummers also took a well-deserved break. I made my way back to the camp and found the boys up and active. After a short visit, we all headed back to the arbor. Trapper quickly found his little friends and was off to play. I looked about the crowd, and in the area of the drums found a familiar face. It was the pipe keeper, Arval Looking Horse. His tall, slender body towered over everyone. I recognized his distinctive stance, his arms folded across his chest, and his head slightly tilted to listen better. It was good to see him again. He wore his trademark black cowboy hat. His long black hair was tied back in a pony tail half-way down his back. His old Levis and brown shirt blended well with his quiet style. While humble in appearance, he bore much responsibility and power as the keeper of the most holy pipe, the Wakan Chanunpa.

I continued watching and listening. It seemed as though more people were present now, maybe seventy or so. My observations were interrupted by the familiar shrill of the eagle bone whistle. This was the signal made by the lead dancer to the other dancers to prepare and line up for the next round. It had been about thirty minutes since the last round ended.

The buffalo dancer performed his duties of smudging. Each dancer was blessed with the sacred smoke. Some almost dove into the smoke to absorb its power. The smoke was like an energizer, both physical and spiritual. The dancers disappeared into the smoke, then reappeared almost glowing.

Once the men were lined up, the women fell into place behind them. When things were set, the buffalo dancer signaled the drummers to begin, and, in single file, the dancers re-entered the Mystery Circle. They circled clockwise once around the sacred tree, eventually stopping at the south side of the arbor. The sun had risen and moved enough to make this location the most powerful in relationship to the sun. As before, the dancers began by dancing in place, raising their arms in a prayerful manner at each verse of the songs.

A personal surprise came during this round. Four more pipes had been identified and the buffalo dancer was on his round to identify the helpers. He walked up to me and pointed, "You come." A surge of power moved through me. I had been selected to help with the pipes, a very important honor. I followed him to the opposite side of the arbor. In our travels he selected three more individuals, an elder man with a cane and two elder women. I did not feel as though I belonged, but I was not about to question his decision. We four removed our shoes and, barefoot, entered the Mystery Circle. Meanwhile the buffalo dancer moved about the arbor collecting the four dancers. They approached the south gate where we stood and then lined up directly in front of us. Across from me was the lead dancer of the ceremony! I could tell from his arms and chest that he had been participating in the sun dance for many years. His duty as lead dancer was another indicator. The other three men already seemed to be dragging a bit, but the elder sun dancer in front of me stepped lively to the drummers. His face of many winters seemed fresh and full of excitement. I found myself being drawn into his presence. I heard the voice of the buffalo dancer asking the helpers, in Lakota, to prepare to receive the pipes. We held out our hands, palms up. The dancers stopped dancing and on the command of the buffalo dancer offered the pipes to us. In traditional manner, the pipes were offered four times, and we accepted them on the fourth offer. The lead dancer released his pipe to me as a mother hands over her child. I felt great honor. The dancers turned and were led to the bed of sage, while we continued with our work as helpers. I took the chanunpa I had to the north side of the arbor, where I lit and smoked its power. I then carried it to the other observers who were gathered in my direct area. Each person smoked, then nodded in respect, handing the pipe back to me. I recall a young man, maybe fourteen years old, looking in awe at the beautiful pipe, which was decorated with four eagle feathers and had colorful quill work on the stem. Holding it as if the Creator himself was in his hands, he was absolutely thrilled. His excitement was so obvious that it made me feel good inside.

Once the tobacco in the pipe had been completely smoked, I joined the other helpers at the south gate. The sun dancers who had carried these pipes were brought there as well. In the usual four stages we returned the pipes. The lead dancer cast a half smile in my direction as he parted; I nodded back in respect. The moment felt good. The dancers placed their pipes on the opposite side of the altar beside the other four from the first round. It was past noon now as the dancers took their second break. It was announced that this break would be a long one, and would include the noon meal.

62. ARVAL'S COUNCIL

Dance Back the Year

I looked toward the drummers. Some had walked out a ways from the arbor and lit cigarettes; others mingled. I noticed that the pipe keeper was gone. I hoped to visit with him later on. I turned to look for Trapper and to my surprise found myself face to face with Looking Horse.

"Hi!" he said with a big smile. "I thought I recognized you a while ago."

We shook hands. "Yes, I saw you too." I was still a bit surprised. Arval turned and looked toward the tree where the kids were playing. "Is that your boy?"

"Yes, he really likes the grasshoppers in these parts!"

"Well there's plenty of them around for sure," he said with a smile.

An uneasy silence followed. I could almost feel his question before he asked.

"How's your wife?" He continued to watch the kids play.

"She's gone, Arval," I said immediately.

"Uh huh," he replied. "I'm sorry for you. She was a very nice lady." Arval removed his wide-brimmed cowboy hat. "She had a sweet smile and a quiet way."

We both watched the children. I replied, "Yes, she was very special."

"How are you and the little one doing?" he asked.

"Oh fine, I guess. It does become a bit difficult when my son asks tough questions. But I work through it." He nodded and I continued, "I miss her more than I thought I would. It hurts more than I thought it would too."

"Oh yes," he noted, "that's to be expected. You will need more time before you will become comfortable."

"How long, you figure?" I asked.

"Whatever it takes. Most of the time, at least a year. It's a good idea that you wait and mourn for a year. Then you will be able to let go and carry on with your life." He made a quick gesture with his hand to the sky and added, "She will tell you when the time is right."

I checked on Trapper. He was fine. "I feel my grief will last forever. A year seems so short now."

"You will miss her and love her forever. That is understood. It is good to look at a year for your healing as a time of renewal, a cycle of life."

We were quiet again, then I spoke. "I would like to talk to you about the pipe bag sometime."

Arval had folded his arms across his chest. "Oh yes. My offer is still there."

"I spoke with Tammy about it and the family as well. I also spoke with other elders and the medicine people. The feeling I get is that the pipe bag has done its work with our family and that it is time to return it to the Lakota's keeping."

Someone from the kitchen area called out for Arval.

"I've got to go but we will talk more later."

"Thanks Arval," I acknowledged.

He replaced his hat and patted me on the back. "She was a nice person and I'm sure she is doing fine."

As he departed, I thought about the pipe bag. It had been a symbol of strength to our family for many years, and now I was holding its fate in my hands. The weight of that responsibility was growing heavier. The dreams and counsels were my guiding lights. I knew what had to be done. The little voices of intuition were speaking louder. The sparks of energy were filling my life. My darling wife had heard those voices and I now listened closely to them. In her pure and beautiful energy-existence she was helping me make life-changing decisions.

I gathered up Trapper and headed for the kitchen. A small crowd had gathered. A number of people, including Arval, were hustling about serving the elders who had taken their seats along the small hill adjacent to the kitchen. Once they had been served, the signal was given and everyone else lined up. As I inched my way forward in the line, I looked at the four or five women who were running the kitchen. I wondered about Shirley Calfrobe, the one-of-a-kind little powder keg who ran the kitchen area on my other visits. It was easy to tell that the kitchen operations were not as smooth as they had been under her rolling-pin control. Once I reached the rather large pot of buffalo stew, I held my bowl out. A young woman filled it up. I asked her if she knew anything of Shirley Calfrobe. "She's around here somewhere," she said, and yelled over to one of the elders enjoying his meal. Even though her question was in Lakota, I could tell she was asking the whereabouts of Shirley Calfrobe. He replied and pointed over his shoulder.

"He says she was here earlier but has gone back over to the old camp."

I looked toward the elder and asked, "How's she doing?"

He replied in Lakota, and got a robust round of laughter from the other nearby elders. I smiled and looked back toward the young woman, who was trying her best not to laugh. I asked, "What did he say?"

"Oh, he's a kidder. He asked, 'Doing what!'" Elder's humor, I thought to myself and laughed.

I added some hard bread and juice to my plate and found a comfortable place to sit. Trapper sat down beside me and dug right into the stew. My thoughts brought forth Shirley's husband, Tom Calfrobe. He had danced every year here, but I had seen neither him nor Shirley. A disturbing feeling welled up in my stomach. I looked up and found a couple of large puffy groups of clouds swirling around. I recalled Tom Calfrobe, the cloud watcher, and remembered his message and teachings. My observations of the clouds seemed to indicate a disturbance of some sort, but I wasn't sure. Lying back on the hillside, I watched even more closely. The sounds of the kitchen seemed to melt away. I saw what appeared to be a foot, rimmed with a black border. It was floating and breaking up slowly. Then it was gone. I wondered to myself what Tom would have said about such a sight. I hoped to see him and Shirley before I left.

The hour-and-a-half for lunch went by quickly. Trapper and I returned to our camp for a visit and then returned to the sun dance arbor. Trapper shuffled off to his friends, who were eagerly awaiting his return.

63. TWO MEN DANCING

Dance Back the Pierced Ones

The sound of the lead dancer's eagle bone whistle announced the beginning of the third round. The drummers began their songs. The buffalo dancer began his work, the intercessor his. The rounds were all very similar, but something unseen, a spirit, a movement, distinguished each round from the others. The wind had picked up, and it made the dancers' work even more difficult.

As I stood among the other observers, I felt blessed. With me on the sidelines were the mothers, fathers, uncles, aunts, cousins, brothers, sisters, and friends of the dancers. I watched the elder, Keven Brown Eagle, as he stepped to the music of the ceremony. I was his supporter, a friend. He had taken the name of my wife with him to the sacred arbor. I could see the small pouch of tobacco I had given to him last night tied to his belt. I thanked him once again in a silent prayer. The observers were absorbed at different levels. Some sat quietly, others stood with me, dancing with the sun dancers. Others seemed to be in a trancelike state, their palms upward, swaying with the strong afternoon breezes.

The moment passed and I saw the intercessor approaching the sacred tree. In his hand he held an eagle-wing fan. The buffalo dancer followed with a buffalo robe. I could see it was beautifully decorated with quill and bead work. Once again he smudged the area. The two men spoke between themselves for a moment, then the intercessor waved one of the dancers to the center with his fan. The middle-aged man approached, dancing slowly. His jet black hair hung across his face and midway down his back. His trim, firm body glistened in the hot afternoon sunlight. Upon arriving at the center of the Mystery Circle, he was immediately smudged and blessed by both elders. The intercessor ran his fan up and down the length of the dancer's body.

Eventually the intercessor directed the dancer to lay down upon the robe. The intercessor got to his knees beside the dancer. He quickly opened a small bundle and it became apparent that this dancer was not going to wait for the usual fourth day before he pierced. His vow directed him to this day, the first day! The intercessor removed a necklace from around the dancer's neck. It contained the two cottonwood piercing sticks that would be used by the dancer. The intercessor placed them both in his mouth for easier access. He then vigorously rubbed sage on the dancer's chest where the piercing would take place. He placed a handful of sage in the dancer's mouth and the dancer bit firmly down on it. Soon thereafter the intercessor pinched a portion of the man's skin about two inches above the nipple and, with a piercing tool, shoved a hole through the skin. He then took the first stick from his mouth and eased it into the hole. After that he tied two pieces of red cloth around the cottonwood sticks, securing them firmly in place. The dancer had not made a single move or sound. He simply clenched his teeth down on the sage. The intercessor, very efficiently, went to work on the other side and within a minute the dancer jumped to his feet and began his dance once again. The buffalo dancer gathered up the dancer's rope and brought it to the intercessor, who attached it to the piercing sticks. He pulled slightly to ensure it was snug, then directed the dancer back out to the perimeter of the circle. I could not help but be amazed at the process: quick and simple, but very powerful. I watched the slack from the rope tightening until the dancer stopped just short of the stretching point. Nothing else had changed, yet the energy of the dancer had increased. The circle had now been consecrated by the blood of a dancer, a warrior.

A few minutes went by. The intercessor and the buffalo dancer quietly talked together. Then a signal was given once again, indicating that another dancer had decided to pierce early. This dancer was younger than the first, probably in his mid-twenties.

His thick, dark brown hair extended down his back. He hustled into position and the two men went to work quickly. Before I knew it, he was up and done, and just as quickly he moved back into position with his piercing sticks in place, hooked up to his piercing rope.

The two men had made an extraordinary vow: to dance, pierced, all four days! Very unusual in the way of contemporary sun dances. It was becoming evident that this was not a routine sun dance.

The intercessor and buffalo dancer secured their tools, then returned to the normal flow of the dance. The next set of four pipes was gathered and identified. The dancers presented them to new helpers at the south gate and retrieved them once they had been smoked. The usual short break followed at the end of the round. All the dancers filed to the rest area with the exception of the two pierced dancers. They remained standing under the ninety-plus degrees of the sweltering sun. There would be no rest for these two men.

It was close to 4:00 PM when the fourth and final round of the day started. The eagle bone whistle sounded and the dancers entered the Mystery Circle once again. I could tell that a few of the young, first-time dancers were already being tested. Their feet dragged a bit and their efforts seemed more labored. As they raised their arms at each up-beat of the song, their heads would bow down before the heat and intensity of the long day. The older men and long-time dancers still exhibited a special strength and stamina. The women dancers were also feeling the strain of the long day of sacrifice.

The dancers made their way to the four cardinal points, always starting and ending with the sun directly facing them. The onlookers now numbered close to fifty. All were very serious about what was going on. Finally, the last set of pipes was taken care of and the dancers were at the end of the first day. I wondered how they would be able to withstand three more days of ceremony. The male dancers approached the sacred tree for final prayers before leaving the Mystery Circle to go to the sweatlodge. The sun was slipping quietly behind the western buttes. A reddish sky saluted the power of the day. I found my boy and we headed back to our camp.

"Is the dance over, Dad?" Trapper asked.

"Yes, for today. They will start again in the morning," I answered him while rubbing his head.

"But what about those guys?" he asked anxiously.

I quickly turned and, to my surprise, discovered the two pierced men still dancing to the spirit drum in their heads.

"Oh, those men are special, Son. They will stay."

64. PAHA SAPA COUNCIL
Dance Back the Black Hills

That evening would be special. It marked the first of the nightly gatherings near the arbor to share stories, messages, music, and good company. It allowed for the elder medicine men and women to speak their words of wisdom and provided a wonderful opportunity to absorb the special and rare voices of the people.

After our evening meal, I gathered up some soap and towels and headed to the river, where Trapper and I took the time to rinse off the layers of dust and dirt that we had acquired during the last couple of days. A peace seemed to settle into the surroundings like the water around our bodies as we went about our duties. It was around 9:00 PM when we returned to the camp. I then joined in with the flow of people heading for the council area. Trapper stayed behind with his brothers.

Upon arriving, I noticed that the fire had been built up almost to a bonfire. The dancers sat and stood inside a marked area and a large number of observers were stationed nearby. A cottonwood round had been set up to serve as the speaker's area. I quickly identified the first speaker as Arval Looking Horse, the pipe keeper. He puffed on a cigarette and was speaking to a couple of men. It was not too long before Arval began talking to the crowd.

"Hello everyone. I am glad you have come to this sun dance. It is very special to us." He paused for a moment and continued, "I would like to open with a prayer. I know that everyone here cannot speak Lakota. That's okay."

I listened with my heart as Arval recited a deeply moving, lengthy prayer. Periodically his prayer was highlighted by a deep grunt or other unintelligible sound from a nearby Lakota.

Once he had finished, he introduced one of the men standing nearby. "My brother-friend, Billy Two Hawks, will do a song now."

Billy nodded politely and then said, "Before I start, I would like to express my thanks to Arval and his family for their work in putting this sun dance together. It is not an easy job. It takes months and months of preparation to do it. It also takes a lot of assistance from a lot of people. I feel very good that I am here and that I am a part of this sacred ceremony." Two Hawks then spoke in Lakota for a moment before beginning his beautiful song, which eventually became a melodic sing along. The night air was filled with an uplifting and refreshing feeling. Two Hawks finished his song, and the pipe keeper spoke again.

"Some of you may be here for the first time. I will tell you that this is a very sacred time for us. It is a holy ceremony that you will see and be a part of. Our sun dance is done in the old way, the traditional way. No water or food is allowed near the dancers. It is important that you keep this in mind. Don't make it harder on these men by tempting them with water or food or anything else. Respect their vows! This is the second year we have had our sun dance here. In previous years it was held near the house on the other side of the river. I was given a vision that this work should be done over here. It is a secluded area and there is less chance for unwanted visitors."

Holding up four fingers, Looking Horse continued, "Our dance is done for four days, not three or two; we go four. That is our sacred number. Everything holy is done in fours." He pointed to the distant buttes. "On the hill there we have men and women on hanbleceya, vision quest. They will be there for four days. They will not come down from their places until four days have passed." The large fire had burnt down some but still crackled in the background as Looking Horse continued. He pointed across the river toward the pipe house. "The symbol of our life and religion is just over there: the Buffalo Calf pipe. It would not be good if we decided to shorten our ceremonies. It would be disrespectful to that power to do such a thing. So we do our work in the old way. By doing it with respect for our traditions we will learn from it. The old knowledge is alive within these buttes.

"I would like to talk to you about another very important subject: the Black Hills. Those hills are sacred to us. The Black Hills have been placed in our protection. It is our responsibility to preserve and protect them. The holy buttes should be returned to the Indian people for that protection. This protection is not on any paper or ordained by any priest. It is not sanctioned by any governmental agency; it is work given to us by the Creator, Wakan Tanka. The Creator designated the natives of this land to keep and protect sacred spots, such as the Black Hills and the Pipestone quarries. I have a friend here who is very knowledgeable about the efforts to return the Black Hills to the Indian people. I will ask him to speak to you now."

An elder stood up and slowly and made his way to the front of the crowd. He removed his large, well used, black cowboy hat. Although most of his conversation would be of a very serious nature, his wrinkled face was lit with a big smile. His eyes seemed to be examining the hearts of the listeners, ensuring that they were paying attention.

"Hello, my name is William Grass. I'm from Standing Rock. I want to tell you my heart, but you must listen with your heart to hear me. The Black Hills are the place where we bury our dead. Bear Butte is where we go to pray, seek visions, and dream. I believe that it is a sin for the white people or any people to go into these areas with their bulldozers and backhoes to dig and destroy the land in the name of progress. They say progress is good. I don't believe that. Not all progress is good. Before my wife died last summer, the doctors told me that her cancer was progressing. That is bad progress, just like the white man's progress in the Black Hills. It is a sin! These days it is very hard to find a place where a man can be alone. Being alone is important to us for ceremonial purposes. We need our privacy in order to be complete and whole beings." His voice rose with strong feelings. "The earth is not our enemy! She is the one who loves us. The enemy is human beings. The people who blindly and deliberately scar and hurt Mother Earth, who line our sacred Black Hills with black pavement. They are the enemy! That is where our fight lies."

He paused to find an attentive audience. "The natives of this land have been here since time began. We are not new to this land. Christopher Columbus did not discover us. We saved his ass!" This got a big laugh from everyone. "We are not the owners of this land, just as my brother-friend Arval is not the owner of that Holy Calf pipe. We are the keepers. If we could look at our work in the same way that the pipe keeper looks at his work, we'd be on the right track. We should all look at this work as a sacred obligation." Again he paused. He leaned over to a younger man to his left and said something in Lakota. The young man quickly pulled out a pack of Camels and offered one to the elder Grass. After getting a light from his assistant, he continued.

"You know it's sort of funny, I laugh!" A short but comical giggle popped out of the elder. "It's funny. The white man came here 300 years ago. He came to escape those people who persecuted him in his old land. He came to escape those evil ones who interfered with his God-given right to worship the way he wanted." His eyes were bright and he giggled again. "It really makes you want to laugh! You know what I mean?"

He looked around, not really expecting an answer.

He took a long drag from his cigarette and moved his arm across the horizon as he spoke. "This country, the earth we stand on, is sacred. It is our altar, our church, our sacred shrine. We don't have to build great monuments; our monuments are the trees and rocks, the four legged and winged ones. Our most sacred monument is the Black Hills. They are our living memorial. I don't think the white man understands that." His voice raised a little. "Our blood, our love is in these hills, the land we stand on. The white man's law tells us that we have no rights to the Black Hills or the quarries. That is their law! It is for their use! It is not our law. Our law is a natural and spiritual law. The enforcers of this natural law are the water, the earth, the moon, the sun, the animals, and the fish. They are the guardians of the natural law. This is the Indian law. The enforcer of the spiritual law is the Creator alone! Not the man with the Bible and fancy suit. Not the government either! Wakan Tanka is the only authority of the spirit law. The white man has many religions. He can't make up his mind, so every now and then he will redo his religion to fit his needs. God, Wakan Tanka, created our religion. It is a religion of prayer, fasting, dreaming, and vision seeking. Our religion is this ceremony, the sun dance. We don't just live our religion on a certain day of the week or day of the year. Ours is a twenty-four-hour-a-day, seven-day-a-week, lifetime religion. Our faith is here in this place. It is represented by the men and women who sacrifice."

He took a last puff from his short cigarette, carefully broke apart the remainder of it, and neatly laid it on the ground. Then he looked up at all of us. "If your hearts are right and your prayers are sincere, you may be visited by the ones from the other side." As he paused once again, I could not help but feel he was speaking directly to me. "Those loved ones will be here. Wakan Tanka is here and those spirit ones will be here as well. She will come to you in the sweatlodge or in a dream. She may even come and sit in the sacred tree." My heart jumped a beat. He used the word "she" and spoke of her sitting in the sacred tree. He continued, "Some of you have had those visits already. At least one I know of, because I saw her too! Open your hearts; don't try to analyze the mystery. That's where you will fail. Just accept it and be happy." I was stunned. I knew my mouth must have been open with amazement. The elder Grass continued, "This ceremony, those Black Hills, the redtail hawk, the rivers are all inseparable. We all coexist with those things. We survive only if they survive! If any part of creation is abused or exploited, then we are abused, and we are exploited. Our spirits suffer.

"You know only ten or fifteen years ago we would have been arrested for doing this work. We would have been beaten for speaking our minds, speaking our hearts. The white man's government finally recognized that we had a God-given right to be who we are, to pray the way we want. But they have still fallen short of a true and complete recognition." He laughed. "It's like almost being pregnant! You are or you ain't." Another big laugh erupted from the understanding listeners. "The government either gives us the rights we deserve, which includes guardianship of the Black Hills and the quarries, or they don't. It's pretty simple, huh?

"Let me tell you something. The Black Hills are not sacred because I said so, or you, or Crazy Horse, or Sitting Bull, or anyone." He slowly raised his right hand into the air. "They are sacred because the Creator said they were!" An almost harmonic "Hau!" was sounded by the crowd. "The Indian people were given their laws, our Ten Commandments you might say, at this holy place. We were given our directions and the procedures that we use to worship. Those Black Hills are sacred, my friends, more so than most people know. My grandfather is buried in the Black Hills, his farther and his father's father."

William Grass looked through the crowd to find someone. He pointed and called out in Lakota. A man in his thirties wearing glasses and braids approached the front of the group. The elder Grass introduced him. "Some of you folks know this man, but for those of you who don't, he is Kenny Good Eagle. He has been very helpful in our efforts to regain the Black Hills. I'm going to take a break here and let him tell you more."

Kenny Good Eagle stepped forward and said something in Lakota. His delivery was very exact and detailed. "During the 1850s and 1860s the U.S. Government made treaties with the Indian people of this region. Among the nations which were party to these treaties were the Northern Cheyenne, the Arapaho, and the Lakota. These treaties were legal documents, drawn up and agreed upon by all parties. They designated more than fifty million acres of land as being Indian territory for use by Indian people. However, in 1874, the world changed for all Indians. That is when the yellow rock, gold, was found in the Black Hills. This discovery occurred only nine years after the last treaty was signed. With the blessing of the U.S. Government, miners and settlers invaded the Black Hills and were permitted to acquire the land that had been legally allotted to the native people. This obviously caused bitter wars and conflicts between the Indian and white worlds. These conflicts have not yet gone away! So here we are, more than one hundred years later, still trying to regain what was rightfully ours from the start."

Kenny motioned vigorously with his hands as he talked. "There is another title that the Indian has to the Black Hills, a spiritual one. My elder, Grass, spoke of it earlier. The white man has a hard time understanding this title. It is an unseen but very powerful title that has kept the Lakota and other nations going on." Kenny Good Eagle stopped for a moment. "You know, in our language the Black Hills are called Paha Sapa or H'e Sapa, which means, 'the hills appear to be black.' They are also known among the old ones as O'onakezin, which means 'a place to take shelter.' Another name by which they are sometimes called is Wamakaognaka E'cante, which means 'the heart of everything that is.' The area surrounding the Black Hills is called Cha' Gliska." Kenny Good Eagle made a hoop with his arms. "This means 'sacred hoop.' So you have a center and a sacred hoop encircling it. The Indian people have been forced to live outside this hoop. It is like going to church and being told that you may worship, but only from outside the church. There are many places within the Black Hills that have special significance, such as the hot springs. Years ago our medicine men would meet there and share stories and medicines. They would sit within the warmth of Mother Earth. Now the place is an amusement park. This, my friends, is what you call exploitation, mistreating and destroying a sacred place. There is another place called the Red Lodge Canyon, where our ancient picture-writings are on the walls. These writings have been vandalized. An awful toll has been taken on them. Within these rock writings are the Seven Commandments of the Indian religion. These coincide with the seven rites of the Lakota. We still go there to fast, to vision quest, to gather sage or herbs, but we always have to get permission!" He laughed out loud causing others to join him. "It's crazy. That's like asking for permission to kiss your own child. It is our right. When we go to the hot springs, it is likely that we will be intruded upon by campers, tourists, hikers, curious onlookers, all asking questions and taking pictures. Our solitude is extremely important, but it is almost impossible to have it now. Kenny Good Eagle concluded, "I've said enough for now. I thank you for listening. I'm sure we'll have more opportunities to talk later. Hau! Mitakuye Oyasin." He looked over to Arval, who then stood and spoke.

"Thank you, Kenny, and you, too, William. I hope their words have found a place in your hearts and you all will take your own steps to help with the struggle." Arval Looking Horse then spoke Lakota to a singer-friend, who stood and recited a prayer in Lakota followed by a closing song. It was a wonderful and enlightening evening. I would take the good words with me and pass them on to others.

Trapper was fast asleep when I returned to the camp. As I climbed into my sleeping bag, I reflected on the incredible events of the first day of the sun dance. As I began to drift off, the images of the two pierced men returned. I said a special prayer for them. Even though it would be a restful night for me, they would not enjoy such rest.

65. DAY TWO OF THE GREENGRASS SUN DANCE

Dance Back the Tree

The fire for the observers' sweatlodge was well underway. I eased my way into the group of waiting people. A jovial and relaxed atmosphere greeted me. I felt very comfortable. I did not know the elder who was leading the sweat, but his big toothless smile and roaring laugh were infectious. The rocks were ready and the elder made his way inside. He then called for four rocks. I could hear him in prayer and song. As we prepared to enter a mother walked up from the nearby campsite. In her arms she carried a small boy, maybe two years old. The little one was not happy; his uproar drew the elder from the lodge. He stuck his head out and asked, "Who's that doing all the yelling out here?" The lady announced her

child and said she had come to steam off the little one. For a
moment the child continued his displeasing performance. The
elder then instructed the young mother, "Hand me the boy!" As
soon as he held him, the child stopped his crying. The elder
spoke softly to him in Lakota. They both disappeared back into
the darkness of the sweatlodge. The boy's mother paced
nervously around the lodge until the elder reappeared about two
minutes later with the little one happily in his arms. The child
was actually smiling. As his mother took him away he waved to
the smiling elder, who then surveyed the group of waiting
adults and announced, "Next!" That announcement got some
giggles from the people. We entered. As I rounded to the west
side I felt a tingling sensation, a warm happy feeling. When we
had all gotten in and settled down, I counted eight men and two
women in the lodge with me. The elder said something in
Lakota that got a laugh from the singers on the north side of the
lodge. He then leaned toward the doorway and called for more
rocks. I was not sure how many he had ordered since he had
spoken in Lakota. After approximately five minute the rock man
passed in sixteen more rocks, all glowing red. The heat
generated from the rocks had already put me into a good sweat.

The door was closed and the singers immediately went into a
song. The elder quickly threw four scoops of cold water onto the
intensely heated rocks. Even so, the majority of the rocks
continued to glow. The brutal heat, moving from the top of the
lodge to my head, my neck, and then down my back, startled
me. I began to pray out loud along with the others. The singers
sang; the elder prayed. I heard more water dance onto the rocks.
Then there was a yell from one of the men, letting us all know
that it was time for him to go. The elder recognized the request
and called for the door to be opened. As soon as it was opened,
the young man jumped over my lap and the others to the cool
outside. Not unusual, I thought to myself. But before the elder
could do anything else, four more men and one of the women
asked and were granted permission to leave.

When the dust and steam had cleared, I counted four still in the
lodge. Oh no, I thought. The elder's previously jovial demeanor
had changed to a more serious and somber one. His long,
gray-black hair hung down in front of his face. He leaned
forward and squinted into the faces of the remaining
participants. He found two former sun dancers, a middle-aged
Lakota woman, and one scared-as-hell Micmac. We repositioned
ourselves around the lodge. He then called for the rock man,
who appeared at the door. To my shock, he called for more

rocks. The rock man quickly hustled into action and before I could say oops, he brought four more rocks into the lodge. The door flap was then closed and tucked in snugly around lodge's base. I knew that this was going to be one of those memorable sweats. The elder sang a soft song that eventually became a loud one. Occasionally, I heard his scooper dip into the large plastic bucket of water and then the sounds of the hissing and popping of the rocks as the water splashed on them. The heat of the sweat was unbelievable! I found myself sprawled out, face down on the good earth. I pinched a small piece of sage from the floor covering and placed it into my mouth. The bitter taste of the sage was a comfort and distraction from the unrelenting heat. I began to pray, deeply and sincerely. I prayed for strength and endurance. My entire body was suffering! The power of the moment exploded into bright white light. I thought I might be near fainting, but I recovered enough to look in the direction of the light source, which appeared to be fluttering, then rotating in a clockwise fashion. As I watched the mystifying event, I lost all concept of sound. The odd light began to shrink into a smaller and smaller circle. Eventually it seemed to split into two separate entities of energy. As the extraordinary event continued to develop, I was shaken once again. The lights zipped into the eyes of the elder! In amazement, I watched. The light source simply went to the elder. I could see his face glowing from the light. A Lakota voice I had not heard before filled the confines of the lodge with a thunderous power. I could now understand the words, words that seemed directed toward me. "Who is it that says he is alone?" Without using my mouth, I answered, "Me." I caught the sound of a bubbling in the background and then the voice again. "The eagle is never alone with the tree!" I pictured an eagle landing gracefully in a tall cedar tree. The voice proclaimed, "The tree is your comfort." I closed my eyes and asked, "Where is my tree?" The rumbling and boiling seemed to intensify as I heard the voice once again, "Seek the tree, not the forest, with the eye of the soul." The energy that had so dominated every part of the sweatlodge dropped away. A quiet and soft space now existed. I felt dazed by what had happened. The light in the elder had faded away. A familiar darkness filled the lodge. It was a quiet moment and my mind rested.

The sweat was good and I felt very energized by it. The sun had cleared the ridge and in the distance I heard the familiar and mystical sounds of the eagle bone whistles being blown by the sun dancers. I made a swing through camp before going to the arbor. I found the boys still asleep.

The dancers were in position and the drummers and singers were deeply involved with their duties. I noticed that there were only twelve people in the observers area, not counting the drummers. None of the pipes had been moved, indicating that the dancers were early in the first round. The ceremony would be very similar to the previous day, consisting of four parts or rounds separated by the pipes of the dancers.

66. WINGED ONE PAYS A VISIT
Dance Back the Brown Bird

It was just before the noon break when we were visited by the winged one. The winds that had been constant since we arrived seemed to let up a bit, almost as if to announce our visitor. At the east gate, a small brown bird made a gliding entry. No human would be allowed to enter that gate but the bird nation was given permission by the Creator himself. It landed gracefully just inside the circle. A number of observers as well as the dancers spotted it quickly. The eagle bone whistles, which continually sounded, all stopped. This caught the attention of the intercessor and he quickly jumped up from his chair. I saw him scan the arbor and then he spotted the bird. He looked for a moment, then slowly raised his right hand in honor of the special blessing, and sat back down. Then the bird began its dance, hopping around the arbor, stopping, then hopping some more. The dancers, too, had begun their dance once again, their whistles singing. It all seemed natural and proper. After a few minutes our bird visitor flew up into the Mystery Tree and then off to the west with a respectful salute from the dancers and observers. I was later told that it was not unusual for such animal visits to take place; sometimes deer or even an eagle would make a visit to the festivities.

67. NOON MEAL
Dance Back the Air

I noticed the observers had increased in number to about fifty. At the completion of the next round, the noon break was announced. The sun dancers made it to the rest area, all but the two pierced men.

I found Trapper and the boys already in line at the kitchen. I joined them with my paper bowl of buffalo stew. As we enjoyed our noon meal, I looked around at the many faces, young and old, that were with us. A feeling of honor and respect for them entered me: a people who had been oppressed and mistreated for many years were at ease in their environment. The drudgery and hard life of the reservation, the material world, were gone for now. This was a sacred time, a time to laugh and to feel good about one's self. It was truly as if we had stepped back in time.

Trapper had quickly finished his cup of red juice and was asking for more. I gave him the rest of mine. As I continued to scan the crowd in hopes of seeing Shirley Calfrobe, the kitchen boss from the prior gatherings, I spotted a middle-aged lady sitting alone. She seemed familiar. I walked over to her while Trapper went exploring.

"Hello, may I join you?" I respectfully asked.

She nodded in approval. I said, "I'm trying to find a friend; I was hoping you might help me."

She raised her head toward me but did not meet my eyes. "Who you lookin' for?"

"She's been in charge of the kitchen area in the past. Her name is Shirley Calfrobe."

"Oh," she answered, "she's around. Her camp is over by the old arbor area on the other side of the river."

"Uh huh, and how's her husband, Tom, doing?" I followed.

This question seemed to disturb her. "Not sure. I think he's in the hospital." She began to get to her feet. I joined her. "You'd better talk to Shirley about Tom."

I thanked her and she smiled. The thought of Tom Calfrobe being in the hospital bothered me. I hoped he was not critically ill and decided to visit with Shirley Calfrobe that evening.

We went by our campsite prior to the afternoon session at the arbor. Jeremiah and James had done a good job with the clean up. I found a note stuck on the tent:

Dear Dad:
James and I are on our way to lunch and then we will be up at the front gate.
Love, Jeremiah

I felt fortunate to have such fine boys with me on this special journey. Trapper and I headed back to the arbor.

There wasn't any activity going on when we arrived. My young son found his little friends and scurried off to play. I took a seat on the ground to wait for the next session. Whenever I sat or was unoccupied for any extended time, thoughts of Tammy entered my mind. They were comforting thoughts that blended well with my present state of being. I smiled into the hot August air.

After about fifteen minutes, I heard the lead dancer call the other dancers to their feet with his eagle bone whistle. It was time for the second half of the day's ceremony to begin.

68. DANCING ON
Dance Back the Respect

More people had made their way to the arbor by this time and with them came ever increasing afternoon winds, blowing strongly from the north, kicking whirlwinds of dust here and there. I wondered if it would pose a problem to the sun dancers.

The male dancers made their way to the south gate, the female dancers to their regular position at the northwest side of the Mystery Circle. The whistles filled my ears with their rhythmic sounds.

Soon after the first segment had been completed, I began to feel strange and uneasy. This seemed to correspond with the ever increasing velocity of the winds. I quickly realized that the force and intensity of the winds were also affecting the dancers. The sun was hot; the world seemed hot. I was attempting to clear dust from my eyes when I saw one of the dancers go down to his knees! The buffalo dancer, as well as a couple of sun dancers, rushed over to him. The buffalo dancer began to pat the downed man vigorously on his back with an eagle-feathered fan, and then guided him to the smoke from his smudge bucket. The other dancers talked to him and encouraged him. Still the dust swirled and blanketed everyone. My attention was on the fallen man but was redirected when, from the corner of my eye, I saw a second man crumble to the ground! Near him in the observation area was his family. A yell went up from that location. I could see the concern in their faces. They all eased up to the edge of the circle but did not dare go in. The buffalo dancer and nearby dancers once again hustled to assist the second fallen man. It did not seem possible, but the winds were even stronger now. I looked for the intercessor and found him standing with his face gazing upward, as if he were searching for something, a sign or reason for these events. Some dancers do occasionally bow to the power and heat of the dance, but this seemed different. Concern etched the faces in attendance. Then the lead sun dancer, an elder of many dances, fell face first into a cloud of dust! The intercessor approached the center of the arbor, a look of concern on his face. He then extended his right hand, which was holding his eagle-feathered fan, out in front of him. His left hand was held toward the ground, palm down. He seemed to be feeling the air, the energy, in an attempt to identify and maybe change what was happening. The dancers shuffled about uncomfortably. I could see other dancers starting to falter. The intercessor started a prayer and waved his eagle fan along the perimeter of the arbor. Before completing a single pass, he stopped and then pointed his fan toward the northern section of the circle from which the wind was coming. He then ordered that entire area cleared. One of the observers protested a bit but quickly left. The chief of security, Harry Charger, was making a round through the northern section and I heard him explain that someone was in their moon. I recalled that earlier Charger had spoken of the power of women during their menstruation period, that they could produce such energy as to cause a disruption. It was obvious that the intercessor felt this was the cause of our problems.

The wind whistled through the cottonwood coverings of the arbor. There were a number of women on that side of the arbor. No one readily confirmed the intercessor's intuition. Everything, with the exception of the wind, seemed to be settling down now. I saw two women depart the area. One of them I would later see in the moontime camp across the river. The wind now died down and amazingly the dancers, except for one, stood back on their feet, whistles singing. The dancer who did not continue the dance was suffering from diabetes. He was not able to continue and was the only dancer that would not finish the four days.

The rest of the afternoon session went rather smoothly. The pipes were presented and smoked, and the dancers completed the second day of the ceremony. Only the two pierced men continued to dance alone with their Creator. Their work was very sacred and blessed. The other dancers were obviously worn down from the hot and windy day. Their arms and heads hung low. Each spent extra time at the smudge bucket. However, the pierced ones seemed a notch or two above. It was as if they had stepped into a different plane of power. You could actually feel their energy and see their spiritual auras.

69. CALFROBE WRAPPINGS
Dance Back the Hey You!

It was around 9:00 that evening when Trapper and I took a long walk to the old arbor in hopes of finding an old friend. As we approached the campsites, I saw a younger woman occupying two little girls with a story book. I scanned the immediate area but was unable to locate Shirley Calfrobe. I interrupted the woman's story. "Excuse me. I'm trying to find Shirley Calfrobe. I was told that she might be here."

The young lady looked me over for a moment and then replied, "Grandmother is over there." She pointed to the far side of the camp, where I spotted a couple of tents and three parked cars. Upon arriving, I looked around attempting to find her but saw no one. I walked a little to the left and then a little to the right, but she was nowhere to be found. I thought it might have been a little late and she had probably gone to bed already. Suddenly my search and questions were gone with a familiar sound, "Hey you!"

I smiled before I turned around. When I did, I found her only about twenty feet away, sitting in the front seat of a small yellow Datsun.

"You look like you're lost, boy!" she laughed out loud at my embarrassment.

"Hello Shirley. How are you?" I asked, while trying to cover up my surprise.

"Oh, fine. Just resting in a comfortable seat. My back bothers me to stand too long now." She then looked at Trapper and commented, "Oh, I remember this little guy. He's not so little now!" She leaned over and summoned him. He walked cautiously to her. "How old are you now?"

"I'm three-and-a-half!" Trapper answered proudly.

"Oh boy, that's good. You are a big one for three-and-a-half."

She rubbed his head and he smiled. Trapper excused himself with the grace of a three-and-a-half-year-old and ran over to the other kids who were waiting for him.

"He's cute," she said as he ran off. "He looks like his mom." With that, she stopped as if she had heard a distant clap of thunder. My gut stiffened as she turned her head toward me and with squinting eyes and an uneasy voice said, "You should have brought her over with you. I'd like to talk to her." An uncomfortable silence filled my ears as the elder sat patiently waiting for my reply.

"She's gone, Shirley," I said softly.

She shuffled in her seat and then slowly began to crawl out of the car. After straightening herself out, she grabbed my shirt with her right hand. "What did you say?"

I knew she had heard me the first time, but she needed, wanted to hear it again. "She's gone. She's on the other side."

She placed her other hand on her mouth and muffled, "Oh no!" Then her eyes began to dart around as if she was looking for something.

"No, no, no! She was too young! Oh God...Oh no!"

The tears began to build in her eyes; she had released my shirt and now both her hands shook uncontrollably. Her eyes rolled upward and she began to cry.

"Oh no, God!" This was a very loud yell and it caught the attention of her granddaughter. The young lady was quickly on her way over to us. Tears now covered Shirley Calfrobe's aged face. I reached to her and placed my hand on her shoulder, but she pushed it away.

She limped toward the back of the car and then back to the front, while exclaiming her disbelief in both English and Lakota. Her steps seemed quicker now and I stood, open-mouthed, trying to figure out what I could do.

Her granddaughter was beside me. A man who had been in one of the tents also appeared. The granddaughter spoke in Lakota, and I could tell by Shirley Calfrobe's response and body movement that she was telling her of Tammy.

"Oh," the young lady said softly. She then looked at me, "I'm sorry."

With this Shirley Calfrobe crumpled to the hard dusty ground. Her tears and emotional anguish poured onto the dry earth. She appeared to be hugging the earth, sobbing and praying in Lakota. I felt responsible for her sadness. Never in my life had I ever observed anyone show such emotion. The young man knelt down beside her and speaking softly to her, tried to help her to her feet. She slapped at him!

"No!" Her voice was trembling but firm.

In a moment her granddaughter, overwhelmed with the grief her elder was showing, began to cry herself. She was soon on the ground with her grandmother. The elder's powerful sadness was pulling on all of us like a magnet. The young man was the next to fall to the earth. Then my shoulders felt heavy and my heart began to cry with Shirley, crying with the loneliness of being without my dear wife. I followed the young man to the ground. The earth was truly our mother. She took into her arms our overwhelming grief and sadness. She held in her bosom the incredible despair that filled our hearts. An almost supernatural feeling rolled across me. Mud had formed on my face from the abundant tears that still would not stop.

By now the little ones had gathered near us and some joined in. Trapper leaned down to me and asked, "Dad, what happened?" His soft and beautiful face revived me. Like a key, he opened me. He placed his hand on my head and ever so gently patted it. "It's okay Dad." This mere three-and-a-half-year-old softened my sadness and eased my discomfort. I worked my way to my knees and hugged him. He squeezed my neck hard.

"Is she sick, Dad?" he asked, referring to the elder.

"No, Son. She is sad," I answered.

He looked at me with his soft brown eyes and asked, "About Mom?"

"Yes, Son. She's sad because Mom had to go."

He was quiet for a moment and then said, "Me too." A single tear rolled down his cheek.

Eventually, with the assistance of the young man, Shirley worked her way to her feet. She got back into the car. Her granddaughter handed her a hankie and she wiped her face, blew her nose and regained her composure. She then reached for a cigarette from the dash board and lit up. It did not look natural for her to be smoking, but she did anyway. After a couple of puffs she looked over to me.

"How are you and the little one handling things?" she asked matter-of-factly.

"Well as can be expected, I guess." I was still a bit stunned by her demonstration of grief which I had just witnessed. This was the first time I had ever seen anyone express such unrestrained grief, such powerful emotions. This was obviously a superior trait of a natural people, an extraordinary way of letting go and surrendering to the heart, as well as protecting and strengthening oneself. If only others could recognize that it is good to do that. Now the elder sat, composed, asking questions.

Shirley Calfrobe was aware of the circumstances surrounding Tammy's death, but she asked me to tell her again, so I did. She listened intently as I relayed the whole story.

She interrupted me at one point. "Did you say the end?" Unfortunately, I had used that word in my description. "Yes ma'am." Her face was stern as she relayed our beliefs: "Our people do not believe in that word, 'end!' There is no ending. Only a point where we start again. What you refer to as the end is simply the beginning." I nodded agreement. "Your darling wife may be physically gone from our sight, but she is spiritually alive and she is working very hard for you and your children. She is working especially hard for herself. Wakan Tanka called her to his side not to merely enjoy the view. She is at work, God's good work. His work is eternal and sometimes very difficult. When there is a hard job, he will call on his special ones, such as Tammy, to assist him. She is special to you and to God too!"

When she was finished, I asked about Tom Calfrobe, her husband.

"He's not doing very good. The sugar has gotten him pretty bad. He's in the VA Hospital in Rapid."

Diabetes, I thought to myself. "Sorry to hear that. Will he have to stay long?" I asked.

"Not sure," she replied. "Probably, but he's not too happy about it!" She paused for a moment. "This will be the first time in ten years that he's missed the sun dance!"

"Do you think it's possible that he'll be here this year?"

She replied, "His foot is in real bad shape. They want to cut it off, but he's fighting the doctors hard."

"His foot!" The thought of the cloud formation I had seen earlier flashed to me, a single foot floating aimlessly along. It indicated to me that he would indeed have to lose his foot, but I was not about to tell that to his wife. It was not my place.

"Well, I do hope I get to see him before the sun dance is over," I added.

Shirley said, "My son is going to see him tonight. I'll tell him to tell Tom that you're here and asking about him."

"Thank you," I replied. "I'd appreciate that."

I changed the subject. "I see you're not running the kitchen this year."

"Hell no!" she said with a laugh. "That's the job of those young girls now!" This really got her going. "I've done my time and I tried to show them girls how to do it right. Some of them listen good but others are just damn lazy." Even though she had put away her gravy spoon, she still took great pride in her former work as the kitchen boss.

Our talk and visit was very nice. Shirley Calfrobe's confident voice was encouraging. She was a special elder who held a unique place with my wife. I worried about Tom Calfrobe and his diabetes. I hoped that I would get to see him, but doubted he could travel.

Trapper and I walked back to our camp and got into our sleeping bags. Tomorrow morning would come awfully early. As I drifted off into the sleep world, I thought of the special time I had shared with dear Shirley that evening and the comfort that I had felt being "wrapped in a Calfrobe."

70. DAY THREE OF THE GREENGRASS SUN DANCE

Dance Back the Rock Man

Day three came as early as I expected. Harry Charger had decided to conduct his morning wake-ups from the front seat of his El Camino utilizing his built in P.A. system.

"Good morning sunshine!" He startled me to the sitting position. His next words were, "Hey! Hey! Hey! is that Little Eagle camp up yet?"

"We are now!" I yelled back at him.

"Okay! All right!" He then drove on to the next campsite. "How about that Augustine camp; you guys up in there?" After their response, I heard him say, "All right! Put some coffee on. I'll be back in a while."

As he drove off he announced to the general ear, "We need some help with the sweats!" I decided to assist with the rocks and do a short steam off this morning. I left the boys at breakfast and then headed for the sweatlodge. I found a young man leaning against a shovel, the same young man who had been working the sweats the previous two days. I offered to run the rocks. He gladly accepted. Fortunately, the fire was blazing well and my job consisted of keeping it going and working the rocks and door.

Within half an hour we had a full house. I was glad to see an elder whom I had met on our first trip out. His name was Harry Long Bear. He would be running the first sweat. His first concern was who was doing the rocks. I introduced myself, not expecting him to recognize me, and he didn't. Pretty soon everyone had entered the sweat and Harry called for seven rocks.

As I raked at the burning coals, I quickly realized that they were very hot. The shovel handle seemed too short and I would occasionally smell the hair on my bare legs singeing from the heat. The deliveries were made. I handed in the large bucket of water and a dipper, after which Harry called for the door to be closed. I then checked my exposed rocks, added some more wood, and took up my post at the door.

I took a lot of pride in serving the elder and participants in the capacity of rock man, a position sometimes misunderstood or even taken for granted. Each rock is a prayer, a life force in itself. Each stick of wood is sacred in its work to prepare the rocks for use. In most traditional Lakota's views, you can only serve as a rock man after you have first proven yourself worthy in the sweatlodge. I have often entered sweats having a specific elder serving in the duty of rock man. No one else would dare touch his shovel or even throw an extra stick of wood on the burning fire. It just was not done. In most cases, you would recognize such a situation. I volunteered knowing that the young man who had been tasked with the duty would understand and be thankful for some relief. He did, and he was.

I listened attentively to the mumbles from within the lodge. A second crowd was already gathering. They sat quietly in respect for the ongoing sweat.

As the minutes quickly turned into hours, I found that I had worked three sweats. Jeremiah and James took their turns in the sweat. Trapper just sort of roamed. He was very comfortable in this environment. Nature and the young boy blended well. Like his mom, they were one and the same.

It was after noon before I steamed off and headed to the arbor. Upon reviewing the pipes, I could tell that the third day's session was half finished. The lead dancer summoned the others to prepare for the next round. All the observers stood respectfully as the dancers entered. The eagle bone whistles picked up their familiar pulse and rhythm.

The afternoon circuits commenced. The dancers seemed fresh and ready to go. Their steps were strong. The winds that had filled the previous two days had decreased to a gentle breeze coming from the north.

Once again, I was given the honor of assisting with the pipes and went about that task in a humble and respectful manner. Prior to the next and final round, a new but routine part of the ceremony was presented. The announcer near the drummer informed us that the people could now approach the east gate for the purpose of healing. I noticed a number of observers hustling off or sending their kids off to their camps to inform families and bring others. We were instructed to form a line around the outside of the arbor. This line would lead to the protected entryway at the east gate.

71. SUN DANCE HEALING
Dance Back the Healing

Obtaining healing was important, especially for me at this time in my life. I knew I would make my way to the east gate to ask for that gift. By the time I stepped into the line, at least twenty people were already there. Another thirty or so soon joined in behind me. Trapper dashed in and out between the nearby play tree and the line.

The people entered the arbor at the east side but stopped short of the flags where the intercessor, Vincent Black Feather, waited with his pipe. The buffalo dancer was at his side to assist and smudge the people. Another elder observer coordinated entry into the arbor. In addition, a number of assistants, including Harry Charger roamed the line. They occasionally stepped in, brought out an elder or certain other individual, and led them to the front of the line.

Before entering we were instructed to remove our shoes and socks. I noticed a number of people carrying bundles, their own pipes, tobacco ties, or other items. I kept nine tobacco ties with me for just such situations.

One at a time, starting with the elders, the people desiring healing proceeded. The dancers had all gathered at the east gate as well, and would be offering their own powerful prayer to each of the seekers. I could tell by the number in the line that this was going to be a long, slow process.

The elder assistant at the arbor entrance would hold the arm of the next person until the intercessor was ready. There were always four people in the staging area. Each person stepped up to be greeted by the intercessor, who immediately began to softly pray with him or her. Each person, no matter how old or young, was received in the same fashion. The intercessor prayed for a few moments, and then softly touched the stem of his pipe to each shoulder four times, and then rested the stem on the person's head, tapping it numerous times with a small stone. If an individual had something to say, Black Feather listened carefully. He sometimes answered a question, but most visits were simple and quick.

Close to an hour had passed when Trapper and I entered the staging area. My young son was just ahead of me, and it was at that point I realized the three-year-old would be visiting the intercessor by himself! I had simply forgotten to tell him about the ceremony. Fortunately, his keen observations during the past hour of other little ones allowed him to prepare himself. In his hand, he clutched the tobacco ties that I had given to him earlier. He walked up to the intercessor with confidence and stopped, his bare feet standing on the bed of sage that had been laid down for this ceremony. My heart leaped with joy and some type of indescribable energy as I watched my little son in prayer. Black Feather leaned way over to perform the healing functions. After he had finished, Trapper held out his nine tobacco ties and said to Black Feather that the gift was for his mom. Black Feather smiled and I heard him tell Trapper that he would put it on the tree. My young son had completed a manly task and I was so very proud of him.

Trapper took off, and the intercessor redirected his attention to see the next person, me. I then proceeded to the healing spot. He immediately began his ritual of prayer and pipe work. I closed my eyes as the pipe went to my head and thoughts of Tammy came rushing in. I prayed for healing, and survival. She was very strong with me, so strong that I felt her presence. It was as if she were standing directly in front of me! I dared not open my eyes, but did not know why. The gentle tap, tap, tap of the elder's stone against the pipe on my head felt good. I recognized a healing in that tap as I stood there, palms upward. I was thankful. I slowly opened my eyes, thanked him, and departed.

It was over two hours before all the people made their way through the healing. The dancers never left their location. The final round of the day then started. The requisite number of dancers' pipes were gathered, identified, and then delivered to the appointed observers for smoking. After they had been smoked, they were returned to the dancers, who replaced them again on the altar. The third day was completed as the dancers departed the arbor. As usual, they left via the sacred tree. I focused once again on the two pierced dancers. I had spent a long day at the fire pits of the sweatlodge, but I felt inadequate in comparison to those sacred men. These dancers would not be breaking for a drink of cool water or bite of food; they would not be able to crawl into comfortable sleeping bags and get a good night's rest. Their work was truly sacred. I said a prayer for their strength prior to departing.

72. COYOTE SMOKE

Dance Back the Pride

Unlike earlier evenings, we four spent this evening together. The older boys had put a lot of hours into the many less glamorous jobs involved with the sun dance. I had often been stopped by Harry Charger or some other member of the security group to be told that both boys were doing a real good job. I was proud to be with them and I realized also that they were both becoming more than boys. With this work they were taking giant steps into manhood. After our evening meal, we all gathered around our small campfire. James announced that he would like to share his family's pipe with us. This was thrilling to me and a great honor. The Old Coyote pipe had received many blessings and was the symbol of a very special love. I knew the pipe as a friend. It had traveled all over the country and now to this place, the place of the most holy Buffalo Calf pipe. I watched the young man as he carefully and humbly prepared his pipe. Once he had finished loading it, he lit it and then handed it to me. I smoked and said my prayers, then touched it to Trapper's shoulders and head. I passed it on to my other son, Jeremiah. He accepted it in correct form, smoked, and said his personal prayers. I must have glowed with a father's pride to see him holding the pipe. I recalled when I had shared in the pipe smoking with my own father. That had been a special moment. Another was the gift of my own personal pipe, and now, I was sharing in that same ceremony with my son, Jeremiah.

73. DRUMMING FOR STRENGTH

Dance Back the Families

Once we finished, James put his pipe away and he and Jeremiah took Trapper for a stroll to visit some new friends they had met. I was straightening up the camp, washing dishes, and in the middle of putting together our large quantity of dirty clothes, when Harry Charger stepped from the shadows into my sight.

"Little Eagle, they're gathering at the drum up at the arbor. Some of the dancers are having troubles and need help."

"No problem," I replied. "I'm on my way!" I really was not sure what he meant by "having troubles" and I was not sure what I could do to help, but I knew I had to go.

As I got closer, I was joined by a number of other men on their way to the same place. I picked up the pulse of the drum and singers as I got closer. I could now see the drummers and about half-a-dozen other people gathered around. The late evening light cast a mystical glow on the arbor. I saw the two pierced dancers both still standing. A number of the other sun dancers had also gathered at the edge of the western gate. The intercessor was sitting in his usual chair. Things looked fairly routine, but I could feel an uncomfortable atmosphere.

I joined the group around the drum. Up close and personal the songs and drumming were even more intense than usual. Sweat rolled down the faces of the drummers. I scanned the group and found Arval Looking Horse among them. The next song quickly followed the last. Very little conversation took place. The urgency of the event was the driving force. Occasionally one man would pass off his drumstick to someone else in the crowd. Everyone was becoming very involved with the music. There were now about fifteen people standing around the seven drummers. I recognized many of the songs and sang along with the group when I could.

About an hour had gone by and I could see the pierced ones beginning to dance again. The other dancers returned to their resting places. The intercessor was still watching from his chair. The power of the drum was working and we could literally feel a more relaxed mood in the night air.

Arval Looking Horse, who had come and gone, was once again at the drum. The man beside him got up to leave between songs and handed Arval the extra stick. He thanked him, then Looking Horse looked between the two men standing in front of me and held out the stick in my direction! The two men between us parted and simultaneously looked back at me, as did a number of others in the crowd. It definitely caught me off guard and I looked back over my shoulder to find no one. He was offering me the extra stick and a seat next to him at the drum. I stepped through the men and accepted it proudly. Looking Horse didn't say or do anything in my direction after that.

The songs were wonderful and familiar. It did not take long before I became absorbed in the melody and movement of the drumming. My entire heart and soul seemed to merge with that energy. Before I knew it, we had done four songs. It was during the fifth song that I was touched with the mystical, once again.

With eyes closed I felt a familiar presence; I saw an image of beauty. With eyes closed I was moved by love; I felt gentle blue eyes upon me. She stood among the people, one in the crowd. I dared not open my eyes for fear that this glorious feeling would vanish. I am sure I stopped drumming and before I knew it, the song was over. I sat for an instant savoring, like the smell of burning sage, that wonderful visit. I finally opened my eyes and quickly focused into the darkness from which that inspiration came. There was nothing, nothing physical. I knew, however, that she stood right there, as though someone had taken the burning sage away but the sweet aroma lingered. I smiled into that darkness.

Another half hour or so passed before I felt Arval Looking Horse stand and pass his stick to the next man. He tapped me on the shoulder. I understood that as to follow him, which I did.

We strolled into the privacy of the nearby darkness. He lit a cigarette, and offered me one, which I respectfully declined. He returned the pack to his shirt pocket. I could tell he had something important on his mind. The drummers were still going strong as he opened the conversation.

"I thought we'd talk about the pipe bag," he said.

"Yes, it's been on my mind a lot," I noted.

He then asked, "What are your thoughts?"

"I've had a lot of thoughts and also dreams. I feel the decision has been made easier by those feelings and dreams." I paused for a moment. Looking Horse stood savoring his cigarette while the drumming sounded in the distance. As he gazed over my shoulder, I continued, "If it's still okay with you, I'd like to accept the offer you made to me last year and place the pipe bag with the most holy pipe for safekeeping."

Looking Horse looked toward the unseeable pipe house. He nodded in approval. "Sure, I see no problem with that." He then looked at me without really making eye contact. "We can do it on the day after the sun dance. We will be bringing the Buffalo Calf pipe out again this year and that would be the best time."

I thanked him and then asked, "Do you think it's the proper decision?"

He was typically quiet again. Then he answered. "It's really not my decision; it's yours. When you make it, you represent your family. So keep that in mind as you do what must be done. I personally feel it is a good decision."

"Me too," I agreed. "I've spoken with my family about this already. They all are very supportive of me and my decisions with regards to this pipe bag." I paused for a moment. "Our family has had some very difficult times in the past; a lot of the ones we loved the most were hurt the most. The passing of my wife was our sign. It was clear in her heart what must be done. The physical limitations that she suffered gave way to the spiritual freedom of the Creator's indescribable love. She, above all, knew what was approaching. Like the green sprouts of grass returning after a prairie fire, it's now time for my family to begin its healing." Arval Looking Horse did not say anything, but I knew he understood. I asked, "What will be the process?"

His eyebrows raised up and a slight smile appeared on his face. "I'm not really sure. It will just happen. You should be there early and be ready for whatever happens." He giggled a bit and then added, "We don't really worry too much about the process." I nodded in understanding.

It was now close to midnight and the drum was still going strong. The pipe keeper, Arval Looking Horse, headed toward his cabin and I toward my tent. The fourth and final day of sun dance was a few hours away.

74. SWEET DREAMS
Dance Back the Love

That evening the sweet fragrance of dream came to me once again: In the distance, alongside a grassy green butte, I saw the object of my love. I saw Tammy. She was apparently at ease as she vibrated into my view. She never looked up to see me. She wore a colorful dress. The distinctive sounds of drumming rose up from the silent prairie. She heard them also and began to dance, an easygoing, slow dance, step after gentle step. Occasionally she extended her arms out from her sides like wings. She threw her head back in obvious joy. It seemed very proper, even through in all the years I had never seen her dance. It just was not her style. It would have drawn too much attention to her. But now she danced happily along with the beat of the drum, blending beautifully with the green grass background. I looked closer and began to notice the details of her dress. It was inlaid with beads and quill work. The pattern was familiar to me. Suddenly I realized that the patterns and style were exactly the same as the pipe bag! It was as if the pipe bag had transformed into a dress. It flowed so freely on her.

The dream stayed with me for a long time. Its meaning, its beauty, and its message would have to wait.

75. DAY FOUR OF THE GREENGRASS SUN DANCE

Dance Back the Sacrifice

Day four came just like the others with Harry Charger making his rounds, having coffee here, eggs there, and biscuits somewhere else. An understandable energy charged the air, more so than the previous three days. It was obvious that the people were ready for this very special day. A larger than normal crowd gathered at the sweatlodge. The rounds were short and the process was much quicker. People in, people out. After my visit, I joined the flood of people heading toward the arbor. Once I arrived I found the dancers up and set to go. The now familiar and mystical music of the eagle bone whistle greeted my ears. The entire observation area of the arbor was practically filled within a half hour after I arrived.

The dancers had made their way to the first location, dancing the mystical dance. For the first time, I saw body paints. All the male dancers had designs painted on their backs, chests, arms, and legs, and their faces were painted with circles and lines. In addition, there were animal designs such as eagles, bears, and thunder beings. The lightning bolts distinguished the medicine men. The primary colors were red and black.

I saw the intercessor making his preparations. The buffalo dancer waited patiently. In a few minutes he called the elder, Harry Long Bear, to come forward. Harry, as usual, was on the south side, near the drummers. He used his bamboo cane to make his way around the outside of the arbor. In time, he made it to the specific location where the intercessor and the buffalo dancer waited. He stopped at the edge of the arbor and slowly removed his well-worn cowboy boots. He left his socks on. He was then assisted to his knees on the buffalo robe, where the buffalo dancer blessed him with the sage smoke and then took up a spot to Harry's left, also on his knees. The buffalo dancer then produced a razorknife and needle. After running the instruments through the sage smoke, he then began to perform the flesh offering ceremony.

Eventually, the elder gave twelve flesh offerings! He never flinched or moved at anytime while the buffalo dancer worked. I could see the rich red blood flowing down both his arms. Each offering was carefully placed into a red cloth. Once the work was done, the elder was once again assisted to his feet. The buffalo dancer bundled up the offerings in the red cloth and set them aside. Long Bear made his way back to his lounge chair. He then gathered up a microphone and proceeded to explain his vow in Lakota, followed by an English translation.

"My friends, the Creator has given us a good day! A day of honor! I am thankful that He has allowed my old eyes to see this day. I have been blessed by the strong will of the men and women who have taken such an important and sacred vow to the sun and God." He paused for a moment, saying something to another person near by him. Then he addressed the dancers, "Today will be your greatest test. You will have to look into yourselves to find strength. You will have to pray very hard to the Creator to have mercy on you, not for yourselves, but so you will be better able to help your families and your people. You are our leaders. We expect you to be leaders of the people, like those who have danced before you! I have made the flesh offering for you and for another very important reason. Yesterday, as we shared in this ceremony, the world was shaken awake by a very serious sign. A sign of war!" He stopped once again, shifting his legs around to get more comfortable. He captured our attention dramatically with the word "war." He then continued, "In the Middle East, the country of Iraq has moved into another country called Kuwait. They have made a killing road of the people of that country."

I really was not sure where this was leading and it seemed a little out of place. However, if the elder felt it was important enough to bring to our attention, it was important enough to pay attention to.

"Believe me, this will eventually change the world. This event is that which the medicine peoples have told us about. The war will not happen today, nor tomorrow, but it will happen soon. It is the responsibility of you dancers out there to pray for peace. It is also the responsibility of everyone who can hear my voice to pray for peace. Everyone needs to take time to pray. Keep in mind those Indian boys who will be going there. Pray for them and their families."

He was quiet for a moment, looking into the silent crowd. "It is a terrible thing but we must not forget the Creator's will. His plan for us all is a good one!"

The buffalo dancer had made his way over to the elder Long Bear's location and said something to him. Harry relayed it to the rest of us, first in Lakota, then English. "Those of you who wish to make offerings now may come up and do so." He then sat back down in his lounge chair.

The drum began again as I watched a line quickly form at the southwest side of the arbor for the flesh offering ceremony. After a few minutes and a few prayers, I found myself in line with the others. My offering would be in memory of my most beloved wife. I watched the procedures carefully as each person ahead of me made their own offerings. Eventually the buffalo dancer signaled me in. I removed my shoes and socks and entered the circle. I stepped onto the buffalo robe and lowered myself to my knees. The buffalo dancer, very professionally and efficiently, went to work on me. He rubbed sage on my left arm, after which he cleaned and blessed the needle and razorknife. It was then that I made my prayer.

"In the name and memory of my dear Tammy I have come here at this time for the purpose of making an offering. I love and miss her with all my heart and spirit and I will forever carry the light of her precious love deep within my soul."

The buffalo dancer first stuck the needle into my skin. He then lifted the skin with the needle causing it to raise slightly. He then cut away a small portion of skin with his razorknife at that location. I felt nothing. He placed the offering in a red cloth, then took a second offering just above the first. He bundled up the second offering and placed it with the first. I stood and thanked him. He simply nodded and then called the next person. Simple and quick. While putting my shoes on, I felt a tap on my back. When I turned I was surprised by the smiling face of Tom Calfrobe accompanied by his wife, Shirley. He held a pinch of sage between his fingers. "Here, this will help with the bleeding."

I was still a bit stunned. He was the last person I thought I would see. I detected an obvious struggle in his efforts to get and maintain his balance as he spoke to me. I looked down at his foot and saw that it had been freshly bandaged. I said, "Tom, it's good to see you again. It's good to see you up and about!"

He smiled, a painful smile, as he went to work with the sage on my two cuts. He placed a small piece in each wound and the bleeding immediately stopped. He explained, "It will also help with the scarring."

Here was a man who probably needed healing more than anyone at the ceremony, and yet he was offering healing to me. Once he had finished, he slowly worked his way around in front of me. His handsome elder's face was sunken in from the toll of his illness, but still it was so intimately familiar to me: long gray braids tied in the usual red cloth and the worn red flannel shirt covering his obviously weakened body. The diabetes had taken a lot of his weight. His jeans were baggy and bunched up inside the belt, which was tightened up to keep them from falling off. "Let's sit down, Little Eagle."

"Sure," I replied, a bit embarrassed that I had not already offered the same. Shirley Calfrobe held his left arm, assisting, and the young man I had met earlier at the Calfrobe camp supported his right arm. Their granddaughter and great-grand children stood nearby. He sat under the arbor's shade, and his wife sat next to him. I knelt down on my left knee beside Tom Calfrobe. Neither of us jumped into conversation. My mind rambled searching for a proper thing to say. For some reason, "How are you?" did not seem to apply to either of us. I started by repeating myself, "Glad to see you here."

"Yep," he answered, "they weren't going to let me come, but I raised so much hell they figured I wouldn't quit until I was gone." I laughed and he continued. "Shirley told me you were here." He listened for a moment. "She told me about your wife too. Sorry to hear she's gone."

I then felt a strange awkwardness. For some reason my face was flushing and felt warm. I felt like I was about to cry like a baby for his mother. But I kept my composure and managed to say, "Yes, thank you. Our family was very strong during the process."

"That's good," he said.

I continued, "Our time together was but a flash of light and I so cherished that warmth of the light."

Tom nodded in sympathy. "You know, Little Eagle, we saw this in the clouds when you were here last time."

"Yes sir," I replied. "We both recognized our destiny. Your gift and help gave us something to hold close to our hearts. It also gave us something that others had neglected to give us: the truth. After we left Greengrass the last time, we both decided to enjoy, as much as possible, the time we had remaining."

I could see a smile on his face. "I'm glad to hear that."

"We traveled; we visited our families; we held each other, and we loved each other with much more power and importance." I looked out toward the tree. "I can say that we did everything we wanted. I feel we left nothing behind or unsaid. I am grateful."

He watched the same tree. "She was a very pretty lady." He then glanced toward Shirley Calfrobe. "Shirley really liked her company."

I, too, looked at Shirley Calfrobe and saw tears running down her loving face. I said to Tom Calfrobe, "It must be difficult to sit on the sidelines and not be dancing."

He nodded his head. "Yep, very hard. This is the first time for me to miss the dance."

I felt the presence of someone behind me. When I turned I found the elder, Harry Long Bear, standing there. I quickly moved and he eased up beside Tom Calfrobe. They had a short conversation in Lakota. He then patted Tom Calfrobe on his back and left. I returned to my original spot beside him.

"Old Long Bear seems to think I'll be back to dance again next year. That's nice of him to say, but the clouds don't tell me that."

"You never know, Tom," I said. "Sometimes miracles happen."

"Oh yes, I know." He looked skyward. "I saw a cabin in the sky just a few days ago. The miracle that is going to happen in my life is an everlasting miracle. The clouds have told me so."

I understood what he meant. I needed no more explanation. Tom Calfrobe smiled at me, knowing that I knew.

The flesh offering ceremony was coming to an end. Our attention returned to the buffalo dancer, who had gathered the many flesh offerings and was taking them to the sacred tree to place them.

The next segment of the sun dance ceremony finalized the vows of the dancers. The intercessor, with the assistance of the buffalo dancer, prepared an area near the tree for the final work of piercing the remaining dancers. Two men would not have to be pierced that day. They had made their incredible sacrifice on the first day, and by some unseen, untouchable power, they still danced, pipes in hand.

The other pipes were all in place at the buffalo head altar and the sound of the eagle bone whistles filled the air with their mystical shrills. Slowly the process began as it had on the previous three days. The dancers were all on the eastern side. The intercessor, Vincent Black Feather, and the buffalo dancer, Rufus Charger, selected four pipes and proceeded down the line of dancers. The owners of the pipes identified them and made their way to the beds of sage near the altar. Eventually, one of these men stood and danced his way to the piercing area near the tree. On the way, he identified his personal pledger rope and brought it with him. He then received his instructions from the intercessor and lay face up the buffalo robe, his pipe across his midsection. The buffalo dancer leaned over the dancer and said something. He then placed a bundle of sage in the man's mouth. The buffalo dancer removed the small pencil-like piercing sticks from the necklace strap around the dancer's neck. The intercessor began to vigorously rub the chest of the dancer with sage. Everything was well organized. There was no wasted motion or time. Every step was planned and quickly executed. The buffalo dancer handed the intercessor the dancer's piercing sticks, which he immediately placed into his mouth, as if he were smoking two cigarettes. The intercessor then unwrapped a small razorknife from its sterile wrappings and leaned closely to the man's chest. He then pinched a good portion of the man's skin between his thumb and forefinger. Then with the knife, he shoved a hole into the skin. Still holding the skin, he took one of the piercing sticks from his mouth and inserted it into that hole. Without hesitation, he went to work on the other side of his chest. Soon the dancer was assisted to his feet. In his chest he carried the two piercing sticks. The man then retrieved his dangling pledger's rope and the buffalo dancer looped it onto the piercing sticks, securing them to the pledger rope with two strips of red cloth. When the buffalo dancer was finished, the sun dancer moved backwards to the stretching point, but not the breaking point, of the pierced skin.

It was not long before the second man was in place receiving his piercing, then the third man, and then the final member of the first four. All four men took up positions at different areas around the tree. Each had received his piercing in an impressive fashion, without an outburst or cry of pain, just endurance and strength.

As the day moved quickly along, all the dancers eventually made their way to the piercing station and then into a position encircling the Mystery Tree. The number of men now dancing was fourteen. I saw Keven Brown Eagle being pierced, and in his hand he held the tobacco offering I had given him earlier for Tammy.

There would be no lunch break today. The work underway would be the food of the spirit for all of us. The crowd watching was the largest it had been at any time during the four days. Close to 200 men, women, and children representing the four colors of mankind were present. In addition, a couple more drums had been added to the southern area. The pledger ropes looked like a spider's web emanating from the tree. As I watched, I could tell that each man was becoming more and more entranced by the activities, by the drumming and singing, by the hypnotic melody of the eagle bone whistles, and by the dance itself! I found myself moved as well. A new and blessed atmosphere covered us like a spiritual blanket.

This portion of the dance involved movement to and from the tree. The dancers, on the upbeat, started slowly moving toward the tree. Eventually they arrived all at the same time. Then each said a short prayer, followed by a gradual retreat from the tree. This procedure continued for the rest of the afternoon.

The time to break away from the tree was finally upon us, and upon the dancers. The intercessor once again selected certain individuals to start the next segment. As the men prepared to release themselves by running backward, I noticed that the families of each dancer preparing to break were now allowed to enter the arbor a certain distance. Grandmothers, parents, wives, brothers, sisters, and children removed their shoes and socks and then entered. They held each other's hands and stood directly behind the dancer they represented, pride in their faces, love in their hearts. In some cases, as many as ten family members supported a single dancer. During this time the women dancers kept their steady pace of dance and prayer.

The unbelievable and dramatic break away was exactly that, unbelievable and dramatic! The first designated man prayed at the tree, then suddenly bolted backwards from it, stopping only after his pledger rope was taut. The skin stretched against the prongs, pulled outward about two or three inches. When the man did not break away, as was the case in the first attempt, he headed back to the tree for more prayer and strength. At each attempt, a gasp arose from the astonished observers. On the fourth attempt, the dancer stayed at the taut point and beyond until the piercing sticks tore away from the chest with a distinctive popping noise. His pledger rope then literally whipped into the air before falling to the ground. Sometimes a rope would fly twenty feet into the air! Once free, he began his victory trot around the interior of the arbor. As the first man passed by me, I saw his wounds and the blood running down his chest. However, he appeared unconcerned about his physical wounds. Instead, a blissful expression spread across his face. That man's family then returned to the observation area and the next pledger was selected.

The next pledger worked through the same process as the first man, breaking free from his bonds on the fourth attempt. Once free, he joined the other dancer in his victory trot around the tree. The remaining dancers continued with their sacred sacrifices. The intercessor, with the assistance of the buffalo dancer, guided the dancers through the remainder of this most holy portion of the sun dance. Occasionally, the distinctive pop of a man breaking free and the gasp from the nearby crowd could be heard. Eventually, most all the men had freed themselves and were dancing slowly around the tree.

A couple of times, dancers had difficulty breaking loose. When this occurred, the dancer's dramatic attempts to free himself were amazing! Jumping up and back, over and over again, his body would literally fly in the air as he strained against the rope. The dancers who had already freed themselves took up a position next to the man who was having difficulty giving him encouragement and prayers. When it became apparent that a man would not be able to free himself, for whatever reason, two men would hold the man's arms and quickly jerk him back, freeing him.

For about an hour and a half the air was filled with the popping sounds, sometimes as loud as a .22 caliber pistol! This, along with the excitement from the crowd, kept me on my toes.

At long last it was time for the two men who had pierced on the first day to break from their prongs. They both approached the tree together and then backed away. On the fourth and final time, with very little effort, they broke loose. They then joined the others. Now all the dancers had gone through the process but one, the lead male dancer. I was not sure what was going to happen to him, but I had my suspicions. The intercessor called for the other dancers to bring a large tree branch. It was maybe eight feet long and eight inches in diameter. They brought it to the circle from the rest area. A pledger rope was tied to the center point of the branch, and the other end of the rope was tossed through a V shape in the sacred tree. The lead dancer then approached the tree, dancing. He was quickly pierced while standing and hooked up to the specially prepared pledger rope. He was not able to dance too far away from the tree because of the limited length of his rope. The tree limb would move with his weight as he pulled back on it. After six or seven attempts the intercessor called for four dancers to man the tree branch. Then a fifth man was summoned to the tree, where he got to his hands and knees. Then, to my surprise, the lead dancer climbed to the back of the kneeling dancer. The other four men on the tree limb pulled the slack out of the rope. The last pierced man then leaned back from his precarious position. His skin stretched and stretched but amazingly would not break. The dancer then gained his balance and yelled something in Lakota toward the four assistants holding the tree limb. With that instruction the men began to pull and walk backwards away from the tree. The slack in the rope quickly disappeared. Then, to the surprise of the onlookers, the dancer began to rise from the man's back, higher and higher, his skin stretching away from his chest. The man who had been the platform jumped up as a couple more dancers gathered under the hanging dancer to catch him when he eventually fell. Still higher he was lifted, at least ten feet off the ground, his arms and legs dangling loosely. His long, flowing gray hair blew in the light breeze. The intercessor, who had stationed himself near the dancers, pointed his fan toward the four men and commanded extra effort. Suddenly, the lead dancer broke loose, falling into the arms of the waiting men. He quickly got to his feet and joined the other dancers in their circular movement around the arbor.

After another ten or fifteen minutes the intercessor re-entered the Mystery Circle and, while waving his fan over his head, called all the dancers to join him. He then pointed to the tree, and, along with the dancers, he approached the center point of the circle.

After four days of continuous dancing in near 100 degree temperatures and on the scorching hot sands of the plains, the Greengrass sun dance was coming to an end. The intercessor worked his way around the tree, touching and talking to each dancer along the way. I heard expressions of joy and happiness all around me. The dancers treated their own wounds, with the assistance of the diligent buffalo dancer, with sage, tobacco, and other types of medicine materials. Then they mingled among themselves for a few minutes, shaking hands, hugging, laughing, and crying. Eventually, all the observers were called to the south side of the arbor and a long line was formed. The drummers had stopped. The intercessor then led his dancers from the sacred circle in a slow and purposeful walk, their heads held high in honor. The women sun dancers had not been forgotten and their efforts were also regarded with respect. They followed the men dancers as they exited the east gate and headed to the south side for greetings from the nearly 200 observers who had gathered there. I knew the dance was over, but only in a physical sense. The four days of dance would never be over in my heart and mind. Such unbelievable, superhuman efforts, set in such an unbelievable and superior land, could not be forgotten.

Each dancer shook the hand of each person in the long line. Sometimes they received a hug or gift of some sort. It was a joyous time full of smiles and laughter. I felt as though I had become a part of each dancer. Seeing and sharing in their sacrifice made me feel close to them. As I shook their hands, I was honored and thankful that I was here and had the privilege to share in this extraordinary, age-old ceremony. The big elder, Keven Brown Eagle, especially felt good. His strong grip and hearty smile spoke of a holiness that had a special and lasting place with me.

I also noticed that each dancer took special time to greet and speak with their brother, Tom Calfrobe. The line of dancers was often backed up at his chair.

After the dancers had made their way through the mass of people, they quietly disappeared into the crowd. Some returned to their camps; others headed for the sweatlodges. The arbor was now opened for visits from the observers. I saw people entering the circle from all directions. As they approached the tree, I could still detect respect and humbleness in their movements. Some said prayers and others simply touched the tree. Some also left offerings. I finally made my way to the circle and the tree at its center. My prayer was short and comfortable.

Upon returning to the shaded area, I found James and Jeremiah. Both boys had been watching the ceremony along with me. I also found Trapper playing, as usual, with his little friend. We all shared some of our feelings and thoughts before heading back to the camp.

76. TWO FEATHERS' COUNCIL
Dance Back the Sage

It was still mid-afternoon. I was not sure what was supposed to take place prior to the pipe ceremony set for the next day. It was not long before I found out. Harry Charger was making his way through the campsites informing everyone of those plans. "We need help in preparing the grounds for the ceremony tomorrow," he told us.

We joined a large number of people gathering near the pipe house and the old sun dance arbor on the other side of the river, the same location where the previous pipe ceremonies and sun dances took place. One of the most important functions of the gathering was to assist with the collection of sage. The sage had a very important purpose in the pipe ceremony. It would make the sacred road over which the pipe would travel. The path would stretch from the pipe house to the altar, about 500 yards altogether. These arrangements were familiar to me, as they were practically the same as the arrangements done during my first visit three years earlier.

About thirty people were scattered over the vast area with both knives and scissors in hand, cutting sage. They loaded garbage bags, paper sacks, and blankets with the sage.

The women were handling the actual placement of the sage for the pipe path. After about two hours, enough sage had been gathered and placed. An announcement was made that a special council would be held at the old sun dance arbor this night. Prior to returning to our camp on the opposite side of the river, Trapper and I walked to a familiar place. I found the exact location where we had camped on our last trip here with Tammy. Our old campsite still felt quiet and peaceful, even with the hoards of people moving around. I gazed up toward the horseshoe-shaped butte that surrounded the area and remembered my sweet Tammy walking up there, the wind blowing her hair, with her little son in her arms. She truly loved this place as much as any place she had ever been.

With all the set up and preparation completed, everyone headed back toward the campsites. A lot of people had moved their tents to this side. The afternoon quickly gave way to the cooling evening. After our evening meal of beans and fried bread, we joined the rather large crowd gathering at the sun dance arbor. Trapper, Jeremiah, James, and myself joined them. Laughter and general feelings of happiness filled the evening air.

Finally, a man I recognized as a sun dancer stepped up to the microphone. "Hello everyone. I'm glad to see so many here. We have asked our elders to share some council with us. Before they begin, I want to personally thank everyone for the strong support you have given me and the other dancers over the last four days. It really means so much to see everyone."

He changed the subject and continued, "Now tomorrow we have more work to do. It's very sacred work and it is important that you understand what is expected of you." He paused for a moment. "The Wakan Chanunpa will be brought out. The holy of all holy pipes will be honored. Treat this time as a blessing for you and for your families. Remember, be very respectful to the ceremony. No pictures, no recordings. You should open your hearts and receive, not take, from the pipe ceremony. The keeper will be conducting the ceremony and we, the dancers, will be assisting. There are certain procedures that we follow. The elders of the Lakota shall be the first in line to visit with our holy pipe. Our brother, Arval Looking Horse, will call on them and others when the time is right. Be patient! There are probably fifty to one hundred families camping here tonight and another hundred will be coming in tomorrow. Those of you who carry a pipe should get it ready tonight. You will be the first called upon to witness."

He leaned down to the elder on his left and asked him something, then continued. "Our first council will come from our good friend, Benjamin Two Feathers." He attempted to hand the microphone to the elder, but the elder refused, shaking his head. He then opened with a prayer in his native Lakota tongue. Once he had finished, he spoke in English.

"Hoka Hey, Kola, It is good to be here! It is good to see so many here. I take my hat off in honor and respect for those men and women who gave up part of themselves for the good of the people. I was born on Pine Ridge in 1919. I have lived a long and good life. This ceremony, the sun dance at Greengrass, is like it was in the old days. You cannot find such respect and tradition anywhere on any reservation like you have seen here. On Pine Ridge they let anyone sun dance as long as they have the frog skins to pay for the right. I have seen non-Indians out to dance. They make-believe in what they are doing. They dance for an hour or two, then they go to their tents for iced tea or a Coke and a smoke. This is wrong!" His anger and displeasure were evident in his tone and body language. Two Feathers continued, "This ceremony is not for sale! Just as the pipe and the eagle feather are not for sale. They pay money for the sweatlodge ceremony. They pay to go on a vision quest. They pay for blessings on pretty crystals and other things which they consider sacred. I have spoken with our elders on that reservation, as well as other reservations, and they are not happy with such abuse of the sun dance and other sacred ceremonies. They feel a price will be paid, but it's not money they speak of, and it will not be a payment made from the white man's fat pockets. The price paid will be from those so-called medicine men, and it will cost them their spirit!" He stopped for a moment and regained his composure. "I know this is very difficult to understand, and I know that there may be some confusion among some of you listening. Let me say this. It's special and it's holy to Indian people. I am very thankful that the Looking Horse family still does this work and does it in the old way, the good way."

"I am just one man who will talk to you this evening. My words are no more important than the next man's or yours. It's just that I am old now and they let me talk first and more than others." A big smile appeared on his face. "I like it that way." His big smile broke into a hearty toothless laugh. He started again, changing the subject.

"I will tell you something else that is on my mind while I can still remember it. My father's father and my mother's mother have been gone now for many years. But they have only been gone from my physical sight." He pointed to his chest with his thumb. "They are alive right here. I still see them and hear them right here in my soul." He pointed to the sky. "They come to me from the other side and talk to me. They give me help and guidance when I need it. I have been given a message from them to give to you." He looked into the crowd of listening hearts. "The spirit world is sad." A couple of people sitting nearby uttered "Hau" softly in recognition of the powerful statement the elder had just made. "They are sad because of the abuse and misuse of the sacred burial places of their bones, Paha Sapa, the Black Hills. These hills have been our most sacred and honored place from our beginning. There are no Indian or white man's words to describe the feeling and power of these holy lands. The Creator's words alone do justice to them. Our ancestors know these words and someday, soon for me, we will all know these words."

77. THE PIPE DAY! RELEASING THE DANCE

Dance Back the Dance

The day started much like the others with Harry Charger making his rounds, the crackling sound of the sweatlodge fires, and the quiet morning talk from the other camps. I could hear a young child crying for his morning attention. The smell of breakfast wafted through our camp.

I participated in the first sweat of the day as the boys enjoyed a little more well-deserved rest. The sweat was a good one and blessed by a number of sun dancers and elders. I felt very honored to share this place and ceremony with so many honorable men and women. The sweat was purposely short to allow more people to participate. The word had, once again, been passed along that all who wished to participate in the pipe ceremony would first have to purify themselves with the sweat.

Once my sweat was finished, I hustled Jeremiah and James from their comfortable bedrolls and headed them toward the sweatlodge. Before going to the pipe grounds, I took Trapper over to have him steamed off as well. He was very obliging. I also decided to break camp before going to the other side of the river. This would be our last day here and our drive home would be a long one. A lot of the other campers had the same idea, and before too long the original campsites were practically deserted.

Once we arrived at the pipe grounds, we joined the crowd waiting for instructions. A large teepee had been erected at the center of the old sun dance arbor. I spotted Arval Looking Horse hard at work with his preparations. The midmorning light caused the path of sage to glow like a silver carpet of honor.

The boys stayed near the car and I got out. I walked closer to the activities to offer help, if needed. It was not long before Arval Looking Horse spotted me and waved me over to his location.

"Good morning, Little Eagle," he greeted me.

"Good morning, Arval. It looks like a nice day for a pipe ceremony," I mused.

"Yep!" he replied. "I will need your help with the ceremony and the pipe bag portion of it."

"Just let me know what you need," I answered.

"Well," he continued, "after I've put the pipe out on the buffalo robe, I will signal you to bring the pipe bag and place it on the buffalo skull that will be set up near the pipe bundle."

I nodded in understanding. It seemed simple enough. He then added, "That will be about it." Arval went about with more preparation, stopping to talk with different people along the way, and making his trips back and forth between the pipe house and the altar.

The altar itself was set up in a traditional fashion. Four chokecherry saplings had been placed in the four directions, making an area eight feet by eight feet in diameter. Tobacco ties, ribbons, flags, and other items had been tied to the branches of the young saplings. That area inside those saplings was now consecrated as holy and blessed ground.

Arval Looking Horse brought a beautifully beaded and quilled buffalo robe and spread it out within the altar area. One of the other medicine men assisting him brought the ancient buffalo skull that Looking Horse had spoken of earlier. It was placed in the southeast section of the altar area. Later, Rufus Charger, the buffalo dancer from the sun dance, smudged the area thoroughly. Every little detail was checked and then rechecked. Finally, after about an hour, Arval Looking Horse stood quietly outside the altar area with a number of men gathered beside him. He studied the surroundings as a teacher would study a student's work. Then he said something to one of the nearby men, who quickly entered the altar area and turned the buffalo skull slightly. I could see Arval Looking Horse nodding his head approvingly. The man then departed.

It was at this time that I went to prepare the pipe bag. All three boys were waiting near the car and assisted me. A strange feeling began to enter me as I smudged myself in preparation for picking up the bag. I thought of the long and mysterious history of this sacred instrument within our family. The first person to enter mind was the good doctor, Alexander Brown. He was the man who befriended a Lakota chief in 1895 by saving his son's life. It was a tragic and historic time for the Lakota people. The great excitement of the Ghost Dance was being crushed by the U.S. Government. Sitting Bull and Crazy Horse were both assassinated. Distrust and fear blew through the plains like the cold winter winds that blew across the grounds of the Wounded Knee massacre. The doctor would not accept payment, but the Lakota chief insisted that he take a gift. That gift profoundly affected the doctor's family for the next hundred years. It was a beautifully quilled and beaded pipe bag that many believe belonged to the Lakota hero, Crazy Horse.

At the doctor's passing in 1948, responsibility for the pipe bag went to his son, Vinson Brown, who received great inspiration from it to write and teach. Along with this inspiration came the tests and difficulties of such lofty responsibilities. These would fill the rest of the days of his life. He would carry and protect the chief's gift for forty years, until October of 1988, when he placed its protection and keeping into my hands, just as foreseen in my sweatlodge ceremony on my first visit to Greengrass two years earlier. With deep respect and humbleness, I accepted the priceless gift. It came into my life and the life of my beloved wife as a healing tool. We used it to call on the same spirit that helped the good doctor save the life of a young boy, to save the life of a young woman.

As life goes, the healing would be given in a different but very powerful way, the healing of a family. Tammy knew this and in her loving way she accepted its true value. A hundred years of illness will need a hundred years of healing. The descendants of the good doctor had prospered and succeeded as surely as they had cried and failed.

The pipe bag was mine to honor and hold, one last time, as I prepared to return it to the first keepers. I felt surrounded by the ancestors, watched by that one who gave all for the love of family. I began my prayers. The sun was near its apex and the heat of the day brought sweat down my face, which mingled with my tears. I felt my beloved's blue eyes upon me. The strength of her spirit supported my frail and hesitant steps.

Gently now, I hold the pipe bag. Gently now, I prepare to return it to the people from which it came. Gently now, I cry out of respect, love, and undying faith.

I looked up the hillside toward the pipe house and spotted the sacred procession. The mother of all pipes was approaching! In the lead was the elder medicine man with his eagle staff. He was followed by four young girls, all dressed in their finest outfits. Behind them was the pipe keeper, Arval Looking Horse. In his arms, wrapped in an ancient buffalo robe, rested the Wakan Chanunpa, the most holy pipe. He carried it with obvious pride and respect. All members of this party walked barefoot, as was the custom. Three elder men and one elder woman followed the pipe. Each person had honored work to do. I was not knowledgeable about that work, but it was not for me to know either.

As the pipe made its way toward the altar, the crowd grew larger and drew nearer to the center. A vibrant energy surrounded the activities. It took me back to the first time I had participated in this ceremony. The visions of the pipe bag in my hands reappeared to me. It did not seem possible, but here it was. I was returning it to its rightful, and now, proper place.

The pipe keeper entered the altar area and laid the sacred pipe on the buffalo robe. The four young girls took a seat near the lodge. The eagle staff was put in place and the elder walked around to the entrance where the pipe keeper had taken his station. He had been joined by his wife at that place. He then gave the signal for specific elders to enter and make their prayers with the pipe. As soon as one would finish another would enter.

Now the signal was given for all pipe carriers to approach and prepare themselves. In my arms was the pipe bag and with my left hand I carried my pipe. One of the elders was directing people and escorting them into position. Elders were brought to the front. The people were lining up side by side in rows of twenty or so. I found myself in the third row back. Once all the pipe carriers had taken their places, I counted nine rows. At least 150 pipe carriers were present.

The energy of the ceremony was putting me in an almost trancelike state. The drum group began its honor songs and the pipe carriers, once again, were transformed into the Greengrass pipe dancers!

I was then surprised by one elder medicine man who grabbed hold of my left arm and said something to me, which I understood to mean, "follow me." I was quickly taken to the entrance of the altar area, where I was greeted by Arval Looking Horse.

I stood there for a moment, not sure of what was happening. It didn't seem appropriate that I should be here first, ahead of the many elders and Lakota pipe carriers. But my confusion was quickly taken away by Arval Looking Horse's next words.

"It is time. Are you ready?"

I realized that it was the pipe bag that was here more than myself. I nodded and he pointed to the buffalo skull, which was next to the most holy pipe.

"There, you may put it there on the buffalo skull and then come back here."

I entered the altar area by turning once, in a clockwise fashion, and then approached the buffalo skull. I could not help but feel the energy of the sacred pipe, which lay just to the right. I leaned down and placed the bag on top of the skull. In that instant, a hundred years of responsibility and care were released. A family's honor, life, and love were reborn in that incredible moment. A feeling of permanence entered my thoughts. The sacred pipe bag of my family was, at long last, being returned to the land and the people from which it came. I felt an urgency in my work. Once the bag was in place, I stared down at it. I closed my eyes to feel the moment, to say a short prayer, and then to say good-bye. I turned slowly and respectfully departed the altar area. As simply as the bag had been placed in my personal trust, it had now been returned. No tears, no remorse, no sadness. I was escorted back to my position with the other pipe carriers. My work, and the work of a good family, was done.

The pipe keeper, Arval Looking Horse, then called on the Lakota elders to come forward. Slowly they made their way to that place to pray, to give thanks, and to seek guidance. One at a time the elders came to that most sacred station. Some prayed for an extended time; others visited briefly. Each person was very respectful. Occasionally, I would see someone inspect the pipe bag. Some would hold their hands against it to feel its energy or to pay respect.

Once the elders had finished their prayers, the pipe carriers were signaled to come forward. Four at a time were allowed to enter the altar area, two on one side of the pipe bundle and two on the other side. Prayers were given, offerings left behind, and guidance and blessings received. Each man and woman would lay their personal pipe on the bundle and it would thereby be energized with an ancient and holy power.

Eventually, I was led once again to the entrance way, this time with three others for the same purpose. As I entered I found myself being drawn to the Buffalo Calf pipe and the pipe bag. Others had left offerings and I discovered that a number of sage bundles and tobacco ties had been placed on top of the pipe bag.

I returned my thoughts and prayers to the most holy Buffalo Calf pipe, absorbed by the moment. In that state of spiritual focus, a voice entered my head and heart, a familiar and beautiful voice of love.

"Yes, Love, this is right."

My eyes were closed, but I could feel her presence in those words. Her soft, shoulder-length, golden brown hair was blowing in the wind and across her face. Her blue eyes sparkled with love and life. Her smile made me smile. It was Tammy. The colorful dress that I had seen earlier was changing. Its vivid colors were giving away to a beautiful and pure white dress. I concentrated on the moment, on the events and prayers. I knelt down and placed my hands on the sacred bundle. I held my personal pipe in my hands and across the length of the bundle. In that deep and prayerful manner, I suddenly felt the presence of others, my guides of the past and the future. The intensity of this event continued to grow.

In a distant dream world, I saw a man on an eastern butte, a young white man standing alone. His dark hair and dark suit seemed out of place but appropriate. In his right hand he held a small black bag, a doctor's bag. He was of medium height and slender in build with a stern expression on his face. He stood silent, the wind and dust whipping his clothes about. I realized that the physical sensation of the pipe bundle and its surroundings were gone and it felt as though I was standing in the middle of a wide open prairie. It seemed proper and in order. I became aware of the ease and simplicity of this place. I no longer had to focus or concentrate. Everything was easy and real!

The young man I watched from across the prairie was the young Doctor Alexander Brown. He smiled at my quiet observation and recognition, then slowly shook his head in affirmation. As I watched, mystified, his appearance began to change. His dark suite gradually gave way to a lighter color, and like Tammy earlier, an almost translucent and pure appearance. He appeared to be released, and a glorious feeling swooped into both of us.

Freedom and love surrounded us. Behind him I saw beautiful lights dancing. Then he slowly raised his left hand and from it the same lights glowed. He made a circling motion, then began to dance, a slow dance. I watched as he looked around and then seemed to find something. He released the light from his hand, which appeared to shoot across the vast prairie as if it was alive. I followed its path to a butte on the southern horizon. There, another man stood silently, watching and waiting. This man was Indian.

He was dressed in simple traditional clothing of browns and blacks. However, there was nothing simple about his presence; it was majestic and powerful. His long, flowing hair danced with the wind. In his hair was a small clump of feathers. He seemed familiar to me, but I was not sure. The dancing lights splashed onto him and the scene came alive with the same feelings I had just felt with the good doctor. As I watched him come to life with the lights, he began to dance. A joyful and peaceful feeling emanated from those actions and again a clarity of presence surrounded me. I recognized this warrior as the holy one, Crazy Horse! He kicked up the lights and dust like a little boy playing. I watched this magical moment with great happiness and amazement. I could feel myself smiling. The sacred one then slowed his steps slightly and raised his left hand. The lights enveloped his hand and with four distinctive motions he sent the magic on.

I once again followed the path of the lights, losing sight of him. The heavenly lights came to rest on the western buttes, rolled for a moment, and then from their midst came my Tammy. The previously colorful dress was completely gone now and in its place was a silky white dress, shimmering with light. I felt my heart stop with the power of the moment. I breathed in deep the love and sweetness of what I was seeing and feeling. She stood silently, as if listening to my fluttering heart, and then in a way I had never seen before nor will again, she smiled to me from across the prairie and the heavens. For the first time since she left, I felt truly at ease. She made that ease come to me with her holy smile and her peaceful existence. I found myself longing to hold her once again. I must have beckoned her in my thoughts, for she raised her hands, palms toward me, to relay to me that it was okay for me to be here and for her to be there. I watched her become more involved with the lights dancing around her. Then, in the same fashion as the two other visitors, she began to dance, a splendid dance such as I had never seen before. Sweet and gentle, with the lights, she danced on. The purity of the moment caused unbridled tears of love and happiness to flow. I smiled as she smiled. I loved as she loved.

I watched as she raised both her arms once again and, with circular motions, stirred the dancing stars around her head. Now with one powerful movement she sent them on to the northern buttes. I felt them pass by me and I tried to follow them but found that I was unable to do so. With that one effort I ceased all further attempts to find the lights. It was apparent to me that I was not supposed to see that fourth destination, at least not at this time. I returned my attention to her and found that she was leaving. Like the breath of the buffalo in wintertime, she was here and then she was gone.

I was left with those wonderful memories and pictures in my heart of our time together and our love. Suddenly everything seemed to flash by me: our first meeting on a warm, sun-kissed beach in California, our travels to her home in Happy Camp, California, a roaring laugh over a joke, a smile of pride over her sons. Another flash brought forward the creative moment of our son, Trapper. His birth, his life. The drive on Highway 16, when we were made aware of the unstoppable. The smiles of love, peace, and joy. These and thousands of other events moved with lightning speed through my thoughts.

The sounds and activities of the pipe ceremony returned to my senses, and I opened my eyes to see the bundle that lay in front of me. I quickly realized that I was the only one at the bundle and the other three people who had come with me were gone. I glanced over my shoulder and found the pipe keeper standing in the same spot as before. A number of others were waiting in the long line to make their visit to the bundle. Everything seemed okay and I was not disturbed during my visit. Now that visit was over and I stood and circled my way out of the altar area. I felt dazed by what had just happened, but I also felt very good and happy about it. My heart seemed to beat in rhythm with the drumming. As I left the altar area my legs moved with that same beat and rhythm. I spotted the pipe house just ahead of me. It was beautiful. I looked to the east, to the south, and to the west. The skies seemed brighter and more alive. I was overwhelmed with the urge to dance. The beat of the drum escorted me into that motion and the steps came to me. I walked alone to the large field between the pipe house and the pipe ceremony grounds. My dance picked up and I felt a celebration of spirit move over me. I danced among the brown-green grasses of Greengrass. Gradually, others came to join me, and, in time, the magic of the moment brought many more. We all danced that Greengrass pipe dance.

After nearly six hours of visitations, the pipe keeper finally closed that part of the ceremony. He carefully went about his work of returning the most holy pipe to its resting place in the pipe house. By this time, the entire altar area was overflowing with gifts and offerings: flowers, beads, sage bundles, even money.

In his work, the first thing the pipe keeper did was to collect the pipe bag from the buffalo skull and lay it lengthwise on top of the pipe bundle. He then lifted both into his arms. The group that had helped him bring the pipe was now summoned to help him return it. They gathered up the offerings.

The elder medicine man took the eagle staff and headed out of the altar entrance area. He was followed by the four young girls, who also had their arms full of gifts and offerings. Arval Looking Horse followed them. As they moved ever so slowly up the path of sage, the people joined them. By the time the pipe keeper reached the pipe house, well over 200 people had joined in the procession. The door to the pipe house was swung open and he quickly entered the cool darkness of its interior. Once he had placed the bundle, and was satisfied with its position, he returned. The elders and others who were carrying the many offerings handed them over to the pipe keeper, who then deposited them in a proper location in the pipe house. After this work was completed, Arval Looking Horse looked about the crowd, smiled, and said these parting words:

"This has been a very good day! A very good week! Our sun dance went well and the dancers brought us honor and pride. I thank them for that. Everyone here has brought honor and pride to this place and I thank you all for that. I hope to see everyone next year. You pipe carriers have a special responsibility. You are expected to live honorable lives and help your families and your communities. Take those pipes, which are all descendants of this Buffalo Calf pipe, and smoke them with your families and your loved ones. Pray with your families. Laugh and cry with your families, your people. Doing this will bring a fullness to your life and the pipe that you carry."

With this Arval Looking Horse turned and peered into the pipe house for a short moment. He then pulled the huge door closed and quickly fastened a large padlock to secure it. He jerked on the lock a couple of times to satisfy himself that the holy pipe was, once again, in safe and secure surroundings. He then returned to the quiet crowd.

"Our work is done. Let's shake hands and share in the potluck and remember what we have seen and heard here. Hau!"

We took part in a wonderful potluck and visited with some of the many people we had gotten to know during our stay. There was a joyful feeling among the people present. Afterwards, we loaded up for our long drive home to Suquamish, Washington.

The dust obscured my view of the pipe house in the rear view mirror as we pulled away, but the memories of those who had been my guides and helpers will never be obscured in my heart and spirit. I thought of them all: the Greengrass pipe dancers, the Looking Horse and Calfrobe families, and the many medicine men and women of the Pine Ridge Reservation, including the Not-Help-Him family. I also reflected on the dance of the good doctor and the sacred warrior, Crazy Horse. But just as she was my first thought, my last and forever thought was a gentle and peaceful lady named Tammy. I will, forever, be in love with the one who so loves me. God speed you, my dear and beautiful Greengrass Pipe Dancer.

EPILOGUE

In my efforts to write *Greengrass Pipe Dancers*, I would often take the opportunity to speak with Vinson about my travels and research for this story. He was always keenly interested in my reports. Of special interest to him were the thoughts and words of the elders and medicine people I encountered. Vinson was always willing to give instruction and guidance in my writing efforts. I had the desire and inner need to write, but lacked the dedication and discipline to carry it through. He gifted me with that and I thank him. This period of time seemed to signal a change, as when the ants cover the holes of their hills in advance of an approaching storm. I realize now that I did not see the storm coming, but I still had to ride it out.

In the last chapter of this book, I attempted to describe the indescribable when I wrote of the dancing lights on the buttes surrounding me at Greengrass. It was a supreme moment of emotion and glory, but at the time it was also incomplete. When the dancing lights moved to the fourth direction on the northern buttes, I was unable to turn and see their ultimate destination, the place that would eventually represent the final and true completion of the story. It was not until the Moon of the Popping Trees, 1991, that I was able to turn my heart and peer into the fourth and final stage of the dancing lights of Greengrass. What I saw there was my elder and teacher, Vinson. Those lights of spirit moved in and about him as they celebrated his homecoming. I did not see distress or despair but rather happiness and completion.

It seems he had planned to take a walk one cool December evening, as he so often did, to commune with nature, to offer his prayers to the Great Spirit, and simply to stretch his long legs. This was a familiar trip, one that he had made many times before. What Vinson did not realize as he set out on his journey was that this evening's adventure would be his last one on this good earth. He had planned to cross over the bridge on Indian Creek; instead he crossed over the bridge of life. Vinson died his physical death on December 17, 1991, but he was born into the spiritual and everlasting dancing lights of eternity.